Purton in the
First World War

Rick Dixon

© Rick Dixon 2018

First Edition: September 2018

Published by: Rick Dixon (Cricklade)
19 North Wall, Cricklade, Wiltshire SN6 6DU

Printed by: Pixartprinting S.p.A. Italy

ISBN: 978 1 9164618 0 2

Contents

Foreword..5
Introduction: Purton & A Great War...6
Part 1: German Unification..8
Part 2: The Rise & Decline of the Ottoman Empire....................................10
Part 3: The Austro-Hungarian Empire...13
Part 4:   Italian Unification - the Risorgimento...15
Part 5: Britain by the early Twentieth Century...20
Part 6: Russia in Late Tsarist Days...23
Part 7: Empire, Entente & Alliance..26
Part 8: Steel, Gunboats & Ironclads..29
Part 9: Libya & The Balkan Wars (1912-13)..31
Part 10: The State of the World - January 1914..33
Part 11: Events January to May 1914..36
Part 12: June 1914: Assassination..38
Part 13: July (and a bit of August) 1914: The Road to War 40
Part 14: War - August 1914...42
My Family's War - My Great Great Aunt and Uncle 45
Part 15:   September 1914..46
Part 16: October 1914...48
My Family's War - George Smith: The Flying Cabinet Maker.....................48
My Family's War - Edward, Ernest and Sidney Holder..............................51
My Family's War - Bonny..51
Part 17: November 1914..52
Part 18: December 1914..55
My Family's War - The Pickled Thumb..57
My Family's War - Captain Mervyn Stronge Richardson 58
Part 19: January 1915...59
My Family's War - Reginald Stevens...62
Part 20: February 1915..63
Part 21: March 1915..65
My Family's War - Roger Moreton...68
Part 22: April 1915..69
Part 23: May 1915...70
Part 24: June 1915...73
Part 25: July 1915...75
Part 26: August 1915...77
Part 27: September 1915..79
My Family's War - Lilian Monks, the Munitionette......................................81
Part 28: October 1915...82
My Family's War - Purton Remount Depot...84
Part 29: November 1915...85

Part 30: December 1915...87
Part 31: January 1916..89
My Family's War - Childhood Memories..........................91
Part 32: February 1916..92
Part 33: March 1916...93
Part 34: April 1916...95
Part 35: May 1916..98
My Family's War - Great Aunts...................................100
Part 36: June 1916..101
My Family's War - The World War One Crocodile...........102
Part 37: July 1916...103
Part 38: August 1916...105
Part 39: September 1916..106
Part 40: October 1916..109
Part 41: November 1916..113
Part 42: December 1916..115
Part 43: January 1917..119
Part 44: February 1917...121
My Family's War - A Deferment of Service....................123
Part 45: March 1917...124
Part 45: April 1917...127
Part 47: May 1917..129
Part 48: June 1917...131
Part 49: July 1917..134
Part 50: August 1917..137
Part 51: September 1917...139
Part 52: October 1917..141
Part 53: November 1917...144
Part 54: December 1917...147
My Family's War - Three Cookery Books.......................150
Part 55: January 1918..152
Woodrow Wilson's 14 Points......................................155
Part 56: February 1918...157
Part 57: March 1918...159
My Family's War - Herbert Dubrey................................164
Part 56: April 1918...165
Part 59: May 1918..169
Part 60: June 1918...173
Part 61: July 1918..176
Part 62: August 1918..179
Part 63: September 1918...181
Part 64: October 1918...184
Part 65: November 1918...189
Part 66: The Immediate Aftermath.................................195

Part 67: Peace Treaties 1919-20...197
Part 68: Elections and Civil Wars...202
Part 68: Greece and Turkey..204
Part 70: Spanish 'Flu...207
Part 71: Weimar and the Rise of Fascism.....................................209
Part 72: Remembrance..212
Part 73: Echoes that Live On..229
Bibliography...234
Acknowledgements...235
Index..236

Index to Maps

Western Front, 1914-1916.....................................Inside front cover
German Spring Offensive, 1918................................Inside front cover
Europe in 1860...7
Growth of Germany, 1807-1871...9
Ottoman Empire at its height, 1609..11
Austro-Hungarian Empire, ethnic map, 1910...................................14
Italy, 1848...17
Europe in 1912..28
1st & 2nd Balkan Wars...32
Europe in 1914..41
Battles of Mons and Le Cateau...44
Battles of the Marne and Aisne, 1914..46
1st Battle of Ypres, 1914...52
Gallipoli Campaign location map...72
Battle of Jutland, 1916...99
German East Africa...106
Partitioning of Germany, 1919..198
Partitioning of Austria-Hungary, 1919-1920.................................200
Ottoman Empire - Treaty of Sèvres..205
Ottoman Empire - Treaty of Lausanne..206
Eastern Front, 1914-1918.....................................Inside back cover
Palestine and Levant, 1917-1918..............................Inside back cover
Mesopotamia Campaign, 1914-1918..............................Inside back cover

All human beings are born free and equal in dignity and rights. They are endowed with reason and conscience and should act towards one another in a spirit of brotherhood

Universal Declaration of Human Rights
Article 1

"Where does it all begin? History has no beginnings, for everything that happens becomes the cause or pretext for what occurs afterwards, and this chain of cause and pretext stretches back to the Palaeolithic age, when the first Cain of one tribe murdered the first Abel of another. All war is fratricide, and there is therefore an infinite chain of blame that winds its circuitous route back and forth across the path and under the feet of every people and every nation, so that a people who are the victims of one time become the victimisers a generation later, and newly liberated nations resort immediately to the means of their former oppressors. The triple contagions of nationalism, utopianism and religious absolutism effervesce together into an acid that corrodes the moral metal of a race, and it shamelessly and even proudly performs deeds that it would deem vile if they were done by any other."

Louis de Bernières, Birds Without Wings

Dedication

I would like to dedicate this book and the original serialisation in Purton Magazine to Mr Peter M. Dodd who taught me History at Calday Grange Grammar School in West Kirby on the Wirral, in Cheshire as it was in those days. His inspirational teaching of my 1967 O' Level course "The History of the Great Powers, 1870-1914" has remained with me all of my life and has put much of the world's subsequent history into perspective.

Rick Dixon

Foreword

Purton in Wiltshire is situated 4 miles west of Swindon, with Cricklade to the north and Royal Wootton Bassett to the south. The village was named for the pear trees that grew there in Anglo-Saxon times when it was called Piritone or Pirigtune. The village has been in existence since early times and includes Iron Age and Roman remains. Purton is mentioned in the Domesday Book which notes that it was then owned by the Abbots of Malmesbury. Abbot Aldhelm had received it in gift from King Caedwalha of Wessex in 688 A.D.

Situated on an easily defensible ridge and with a good supply of water from wells, the village occupies a strategic position which has assured its continuous development. The buildings of the High Street date from the 17th century. Today the parish has a population of 3,897 (2011 census). The 1911 census shows the population before the Great War was 2,578 and had reduced by 1921 to 2,458, a fall of 120 and the only recorded fall since the start of census records in 1801.

It is a relief and a sense of pride to have achieved the goal of the 72 monthly articles I set myself to write for Purton Magazine back in 2013. It has also been an interesting journey for me and has reminded my during my research of much that I had forgotten, never knew or had posted to the back of my memory.

I hope I have achieved my initial aim of memorialising those who gave their lives in the Great War set within a narrative that puts their sacrifice into a time frame of the events that occurred. My intention was neither to glorify war, nor to create a comprehensive guide to the War in any of the theatres, campaigns, battles and actions that took place; simply to put those men's actions and sacrifices into context.

Photographs of servicemen have been used where they exist and mostly come from the archives of Purton Museum. They are of course over 100 years old and the quality is not what you would hope for today. Nor are they complete; we only have photographs of 26 of the 91 men who died.

Purton men served in most theatres of the war, so some campaigns are included that might seem beyond the scope of the present work but eventually we find that someone served there.

All profits over and above the printing and postage costs of this book will be donated to Combat Stress, a charity set up in 1919 as the Ex-Servicemen's Welfare Society. Their work is summarised in the final part of the present work.

Rick Dixon, 2018

Introduction: Purton & A Great War

Reproduced form Purton Magazine July 2013 issue:

I'll tell you straight … I'm quite scared. I'm taking on a huge project which will take six years to complete and I'll be nearly 70 when it's done.

Over the years since 1999, I have produced an Exhibit of the Month in this Magazine, usually using the "exhibit" to tell a story that it represented. Often, you might have guessed, I've not necessarily let a fact stand in the way of a good story! My themes have always been social history, though political history can never be ignored as that is the framework within which the ordinary person has to live.

I'm going to stop the "Exhibit of the Month" series to report on an overwhelmingly important piece of social history … variously known as the First World War, the Great War, the War to end all Wars but, whatever you care to call it, one of the worst disasters that mankind has inflicted upon itself.

As we approach the 100th anniversary of the start of the Great War, there will be loads of Memorial items in books and on TV about it. But I want to talk about the effects the Great War had on Purton and her young people who fought, died, and even survived in far-flung places most had never even heard of. RAF Mechanic Bob Lloyd who has published two books on Purton and the Great War has kindly agreed to help me with this project and I will be drawing heavily on his research. His most recent book *Purton & The Great War 1914-1918* is being updated and Bob plans to have it available in 2014*.

History books, certainly in the "old days", used to talk about the Great War as the 1914-18 War, but those dates are rather misleading. They only cover the period of armed hostilities between the Great Powers, those countries being mainly the old empires and powers of Europe: Britain, Germany, Austro-Hungary, Russia, France, the Ottomans … and the United States from 1917. However the War itself was perhaps only the most deadly phase of a virus of conflict that started way back in the 1800s with the creation of Germany between and after the Austro-Prussian and Franco-Prussian Wars and the progressive decline of the Ottoman Empire especially in its inability to hold onto its European territories in the Balkans. There are seeds that go back even further.

Then again, the War didn't really stop in 1918. White Russians were still fighting Red Russians well into the middle of the 1920s. The 1918 Armistice terms led to the rise of Hitler and the Second World War, and the end of that War resulted in the Cold War. The collapse of the Ottoman Empire led to the creation of states in the Levant and North Africa that are now in conflict internally and with their neighbours: Syria, Iraq, Lebanon, Libya, Tunisia, Palestine … While the abrupt retreats from Empire have caused the problems we see today in Mali, Algeria, and earlier in Malaya, Aden, Kenya, Vietnam …

In Europe, lands of the Austro-Hungarian Empire were carved off to form new states based on a perceived "ethnicity" such as Yugoslavia (the land of the southern Slavs), Czechoslovakia (the land of the Czechs and Slovaks). Neither

* Yes, it was published in CD form in 2014 and copies may still be available.

of these is one country still today, but thank heavens the Czechs and Slovaks parted company more peacefully than the Yugoslavs.

Anyway, we're getting ahead of ourselves.

What I would like to do over the next six years (gosh!) is to talk about the War on a month-by-month basis.

- As the Great War started in August 1914, I will start next month (August 2013). Until spring 2014 (1914), each month I will cover a facet of the causes of the Great War. There are quite a lot of them and I feel that would take us up to the beginning of 2014.
- From 2014 to 2018 (1914-1918) I will tell the story as it happened, month-by-month … and how Purton people were affected.
- In 2019 we get the summing up.

I will be most grateful to hear, from anyone, stories and anecdotes with a Purton connection, however serious or trivial, and I will try to fit them in. I will try to deal with them as they relate to the Purton Story so, if you send me something in 2015 (1915) that relates specifically to 1917, it will be included but will have to wait to the appropriate issue for the 100th anniversary of that story.

Your support in this project is anticipated with grateful thanks. And if anyone wants to help take over the "torch" in the coming years, that person's hand will be grasped and not let go of!

Rick Dixon, 2013

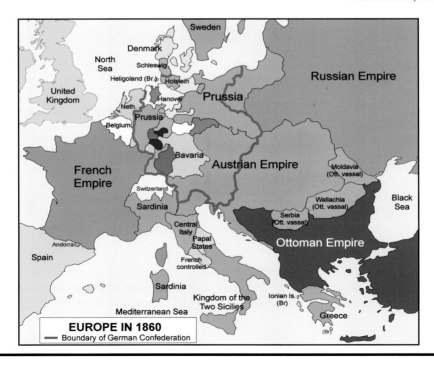

Part 1: German Unification

The world in 1914 didn't look much like it does today ... and the world in 1914 had very little resemblance to what it looked like when Queen Victoria came to the throne in Britain in 1837. Looking at a map of Europe, one of the major differences you would spot right in the middle would be the absence of Germany. We have to go back a little way to find out how Germany came into existence.

Following the collapse of the Roman Empire and during the Middle Ages, the Holy Roman Empire (the Empire) came into prominence in central Europe. This was a confederation of hundreds of small kingdoms, principalities, dukedoms and bishoprics and as such was not a State in the way we would consider one today. Although there was an Emperor, who had some lands he owned directly, the Emperor could not govern the Empire directly. This severely limited his powers and ultimately the strength of the Empire itself. The fragmented nature of the Empire also goes some way to explain why German fairy stories and folk tales are full of Princes, Princesses and castle towers.

The French Revolutions put France at odds with most of its neighbours and, from 1792 onwards, France was at war with various parts of the Empire for numerous reasons - some ideological, some political and some territorial including wanting to retrieve Alsace from the Empire's control. Following the accession of Napoleon Bonaparte as Emperor of France in 1804, a series of military defeats caused the Holy Roman Emperor Francis II to abdicate and the Empire was dissolved on 6 August 1806. In 1807, Napoleon reorganised much of the Empire into the Confederation of the Rhine, which became a French puppet. Francis' Royal House of Habsburg-Lorraine survived the demise of the Empire, continuing to reign as Emperors of Austria and Kings of Hungary.

After the defeat of Napoleon at Waterloo in 1815, the Confederation of the Rhine was replaced by a new union, the German Confederation, with Austria as one of its guarantors.

Meanwhile the kingdom of Prussia allied with Brandenburg, both to the east of the Confederation, were becoming more powerful in the political vacuum left by the demise of the Holy Roman Empire and of French power. King Friedrich Wilhelm IV of Prussia (House of Hohenzollern) died in 1861, and his son and regent became King Wilhelm I. In 1862, Wilhelm was in political and financial conflict with the Prussian Diet, a parliament chiefly of nobles and landowners, especially over reform of the army; he threatened to abdicate. However his son opposed the abdication and believed that Otto von Bismarck was the only politician capable of handling the crisis. Bismarck had in fact been sidelined in politics and was currently the Prussian ambassador to the Russian Empire in St Petersburg. Wilhelm recalled Bismarck and appointed him Minister-President and Foreign Minister with sweeping powers in foreign affairs. Bismarck, together with Helmuth von Moltke, the new Army Chief of Staff, and Albrecht von Roon, the Minister of War, also pushed through the major army reforms.

Growth of Germany 1807-1871

© 2013-18 Rick Dixon

Denmark

Nether-lands

Belgium

France

Russian Empire

to Prussia 1849

Austro-Hungarian Empire

	Prussia in 1807
a	Gained/regained 1815
b	Gained after Danish and Austrian Wars
c	Joined Empire in 1871
d	Annexed from France in 1871

Frederick VII of Denmark died in 1863 and the ownership of the German-speaking duchies of Schleswig and Holstein, loosely tied to Denmark, were claimed by the new Danish king Christian IX, but also by a German duke (Frederick von Augustenburg). Denmark acted to annexe Schleswig and, after a Prussian ultimatum was refused, Austria and Prussia invaded. Denmark sued for peace and ceded Schleswig to Prussia and Holstein to Austria.

Then in 1866, Austria demanded that the German Confederation should decide ownership, rather than Prussia. This back-tracking allowed Bismarck an excuse to declare war on Austria, and Prussian troops occupied Holstein. The newly-reorganised Prussian army quickly defeated Austria and its allies in the German Confederation in the Austro-Prussian War.

Prussia dominated German politics from that point on. The German Confederation was dissolved being replaced by a North German Confederation in 1867, including Prussia and several other North German states. King Wilhelm I became its President, and Bismarck was appointed to be its Chancellor. Prussia also annexed Schleswig, Holstein, Hanover, Hesse-Kassel, Frankfurt and other former Austrian allies. Austria also accepted Prussian demands to keep out of German affairs.

Prussia's victory over Austria increased tensions with France who saw a new great power emerging. This was heightened in 1870, when a German Prince of the same House as Wilhelm I (Hohenzollern) was offered the vacant Spanish throne. France saw the threat of Hohenzollerns on its eastern and south-western borders and demanded that no member of the House of Hohenzollern become King of Spain. Bismarck provoked France into declaring war with Prussia which it did in July 1870. The Franco-Prussian War (1870-71)

Pre-War

saw a total defeat for France who had to surrender Alsace and part of Lorraine, and also pay reparations to Prussia for the cost of the war. Bismarck acted immediately to secure the unification of Germany while the war with France was closing. Wilhelm I of Prussia was proclaimed German Emperor on 18 January 1871 at Versailles which his forces had occupied. The new German Empire was a federation with each of its states keeping some autonomy.

Before 1600 the small kingdom of Prussia had been in modern day Poland. By 1871 it had grown to become the leading force in a new German Empire with its capital in the Brandenburg capital of Berlin.

With the unification, we also see at least three major tensions which would have repercussions on politics in the years up to the Great War, and in its aftermath:
- France's loss of face and payment of major war reparations in the catastrophe of the Franco-Prussian War combined with a desire to gain back Alsace and Lorraine;
- The unresolved issue of Schleswig and Holstein;
- A new and powerful Empire in the middle of Europe sandwiched between Russia to the east, France to the west and Austria to the south.

Part 2: The Rise & Decline of the Ottoman Empire

By 1430, the Byzantine Empire (Eastern Roman Empire) had lost all its cities in Asia Minor and was reduced to a small area around its capital Constantinople (Istanbul) plus the Despotate of Morea (Peloponnese, in Greece). In 1453, the Ottoman Turks captured Constantinople which led to a fast expansion of their empire under a succession of strong Sultans including Suleiman the Magnificent

(1520-1566).

1460 Morea	1521 Serbia
1461 Trebizond (northern Turkey)	1529 1st siege of Vienna (failed)
1463 Bosnia	1533 Iraq
1478 Albania	1547 Hungary (divided with Austria)
1516 Syria and Palestine	1551 Libya
1517 Egypt	1570 Cyprus
	1574 Tunisia

1590 The Caucasus and western Iran

These successes led to an empire that dominated the eastern and southern Mediterranean and stretched to the Persian Gulf *(see map)*. However that era was followed by a period of weak Sultans. Also, as a response to the might of the Ottoman army, European technology had advanced ... Leonardo da Vinci for example was at the height of his career between 1476 and 1513. The Ottomans began to fall behind militarily. The Turks' monopoly of the Mediterranean led Europe to seek new trade routes to Asia, with the Portuguese discovering the Cape of Good Hope route (southern Africa) to India and China. The new Spanish and Portuguese empires in South America were also bringing in large amounts of gold and silver to Europe with a knock-on

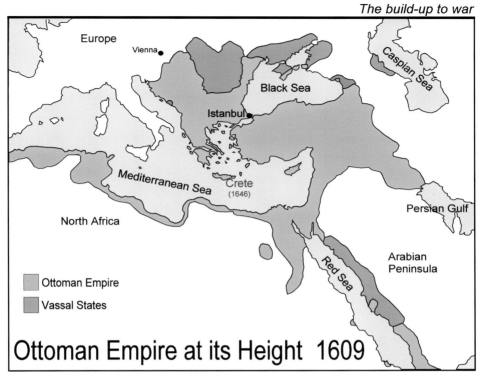

Europe

Vienna•

Black Sea

Caspian Sea

Istanbul•

Mediterranean Sea

Crete
(1646)

Persian Gulf

North Africa

Arabian
Peninsula

Red Sea

█ Ottoman Empire

█ Vassal States

Ottoman Empire at its Height 1609

effect of massive inflation of the Ottoman currency.

Two Ottoman defeats led to a western realisation that they were not invincible. In 1571, a Spanish-led fleet destroyed the main Ottoman fleet at the Battle of Lepanto (western Greece). This was mostly of symbolic importance as ships could quickly be rebuilt. Then in the Great Turkish War (1683-87) a large Ottoman army laid siege yet again to Vienna, but at the Battle of Vienna (1683) the Ottomans were overwhelmed by combined armies of the Holy Roman Empire and Poland under the Polish King Jan III Sobieski. The Ottomans surrendered several significant border territories.

Russian expansion was the next big threat to the Ottomans. Sultan Ahmed III declared war on Russia (1710), but Russia under Peter the Great invaded Moldavia (now Moldova) and Wallachia (now part of Rumania). The Ottomans defeated the Russians in the Pruth River Campaign of 1710-11, but later lost the Austro-Turkish War (1716-18) and ceded Serbia and Oltenia (now south-west Rumania) to Austria. In the Austro-Russian-Turkish War (1735-39), the Turks regained Serbia and Oltenia, but lost Azov, a strategic Black Sea port north of the Crimea, to Russia.

The rise of Prussia took the Russians' and Austrians' minds off Turkey for several decades, but eventually several defeats by Russia showed that Peter the Great's reforms had put Turkey at a disadvantage and that modernisation was needed. But reforms of the army were not made possible until the elite but

Pre-War

politically powerful Janissary army corps was abolished in 1826.

Meanwhile in the early 1800s nationalism arose in the Balkans. First the Serbian rebellion against Janissary cruelty (1804-15) resulted in its virtual independence in 1830. The Greeks rebelled in 1821 (Greek War of Independence 1821-32). The poet Lord Byron had actively funded and campaigned in this war and died of wounds in 1824. Eventually through the Treaty of London (1827), Britain, Russia and France forced Turkey to grant the Greeks autonomy within the Empire and the allied powers sent a combined fleet to the area to ensure that the treaty's terms were complied with.

Later that year, the commander of the Ottoman Mediterranean fleet stationed at Navarino Bay, on the western coast of the Peloponnese, demanded that the allied fleet withdraw. When they did not, the Turks opened fire on the allies but the Turkish fleet was destroyed by superior weaponry. Navarino was the last major naval battle fought entirely between sailing ships and it saved the new autonomous Greek Republic, though the war carried on until 1832 before Greek independence was secure and Ottoman forces were repelled form the Peloponnese. By this time the Ottoman Empire had acquired the nickname of the "sick man" of Europe.

Modernisation and secularisation were gathering pace in the mid to late 1800s with constitutional, legal, banking and army reforms. The Ottoman Ministry of Post was set up in October 1840 only a few months after the Penny Black postage stamp was issued in Britain (May 1840).

The decline of the Ottoman Empire caused Austria and Russia in particular to set their sights on influence over territories in the Empire adjoining their own borders. The Crimean War (1853-56) was part of this, where Russia demanded the right to safeguard the orthodox Christian population of the Ottoman Empire. Britain and France sought to support Turkey in order to preserve the status quo. During the Crimean War at the Siege of Sevastopol (1854-55) British engineers laid a railway line to transport field guns and ammunition from the port. Troops dug earthworks to enable them to get closer to the Russian defences and, in response, the Russians dug rifle pits to protect their snipers firing back. This was a foretaste of the more developed trench warfare that was to become a key ingredient in many sectors of the Great War.

Although the Turks and their allies were ultimately the victors, the cost of the war was crippling to the Empire and led to major foreign debt and population turmoil including emigration, ethnic cleansing and exile. Numbers from different sources vary but perhaps a million or more were deported, exiled or killed.

By 1870, Wallachia and Moldavia were independent and Montenegro virtually so.

A few years later Russia won the Russo-Turkish War (1877-78) and the Ottoman Empire lost control of Bulgaria. Serbia achieved full independence as did Montenegro and Rumania - although Transylvania (the north-western part of modern Rumania) was still part of the Austrian Empire. Austria annexed Bosnia-Herzegovina and the Sanjak of Novi Pazar, a strategic strip of land between Serbia and Montenegro, and defeated an Ottoman army sent to recover them within three weeks.

Always trying to restore the status quo, Benjamin Disraeli, the British Prime Minister, argued at the Congress of Berlin (1878) that the Ottoman territories in the Balkans should be restored to the Empire. Though Britain's view failed, the Sultan in gratitude allowed Britain to take over the administration of Cyprus. Then in 1882, Britain was invited to send troops to Egypt and Sudan to put down a revolt but ended up controlling those countries - strategically very important in securing the independence of the Suez Canal (opened in 1869) and the sea route to British India.

- - - - -

A major power before the late 1600s, the Ottoman Empire had become weak and was disintegrating both from revolt within and from the rise of technologically superior powers surrounding it. The scene was being set for major conflicts of interest in the Balkans as Britain and France tried to create trade routes through the Mediterranean while Russia and Austria sought increased influence in the fledgling states.

In this period we have seen:
- Revolt in the Balkans and positioning by the Great Powers;
- The last naval battle under sail power;
- Advances in military transport and weaponry plus new tactics to fight wars under those conditions including early forms of trench warfare;
- Attempts at modernisation of the Ottoman state in response to changing conditions outside.

Part 3: The Austro-Hungarian Empire

From the History lessons of my schooldays, I seem to remember the Austro-Hungarian Empire being referred to as the "Empire of a Thousand Tongues". I've 'Googled' it more recently but can't find the term being used. But it fits that rather strange empire very well.

We first met Austria in Part 1, when we found that it was a survivor of the Napoleonic wars against the Holy Roman Empire, being Emperor Francis II's personal lands. With the emergence of Prussia after Waterloo, Austria was marginalised from the "North German" mainstream and went its own way … south and east.

From the English spelling, Austria is very confusable with "Australia" and the idea of "South" - from Latin *australis*. But it is more understandable from the German: Austria is an English mis-hearing of Oesterreich (Österreich) meaning "Eastern land".

Much of the politics, confrontation and agreements between the neighbouring empires has been covered in the first two parts, so it may suffice to summarise the Austrian position. In the Napoleonic Wars, coming out of the defeated Holy Roman Empire in 1805-6, the Austrian Empire, with its capital in Vienna, lost its surviving territories in the northern German area of Hanover which became a

Pre-War

The Austro-Hungarian Empire

A map of the different ethnic groups in Austria-Hungary around 1910

separate kingdom under the political control of Britain whose king was George III (House of Hanover, of course) and this control survived into Victorian times. By 1866 after various wars with Prussia and Italy, Austria left the stage of northern German affairs and started looking to cementing an empire with Hungary, large amounts of whose lands the Austrian king already owned as personal possessions, but which were in revolt against their Austrian overlord, culminating in the "Year of Revolutions" (1848). 20 years of instability led to a Union agreement in 1867, known by the German word *Ausgleich*, under which the Austrian Empire became the Austro-Hungarian Empire, and Hungary and the Hungarian lands obtained equal status with the rest of Austria as a whole. Emperor Franz Joseph I of Austria (grandson of Francis II) was crowned King of Hungary, thus it was also known as The Dual Monarchy.

Austria and Hungary shared a common currency (the krone) but otherwise they operated completely independently from one another. Also as an Empire with hugely different ethic groups its internal politics were mainly those of dispute. With twin capitals at Vienna and Buda (Pest was the other side of the Danube), the Empire contained Bosnians, Croatians, Czechs, Germans, Hungarians, Italians, Poles, Rumanians, Serbs, Slovaks, Slovenes and Ukrainians all speaking different languages or dialects and with different ethnic ambitions. It was often regarded more as a "Prison of Nations" than a nation.

The Dual Monarchy, after the Prussian and Italian wars, turned its attention to the Balkans. Here the lands were in turmoil as local nationalists sought to end the rule of the Ottoman Empire. In this region Austria came into political conflict with Russia. Since before the Crimean War, Russia had taken on the self-appointed role of "Protector of Orthodox Christianity" and now was looking to add "Protector of the Slavs" to its title. Meanwhile Austria was on the path towards a multi-ethnic empire which would be as religiously varied as its cultures - Catholics, Protestants, Orthodox Christians, Jews, Muslims. Gyula Andrássy, a Hungarian, was Foreign Minister of the Empire (1871-79) and he opposed Russian plans in the Balkans. He also blocked Serbia's ideas of domination in a new southern Slav federation. The third plank of his diplomacy was that he wanted Germany to ally with Austria, not Russia.

Russia defeated Turkey in the Russo-Turkish War (1877-78); Austria felt that the Treaty of San Stefano, which ended it, favoured Russia. As part of a series of international treaty summits, the Congress of Berlin in 1878 allowed Austria to occupy the province of Bosnia and Herzegovina, a predominantly Slav area. It specifically did not allow Austria to annex Bosnia ... but that is another part of the story.

Here we see:
- An empire which is a hotchpotch of nationalities ...
- ... all with their own ambitions
- the empire seemingly seeking even more diversity in Balkan affairs.
- A policy of rapprochement with Germany.
- A recipe for regional instability as we shall later find.

Part 4: Italian Unification - the Risorgimento

When Charles II of Spain died childless in November 1700, he left the crown to Philip, the grandson of the Bourbon king Louis XIV's of France. He was proclaimed Philip V of Spain. However there was another potential heir to the throne from the Austrian Habsburg side of the family. Spain's large possessions in Europe, including much of Italy, together with an overseas empire caused concern. A Bourbon on the throne was seen by Britain (England and Scotland to 1707) and the Holy Roman Empire (the Empire) as a threat to the balance of power if French influence were to stretch from South America to the Adriatic.

The result was the War of the Spanish Succession (1701-1714) with Britain, the Empire and the Netherlands supporting a Habsburg heir and France, Savoy and Bavaria supporting Philip. The allies under the leadership of the Duke of Marlborough were successful against France and the Spanish European territories, but made little headway in Spain itself. By 1714, in the Treaty of Utrecht, Philip V was confirmed king of a united Spain but renounced all rights to the throne of France. The Spanish territories in Europe were partitioned. Austria received the Spanish Netherlands (mainly Belgium and Luxembourg), Naples, Milan and Sardinia. Savoy gained Sicily and Britain received Gibraltar and Menorca.

Philip didn't let things lie and tried to retake the lost Italian territories. The

Pre-War

War of the Quadruple Alliance (1717-1720) saw the defeat of Spain by an alliance of Britain, France, Austria and the Dutch Republic. Savoy later joined the coalition as the fifth ally. After that war, Victor Amadeus II, Duke of Savoy, Prince of Piedmont and King of Sicily, ceded Sicily to Austria and received Sardinia in exchange (1720). The kingdom of Sardinia had existed since the 14th century, so Victor Amadeus retained the title of king and renamed his lands the Kingdom of Sardinia although Savoy was still the more important part.

Following the French Revolution, a monarchist coalition, led by the Empire, Prussia, Great Britain and Sardinia (the First Coalition) invaded France in 1792 with the aim of stemming the spread of revolution outside France and perhaps reversing the revolution itself. By 1796, a French army under Napoleon Bonaparte invaded Italy to take Sardinia out of the war but went on the conquer the whole of the Italian peninsular. Later, as Emperor of France, Napoleon styled himself King of Italy.

After the Battle of Waterloo (1815) and the end of the Napoleonic era, the separate kingdoms within Italy were restored except for Austria's annexation of the Republic of Venice (including its Istrian and Dalmatian coast territories), and the incorporation of the Republic of Genoa into the Kingdom of Sardinia. Pope Pius VII expelled from the Papal States by Napoleon was restored.

Harsh French rule had stirred popular opinion for a change in governance and the just restoring the old semi-feudal kingdoms was not the answer. Dreams of a united Italy under local rule were reignited.

Insurrections (1820-21) in the Two Sicilies against King Ferdinand I, and in Piedmont and Milan to remove the Austrians were all put down. However, the revolutionaries flew the green, white, and red tricolore of the Cisalpine Republic that had existed in northern Italy in the time of Bonaparte.

The Duke of Modena, Francis IV, hoped to become king of Northern Italy but needed to increase his territory to do so. He stated (1826) that he would not prosecute any faction that was in favour of the unification of Italy. France had another revolution in 1830 and Charles X abdicated to be replaced by a constitutional monarch Louis-Philippe. France said it would intervene if Austria tried to interfere in Italy with troops. When an uprising occurred in Modena, Louis-Philippe didn't intervene, the Duke of Modena abandoned the revolutionaries and executed the leaders.

Insurrections arose in the Papal Legations regions of Bologna, Ferrara, Ravenna, Forlì, Ancona and Perugia all adopting the tricolore. These together with other regions of the Papal Legations proclaimed the creation of a united Central Italian nation. Revolts in Parma caused Duchess Marie Louise to leave the city. All these provinces planned to unite as the *Province Italiane Unite* (United Italian Provinces). The Pope (now Gregory XVI) asked for Austrian help against the rebels. Austria warned France it could not ignore the Italian situation and would not tolerate French intervention. The Austrian army marched across Italy in 1831 crushing resistance.

Attilio and Emilio Bandiera, brothers and members of the *Giovine Italia*, a political unification movement founded in 1831 by Giuseppe Mazzini for Italian youth (under age 40), made a sea raid (1844) against the Two Sicilies in support of Italian Unification. The promised local support was not there and they were betrayed and executed. The authorities were widely condemned for this action.

Yet another revolution in France overthrew Louis-Philippe and established the Second Republic.

Further tensions in Lombardy in 1848 included a civil disobedience strike: citizens stopped smoking cigars and playing the lottery, both sources of Austrian tax revenue; there were revolts in Milan and Venice against Austria. Charles Albert, now King of Sardinia declared war on Austria in 1848 (1st Italian War of Independence): Sardinia's defeat at Custoza meant Austria regained control of all of Lombardy and Venetia except for Venice itself which was set up as the Republic of San Marco.

When a revolutionary band, including Giuseppe Garibaldi and Mazzini, arrived in Rome in late 1848, Pius IX fled from the city. Elections in 1849 created a Roman Republic. France still occupied most of the Papal States and wanted to restore the Pope. After a two-month siege, Rome capitulated in 1849 and the Pope was restored. Garibaldi and Mazzini fled into exile, Garibaldi to New York City.

Meanwhile, Charles Albert of Sardinia renewed the war with Austria but was quickly defeated on 23 March 1849. Austria besieged Venice, defended by volunteers, and took the city in August. 1849. They conducted a mass hanging of independence fighters and set off to quell the rebellions in central Italy. Charles Albert abdicated in favour of his son, Victor Emmanuel II.

If the unification of Italy was going to happen, it needed a strong leadership. Republicanism wasn't providing it and the strongest Italian monarchy was still Sardinia, and specifically Piedmont. But none of them was a match for France and Austria. As the only potential ally, France needed to be offered whatever was necessary for military assistance in pushing Austria out. Victor Emmanuel ceded Savoy and Nice to France in 1860.

The Sardinian Prime Minister Count Cavour signed a secret alliance with Napoleon III, Emperor of France during the Second Empire period. Cavour also provoked Austria with military manoeuvres and effectively manufactured the 2nd Italian War of Independence in April 1859, calling on volunteers to enlist for

Pre-War

liberation. The Austrians hopes of beating Sardinia before the French could come to their aid were dashed by incompetence slowing their advance. They retreated in the face of the combined French and Sardinian forces and were then defeated by the French at the Battle of Solferino. Lombardy was annexed by Sardinia but Austria retained control of Venice.

Giuseppe Garibaldi, born in Nice, deeply resented the French annexation of his home city and hoped to use his supporters to regain the territory. Cavour feared a war with France and persuaded Garibaldi to use his forces in Sicilian rebellions instead. In May 1860, Garibaldi and his Italian volunteer force of about a thousand men (known as *"i Mille"*) landed on the west coast of Sicily.

Garibaldi's army grew as bands of rebels joined him and he proclaimed himself "Dictator of Sicily in the name of Victor Emmanuel". He laid siege to the Sicilian capital, Palermo, which caused a mass uprising in the city in his favour. The army of the Two Sicilies bombarded the city causing severe ruin. The Two Sicilies forces withdrew, after an armistice, leaving Garibaldi holding the capital. Messina fell to Garibaldi a few weeks later giving him complete control of the island of Sicily. As Garibaldi crossed to the mainland, Basilicata and Apulia, cities of the Two Sicilies, declared their annexation to the Kingdom of Sardinia.

By September 1860, Naples (capital of the Two Sicilies) declared a state of siege and its king retreated from the city with the 4,000 troops of the city garrison. The next day, Garibaldi entered Naples by train and was openly welcomed by the people.

Garibaldi's irregulars now amounted to some 25,000 men but they did not have the strength to match the Neapolitan army nor take the fortresses of Capua and Gaeta. To do so required help from the Sardinian army but Rome and the Papal States lay between the two territories. Garibaldi made known his intention to proclaim a "Kingdom of Italy" from Rome, but Pope Pius IX saw this as a threat to Catholicism rather than an advance of Italy and threatened excommunication for any who supported it. The stand-off was resolved when Napoleon III allowed the Sardinian army free passage to take Naples and Umbria as long as Rome and the "Patrimony of St Peter" were untouched. A Sardinian force of two army corps advanced into Papal territories and were met by the papal army, but after a brief conflict the papal forces surrendered. On 9 October 1860, Victor Emmanuel II arrived and took command, and the march south proceeded. Garibaldi willingly handed over his dictatorial power to Victor Emmanuel II, greeting him with the title of King of Italy and they entered Naples side by side. Garibaldi then retired to the island of Caprera, off the north coast of the island of Sardinia, leaving Victor Emmanuel to complete the unification of Italy, but only Rome and Venice remained outside the union.

The first Italian Parliament met in Turin in February 1861 and, in March, proclaimed Victor Emmanuel as King of Italy. On 27 March 1861 Rome was declared the capital ... even though it was not yet in the new kingdom.

There good reasons not to attack the Papal States. International Catholicism was wary of it and there were still French troops in Rome. Victor Emmanuel pulled back on support for revolutionary action. Garibaldi was frustrated by this and came out of retirement. In June 1862, he landed again at Palermo proclaiming *"o Roma o Morte"* (either Rome or Death). He landed with a force of some 4,000 on the mainland in August and marched into the Calabrian mountains. This territory, once part of the Two Sicilies, was by now of course part of Victor Emmanuel's new Italy and the Italian government disapproved, sending a division of the army against Garibaldi. On 28 August the two forces met in the Aspromonte where one of the Italian regulars fired a chance shot, and several volleys followed. Garibaldi told his men not to return fire on fellow Italians. Garibaldi's volunteers suffered casualties and he himself was wounded. He was imprisoned for a while but then released.

Victor Emmanuel negotiated with Napoleon III for the removal of French troops and in September 1864 Napoleon agreed to do so within two years, but the Pope would be allowed to increase his own army in that time. In December 1866, the French troops left Rome. There were now no foreign troops in Italy apart from those in Venice and Savoy. The parliament was moved to Florence in 1865 from the old Sardinian capital of Turin.

By this time Austria was contesting the leadership of the German states with Prussia (Austro-Prussian War, 1866). Italy saw a chance to regain Venetia from Austria so allied itself with Prussia, signing an agreement that supported Italy's acquisition of Venetia. Even though Austria offered Venetia in exchange for non-intervention, Italy declared war on Austria (3rd Italian War of Independence, 1866).

Victor Emmanuel led an army to invade Venetia, while Garibaldi invaded the Tyrol with his Hunters of the Alps. Austria defeated the Italians at Custoza and Lissa, but Garibaldi's volunteers were successful at Bezzecca and advanced to Trento. After Prussia's own aims had been met, Otto von Bismarck signed an armistice with Austria on 27 July and Italy ceased fire 16 days later. However, Prussia's success in the north meant that they could honour their alliance with Italy and obliged Austria to cede Venetia to Italy.

In 1867 Garibaldi made a second attempt to capture Rome but was defeated by the Papal army and French forces. But with the start of the Franco-Prussian War in July 1870, Napoleon III recalled his garrison from Rome. Victor Emmanuel II waited until the collapse of France before advancing on Rome. Pius IX commanded his troops to put up a resistance but after a three-hour cannonade the Italian force breached the city walls and the Italian army entered Rome on 20 September 1870 and marched down Via Pia, which was subsequently renamed Via XX Settembre. Rome and Latium were annexed to the Kingdom of Italy after a plebiscite held on 2 October. The unification of Italy was complete and the capital was moved from Florence to Rome in July 1871.

Unification as it had happened was really the creation of a "Greater Piedmont" as the new Kingdom of Italy was made by renaming the old Kingdom of Sardinia and annexing the new provinces into its structure. The first King of Italy was Victor Emmanuel II, who kept his old title. However, the first ten years of the new kingdom were marred by civil wars especially in Sicily and Naples with both peasant and conservative Catholic protest against the liberalism of

Pre-War

the new country. The north-south divide remains an issue to the present day.

Massimo Taparelli, Marquess of Azeglio (1798-1866), a Piedmontese politician and Prime Minister of Sardinia from 1849 to 1852, said in his memoirs, *"L'Italia è fatta. Restano da fare gli italiani"* ... "We have made Italy. Now we must make Italians."

Part 5: Britain by the early Twentieth Century

Queen Victoria's reign and the period just before it was one of major change. In the 18th century, Britain was largely an agricultural nation, although the Agricultural Revolution had mechanised many parts of it. The first national census of 1801 showed that, of a population of around 10.5 million, only 25% lived in towns and cities.

Supposedly to "solve" resentment and rebellion in Ireland, the British government passed the Acts of Union of 1800-01 and Ireland was incorporated into the United Kingdom. St Patrick was added to the Union

Queen Victoria

Flag to give the flag we know today. Problems from this union will be covered later.

In the 1790s, during the French Revolution, many of the aristocracy that controlled France had been guillotined including King Louis XVI. France descended into chaos. To avoid the same fate, things would have to change in Britain.

Our political system was based on government by the Houses of Commons and Lords made up solely of men and the Lords could overrule any law passed by the Commons. Only men with money and property could vote but no women regardless of their wealth or standing.

Population shifts to the towns showed up the absurdities of the old system. Larger towns and cities were hardly represented in parliament but in "rotten boroughs", hardly anyone could vote but they returned Members of Parliament. Of the most ludicrous, the village of Dunwich on the Suffolk coast had mostly fallen into the sea but returned 2 MPs.

In 1819 a mass meeting at St Peter's Field in Manchester heard speeches demanding parliamentary reform. Halfway through, magistrates declared the meeting illegal and sent cavalry in to break it up. In the confusion the cavalry charged the crowd with 11 killed and 400 wounded. The "massacre" was sarcastically called "Peterloo" after the British victory at Waterloo 4 years previously.

A year later, in the "Cato Street Conspiracy", radicals planned to overthrow

King William IV

the government. They were caught: five were hanged and another five transported to penal colonies in Australia. New farm and industrial machinery also threatened labourers' jobs and in the "Swing Riots" of 1830, nine men who had wrecked machines, were hanged and others transported.

Under pressure for political change in the reign of King William IV, the Great Reform Act (1832) swept away the rotten boroughs, gave more MP seats to industrial cities, and the middle class was given the right to vote. Even so, no women could vote and only one in seven men could … and voting was still done in public. The new Parliament passed acts promoting factory and mine safety and forbidding the abuse of child and women workers.

Queen Victoria came to the throne in 1837. Industry flourished in this period with the development of railways which brought a standardised time system to the country as well as improving transport. Purton got its two railways in this period: Purton Station on the Cheltenham & Great Western Union Railway opened in 1841; Blunsdon Station on the Swindon & Cheltenham Extension of the Midland & South Western Junction Railway opened in 1881.

A new postal service brought in a flat price regardless of how far the letter was going within the country - the Penny Black postage stamp. Cinema, telegraph, telephones, cars and aircraft, were also developed later in the Victorian era as well as photography whose pioneers included William Fox Talbot at Lacock.

Many of today's sports were formalised in this period: cricket, cycling, croquet, roller skating, horse riding, modern tennis and football with the Football League being set up in 1888. Swindon Town Football Club was founded in 1879 and turned professional in 1894.

Back to the political front: the 1840s saw the Opium Wars where Britain fought to preserve the right to sell opium to the Chinese and resulted in the acquisition of the New Territories of Hong Kong; Britain was at war in Afghanistan; the Irish Famine and land clearances saw mass emigration from Ireland and Scotland; and the Corn Laws were repealed - they had artificially raised the price of grain by imposing high import duties putting the price of grain products such as bread above the reach of many.

Then in the 1850s came the restoration of the Catholic Church in England and Scotland; the Great Exhibition (1851); the Crimean War (covered in Part 2); and Charles Darwin published *On the Origin of Species.*

Having lost an empire with the American War of Independence (1775-82), a new empire was being created. At the start of Queen Victoria's reign, New Zealand became a British colony (1840). Exploration and mineral finds in Africa were feeding a land grab there while the power of the Royal Navy at sea

Pre-War

brought many islands and coastal nations under the Crown. The Indian Mutiny (1857-58) showed that the British East India Company was incapable of ruling the subcontinent ... the company was abolished and India brought under direct British rule. It is really only after the acquisition of India that the term British Empire can truly be applied and the term *Indiae Imperatrix* (Empress of India) was added to Queen Victoria's title and *Ind. Imp.* to all coins up until the death of King George VI.

Victoria's consort, Prince Albert, died in 1861 leading to a long period of mourning by the Queen but, since Britain was, and is, a republic in all but name, political life went on even without the Queen's active participation. The colony of British North America became the Dominion of Canada in 1867. In 1875 Britain purchased Egypt's shares in the Suez Canal guaranteeing the sea-route to India and the East; Egypt became a British Protectorate in 1882. Under the Treaty of Berlin of 1878 (see Part 2), Cyprus became a Crown colony.

Southern Africa became a battlefield. In 1879 the Anglo-Zulu War broke out with the Battle of Isandlwana. In 1881 British forces were defeated by Boer farmers at the Battle of Majuba Hill, resulting in the reinstatement of the Afrikaner South African Republic, and ending the First Boer War.

Back at home, social reform continued: the Elementary Education Act of 1870 made basic State Education free for every child under the age of 10. Trade Unions developed for all workers and led to the birth of the Labour Party.

On the political front, between 1867 and 1872 the Second and Third Reform Acts moved more constituencies from rural areas to towns and cities and brought the electorate up to 5 million though suffrage, the right to vote, was still restricted to wealth and being a man. The total population at the time was about 30 million - 3 times that of 1801. In 1872 the Secret Ballot Act allowed people to vote without risk of recriminations from landlords and employers. Women demanded the right to vote and the Suffragette movement was born ... more on this in a later article.

County councils and county borough councils were created in England and Wales in 1888 and in 1894 Parish Councils took over civic duties in rural towns and villages from the ecclesiastical parishes. These civil parishes, including Purton Parish Council, were grouped into rural districts - Purton was part of the Cricklade & Wootton Bassett Rural District.

The century ended with more military activity. In 1898, at the battle of Omdurman, British and Egyptian troops led by Horatio Kitchener defeated an uprising against Turkish-Egyptian rule in the Sudan and brought the Sudan under British control. Winston Churchill took part in that battle and there is a wonderful military depiction of the battle in Purton Museum.

Further south again, the Second Boer War started in 1899 between Britain and the independent Boer republics. The 2nd Battalion of the Wiltshire Regiment (2nd Wilts) was stationed in Guernsey but was dispatched to South Africa, brigaded into the 12th Brigade and assigned to garrison the town of Rensburg, where the 2nd Wilts lost 14 men killed, 57 wounded, and more than 100 prisoners taken. The Wiltshires were pulled back to prevent a Boer break-through, but two companies, on outpost duty, didn't receive the order to retreat. They got back to their battalion's main camp to find it occupied by the Boers and were taken prisoner.

The 2nd Wilts, with the 12th Brigade were sent to capture Christiaan de Wet's Boer commando stronghold at the town of Bethlehem. The town was captured and the brigade followed de Wet to Slabbert's Nek (July 1900) where, with the Royal Irish Regiment, two companies of the 2nd Wilts took 4,000 prisoners. De Wet and a few of his men managed to escape and the Boer War moved into a guerrilla phase. The 2nd Wilts were reassigned to patrol areas north of Pretoria and later to defend the Pretoria-Pietersburg railway line. In early summer 1901, the Wiltshires helped capture 229 Boer commandos and 18 wagons.

In 1902, the Second Boer War ended with the defeat of the Boer commandos and the signing of the Treaty of Vereeniging. The 2nd Wiltshires returned to England in 1903. There must have been Purton men in the Boer War and I would love to know if anyone in Purton has family memories of the Wiltshires' time in South Africa.

In the meantime, Queen Victoria had died in 1901 and the British Royal House changed from Hanover to Saxe-Coburg Gotha with the accession of her son King Edward VII. A new era had begun.

Part 6: Russia in Late Tsarist Days

The Russian Empire played a leading political role in the 19th century but its retention of serfdom (feudal slavery) made economic progress impossible. While the West grew during the Industrial Revolution, Russia lagged behind, stifling its potential as a great power. It had inefficient government and an isolated population due to its sheer size; it was backward economically and in education. Tsar Alexander I had discussed minor constitutional reforms, but only a few had been introduced.

Napoleon had invaded Russia in 1812, a campaign which turned to catastrophe, and his forces were chased back to the gates of Paris by Alexander's troops. Alexander I died of typhus in 1825 and was replaced by his younger brother, Nicholas I (1825-55). A number of educated Russian officers had travelled in Europe in the Napoleonic campaigns, and seen the strength of Western liberalism and sought change in autocratic Russia. In the Decembrist Revolt (December 1825), liberal nobles and army officers moved to overthrow Nicholas and install his brother, Grand Duke Constantine Pavlovich, as constitutional monarch. The revolt was put down and Nicholas turned even further from modernisation. State retaliation made "14th December" stick in the memories of later revolutionaries. Censorship intensified, textbooks were strictly regulated and police spies were everywhere. Hundreds of thousands of revolutionaries were sent to prison camps and exile in Siberia.

Russia's involvement in the Crimean War (1853-56) showed that the country, previously felt to be invincible, had declined against the West and

Pre-War

Nicholas died in 1855 with the future direction of Russia in turmoil.

Alexander II acceded in 1855, with a widespread call for reform in the air: more than 23 million serfs lived under atrocious conditions of poverty. The emancipation of the serfs in 1861 by the Tsar's decree was perhaps the single most important event in 19th century Russian history: it set in train the end for the aristocracy's monopoly of power, as it brought a supply of labour to the cities which stimulated industry and the growth of a middle class. Although serfdom was abolished, revolutionaries felt that the newly freed serfs were merely sold into wage slavery in the industrial towns, and that the bourgeoisie had replaced the landowners' yoke.

Meanwhile, in the east, Alexander II occupied Chinese Outer Manchuria (1858-60) but sold Alaska to the USA in 1867 believing it worthless. There were many clashes from the late 1870s between Russia and the Ottoman Empire covered in Part 2. Russia was taking on the mantle of Protector of the Slavs within the Ottoman domains.

Alexander was assassinated by anarchist terrorists in 1881, and his son became Tsar Alexander III (1881-94). He believed Russia could only be saved from turmoil by cutting itself off from the liberal politics of the West. During his reign Russia sealed an alliance with republican France (1894) to contain the growing power of Germany, completed the conquest of the Central Asian khanates (tribal regions) and demanded important territorial and commercial concessions from a very weak China. A policy of Russianisation was carried out throughout the Empire.

In 1894, Alexander III was succeeded by his son, Nicholas II, who was as autocratic as his father. Industry continued to grow and, in that climate, socialist and revolutionary parties were formed: the Socialist-Revolutionaries proposed the distribution of land among those who actually worked it - the peasants. The Social Democrats, followers of Karl Marx, believed a revolution must rely on urban workers, not the peasantry.

The Social Democrat party's 2nd Congress was held in 1903 in London as it was impossible to do so in Russia. At the Congress, after bitter disagreement, the party split into two wings - the gradualist Mensheviks (literally 'minority'), and the more radical Bolsheviks ('majority'). The Menshevik liberals believed the Russian working class wasn't politically aware enough and that socialism could be achieved only after a period of bourgeois democratic rule. The Bolsheviks, led by Vladimir Lenin, believed a small elite of professional revolutionaries, subject to strong party discipline, could act as the spearhead of the workers (proletariat) in seizing power by force.

As though that wasn't enough, the Russo-Japanese War (1904-05) was "the first great war of the 20th century." It grew out of rival ambitions of the Russian Empire and the Empire of Japan over Manchuria and Korea.

Russia had long sought a warm water port on the Pacific Ocean, for their navy as well as for trade. Vladivostok was frozen up in winter but Russia had leased Port Arthur (modern-day Lüshunkou), a naval base on the Yellow Sea coast across the sheltered sea from Beijing; its waters were open all year. From

1903, negotiations between Russia and Japan proved impractical. Japan offered to recognise Russian dominance in Manchuria in exchange for recognition of Korea as a Japanese sphere of influence. Russia refused and in 1904 the Japanese Navy attacked the Russian eastern fleet at Port Arthur. The Japanese defeated the Russians in a series of battles on land and at sea.

Construction of the Trans-Siberian Railway had started in 1890 to connect Moscow with Vladivostok. Its design was a major cause of Russia losing the war as the single track only allowed trains to move in one direction at a time. Russian supply trains taking men and munitions towards the eastern front had to wait while troops and casualties went from east to west along the line. The Japanese advanced quickly while the Russians waited for troops and supplies.

The Japanese military successes over the Russians, startled the rest of the world. The balance of power in East Asia was shifting as Japan entered onto the world stage. The U.S. President Theodore Roosevelt negotiated the Treaty of Portsmouth (New Hampshire) which brought the war to an end and for which he won the Nobel Peace Prize in 1906. Defeat was a major blow to the Tsarist regime and further increased the potential for unrest.

A religious teacher at a children's orphanage, Father Gapon, had been active with factory workers and families impoverished by unemployment. In January 1905, Gapon led a huge crowd to the Tsar's Winter Palace in Saint Petersburg to present a petition. When the procession reached the palace, Cossacks opened fire on the crowd, killing hundreds, and the incident went down in history as "Bloody Sunday". A general strike was declared against the massacre, demanding a democratic republic and beginning the Russian Revolution of 1905. Soviets (councils of workers) appeared in most cities to direct revolutionary activity. Russia was paralysed.

Under pressure, Nicholas reluctantly issued the October 1905 Manifesto, creating a national Duma (parliament), extending the right to vote and decreeing that no new law could be enacted without ratification by the Duma. Moderates were satisfied but the socialists saw the concessions as too little and tried to organise new strikes. By the end of 1905, there was disunity among the reformers, and the Tsar's position was strengthened … for the time being.

In 1904, Nicholas and his wife, Tsarina Alexandra had their first son, Alexei. However, Alexei inherited haemophilia from his mother. The search for a cure for Alexei led to the rise of the Siberian peasant Grigori Rasputin at court; though semi-literate he was said to have healing powers. He gained increasing influence on the court, especially the Tsarina, and hence over the Tsar himself. This was to have major repercussions as we shall see later.

By the early 20th century, the size of the Russian Empire was about 22.4 million km^2 (8.6 million sq miles) or almost one-sixth of the Earth's landmass; its only rival in size was the British Empire. The Empire comprised more than 100 different ethnic groups, with ethnic Russians comprising about 45% of the population. However the majority of the population lived in European Russia.

Pre-War

Part 7: Empire, Entente & Alliance

So far we've looked at the major powers of Europe, individually and in context with their neighbours. It's now time to put their relationships together. Frictions between these large empires brought a major European War ever closer.

Looked at from the German and Austro-Hungarian perspective, they were pretty much tied to Europe while Britain and France had developed empires around the world in Africa, Asia, the Pacific and, in Britain's case, Canada, India, Australia, New Zealand, strategic island bases in every continent and ocean, plus South Africa and virtually the full length of Africa from Cairo to Cape Town apart from a gap at German East Africa (modern-day Tanzania).

Russia was gaining spheres of influence in the south-east of Europe and in Asia, while even little Belgium owned the huge territory of the Congo in Africa.

Germany had little access to the sea. It had a long Baltic coast but this was inaccessible to the outside world without the tedious circumnavigation of Denmark. Its North Sea coast between Holland and Denmark was short, low-lying and too close to Britain for comfort. A canal linking Kiel on the Baltic to Brunsbüttel on the North Sea was opened in 1895, but mainly as a commercial link.

The German Foreign Minister, Bismarck saw threats of war especially from Russia and set up a system of alliances to prevent war or at least limit its effects. In 1879, Germany and Austria-Hungary signed the Dual Alliance agreeing to aid one another in case of an attack by Russia. It was quite a surprising alliance: though both countries spoke German, they were culturally very different. With a mix of nationalities within its borders, Austria felt that nationalism would destroy it; Germany was nothing if not nationalistic. But a common fear of Russia brought them together.

In 1882 this was extended into the Triple Alliance between Germany, Austria-Hungary and Italy, each promising support in the event of attack by any other great power. Germany separately agreed the same terms with Italy in the event of an attack by France. Italy however specified that the Alliance would not be regarded as being directed against Britain.

This alliance left Russia feeling vulnerable. Also France, isolated since defeat in the 1871 Franco-Prussian War, needed a friend. From 1888, France provided cheap loans to Russia to allow it to rebuild its military and to build strategic railways that could bring troops to Russia's German border. The Franco-Russian alliance (1894) agreed that if one of the countries of the Triple Alliance attacked France or Russia, the other ally would attack that aggressor so, if Germany attacked either France or Russia, it would be fighting a war on 2 fronts.

Britain had maintained a state of "Glorious Isolation" from mainland Europe for many decades, but had a national loss of confidence after the long drawn-out Second Boer War ... an Empire struggling to conquer farmers. She was also feeling isolated against the growing power of Germany. At the same time, relations had been improving with the "old enemy" France. In 1904 the Entente Cordiale was signed between UK and France. This was not an Alliance but a

"Friendly Agreement" though it settled many long-standing issues including France recognising British control over Egypt, and Britain accepting French control in Morocco.

In response to the Entente, in 1905, Kaiser Wilhelm II of Germany landed at Tangier in Morocco declaring he supported the sovereignty of the Moroccan Sultan Abdelaziz, a major challenge to French influence. The Sultan invited the world powers to a conference to advise on reforms. Germany approved of the conference but Théophile Delcassé, the French Foreign Minister, declared it wasn't needed. The German Chancellor, Count Bernhard von Bülow threatened war, France cancelled all military leave, and Germany declared it would sign a defensive alliance with Morocco. The French Prime Minister, Maurice Rouvier, couldn't risk war with Germany, so Delcassé resigned, and France attended the conference at Algeciras, in Spain. Even as the conference started, Germany was calling up reserve units and France moved troops to the German border. With only Austria-Hungary supporting them, Germany accepted a compromise (1906), whereby France lost authority over the Moroccan police, but otherwise retained control of Morocco. Tensions between the Triple Alliance and the Entente were heightened.

This First Moroccan Crisis showed that the Entente Cordiale worked, as Britain had defended France's interests. Russia had also backed France leading to a thaw in relations between Britain and Russia. The Anglo-Russian Convention (1907) solved long-standing issues between the two in Central Asia, particularly over Russia's involvement in the Caucasus and its relationship with British India. It also created a political alliance against the growing strength of Germany. And it did little to calm a still-angry Kaiser Wilhelm II.

Since France was already in alliance with Russia, it was an obvious step to conclude the Triple Entente linking Russia, France and Britain, with additional agreements with Portugal and Japan. However ententes aren't alliances and those counties mainly agreed they would support each others' interests and wouldn't go to war against each other. But it was still seen as a strong political response to the Triple Alliance of Germany, Austria-Hungary, and Italy.

In 1911, a rebellion broke out in Fez, the capital of Morocco, against the new Sultan, Abdelhafid, elder bother of Abdelaziz. In April, France sent troops to put down the rebellion and protect European lives and property. In June, the Spanish army occupied Larache and Ksar-el-Kebir. In July, Germany sent the gunboat Panther to Agadir supposedly to protect German trade interests.

Britain's Foreign Secretary, Sir Edward Grey, believed that the Panther's presence showed German ambitions to turn Agadir into a naval base on the Atlantic as a provocative challenge to the Royal Navy's base at Gibraltar and sent battleships to Morocco in case war broke out. While this was going on, a German stock market crisis resulted in a fall of 30% in a single day, there was a run on the banks and the Reichsbank lost a fifth of its gold reserves in one month. The crisis at home forced Germany to back down and let France take over most of Morocco.

In 1912, the Treaty of Fez recognised Morocco as a French Protectorate

Pre-War

while Germany received French territories in Africa: Middle Congo (now the Republic of the Congo or Congo-Brazzaville), New Kamerun and Togoland. Abdelhafid was far from happy.

Britain and France made a naval agreement with the Royal Navy promising to protect the northern coast of France from German attack, so France could concentrate her fleet in the western Mediterranean and protect British interests there. France was better able to support her North African colonies, and Britain could concentrate more force in home waters to oppose the German High Seas Fleet. Abdelhafid abdicated.

By 1912, the world was split into 2 major power blocs: Germany, Austria-Hungary and Italy were bound into the Triple Alliance of Central European Powers, with only a few overseas possessions to give them a presence outside Europe. They saw themselves surrounded by the alliance of France and Russia … and their friend Britain … together with substantial worldwide territories.

Each side's international treaties were seen as a threat to the other … and vice-versa! War had been narrowly averted in 1906 and 1911, but the world was still living on a powder keg.

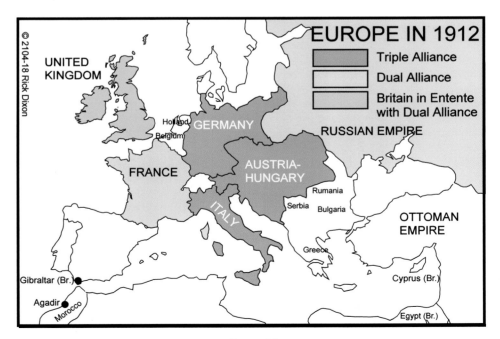

Part 8: Steel, Gunboats & Ironclads

We have looked at the world politics of the early 20th century. What lay beneath that at the industrial and military level?

Industrialisation in the 19th century had made major changes to people's lives in much of Europe but it had also added to the engineering capabilities of those countries. Steel-making in particular saw major advances with the Bessemer furnace process of the early to mid-1800s being replaced by the open hearth process enabling the manufacture, in vast quantities, of steel cable, steel rods, sheet steel and products from them such as high-pressure boilers and high-tensile strength steel for machinery which enabled much more powerful engines, gears and axles than were possible previously. These new products fed into railways as well as the military uses of more powerful guns and carriages, tanks and naval ships.

Naval ships built entirely from wood had been shown to be completely out of date in the face of advances in big gun technology. Armoured warships, or ironclads, were developed in the 1850s. They were steam-propelled and protected by iron or steel armour plates. France launched its first ironclad battleship, *Gloire*, in 1859. The Royal Navy started building two iron-hulled armoured frigates the same year and by 1861 had decided to construct an all-armoured battle fleet. The first naval clashes of the American Civil War (1862) showed that the ironclad was the way forward. By end of the 1890s new ships were increasingly constructed to a standard pattern and designated as battleships or armoured cruisers.

The Royal Navy's *HMS Dreadnought* (launched 1906), made such a strong impression on people's minds that similar battleships built afterwards were called "dreadnoughts", and earlier battleships became known as pre-dreadnoughts. Dreadnought's design had two revolutionary features: an "all-big-gun" armament scheme, with an unprecedented number of heavy-calibre guns, and steam turbine propulsion. The construction of these new warships renewed the naval arms race between the United Kingdom and Germany.

I briefly mentioned the Kiel Canal in Part 7. It was widened for military purposes between 1907 and 1914 specifically to be able to take Dreadnought-sized battleships.

Railways had flourished across Europe from the 1820s. The military benefits were seen very quickly and rail transport was an important factor in many conflicts including:
- the movement of Prussian Troops in 1848 to put down a revolution;
- munitions movements by Britain in the Crimean War;
- massive troop movements by train in the American Civil War;
- and again in the Boer War.

From this, and with fear of a war on two fronts, Kaiser Wilhelm II commissioned Count Alfred von Schlieffen to prepare a military plan for a potential attack on France. Schlieffen's Plan was heavily dependent on railway logistics: to win a two-front war needed a quick defeat of France in the west - 39 days were allowed

Pre-War

for the fall of Paris and 42 for the capitulation of France. Then the attack would go east: Germany intended to turn on Russia, before they were ready.

The Schlieffen Plan (1906) reversed the ideas of his predecessor, Helmuth von Moltke the Elder, whose experiences in the Franco-Prussian War had made him doubt that a swift success could be achieved. But the Japanese victory in the 1904-05 Russo-Japanese War had discredited the Russian military, and the Schlieffen Plan took Russian failure into account. The key would be a rapid German mobilisation, with disregard for the neutrality of Luxembourg, Belgium and the Netherlands and an overwhelming sweep of the powerful German right wing southwest through Belgium towards France.

Of course railway technologies took other guises in this period. In 1901 the Wuppertal Suspension Railway *(Schwebebahn)* was opened as the earliest electric elevated railway in the world with hanging cars and it is a unique system still moving 25 million passengers a year. The suspension railway runs 23 kilometres at about 12 metres above the River Wupper and was a German realisation of a British horse drawn plan of Robinson Palmer (1824). It was seen as a major advance in railway technology of its day, but was never repeated. Having travelled on it, I can recommend the experience especially if you can book into the *Kaiserwagen* in which Wilhelm II travelled on its opening run.

We saw in Part 6 that the protracted conflict of the 2nd Boer War had caused much concern in Britain - the greatest empire the world had ever known had struggled against a militia of farmers. Between 1906 and 1912, the British Secretary of State for War, Richard Burdon Haldane set in place a series of far-ranging reforms of the British army. An Expeditionary Force was formed, specifically prepared and trained for deployment in a major war. This force would have a permanent peacetime organisation and a full complement of supporting troops. Reserve forces were restructured and expanded; the Special Reserve, Volunteer Force and Yeomanry were reorganised into a new Territorial Force for home defence. An Officer Training Corps was established and military strategy was unified across the Empire and Dominions.

Major advances were also being made in the chemical industry, including the development in Germany of the Haber-Bosch process for the manufacture of ammonia, useful peacefully in the manufacture of fertilisers (ammonium nitrate/sulphate) but also as a precursor to nitric acid and its uses in pigments, inks, dyes … and military explosives.

But if engineering had thought itself supreme, it had another think coming when the *RMS Titanic* sank on her maiden voyage on 15 April 1912. So well designed, so unsinkable that it didn't need more than a few lifeboats.

The arms race and its new-fangled weaponry had brought concerns to the fore in terms of how mechanised warfare would be conducted. In 1863, during the American Civil War (1861-65), President Abraham Lincoln signed into force the Lieber Code dictating how soldiers of the Union Army should behave in wartime and covering the treatment of spies, deserters and prisoners of war. It was one of the building blocks of the Hague Conventions of 1899 and 1907. The 1899 Hague Conference defined the conditions of a state of war and the practice of war on land and sea. It also prohibited the use of asphyxiating (poison) gases, expanding bullets (dumdums) and the discharge of projectiles or explosives from balloons. It also set up a Permanent Court of Arbitration.

U.S. President Theodore Roosevelt proposed a new conference at The Hague in 1907, which was officially convened by Tsar Nicholas II of Russia and attended by representatives of 44 states. Agreements were passed concerning:

- the rights and duties of neutral powers and of participants in war on land and sea;
- the laying of automatic submarine contact mines;
- the status of enemy merchant ships;
- bombardment by naval forces in wartime;
- renewal of the declaration prohibiting the discharge of projectiles from balloons;
- acceptance of the principle of compulsory arbitration;
- recommendation that another conference be summoned in eight years, i.e. 1915; this did not happen because of the outbreak of World War I, but it influenced the creation of the more highly organised League of Nations after the war.

The Conference did not reaffirm the declarations prohibiting poison gas and expanding bullets.

Part 9: Libya & The Balkan Wars (1912-13)

Aristotle (384 - 322 BC) said that "nature abhors a vacuum" and a power vacuum was certainly around in the Balkans in the early years of the 20th century. The Ottoman Empire (Turkey) was in retreat from its European eylats (provinces) which had been under occupation for 400 or so years. The people of the Balkans were sensing freedom at last but still trying to work out who they were: Rumanians, Bulgars, Greeks, Croats, Serbs, Kosovars, Albanians … Orthodox Christians, Catholics, Muslims. And where did they live? The old Turkish eylat boundaries had little to do with population movements over several centuries.

Before all this could come to a head, Italy decided it was time to show her hand. As far back as the Congress of Berlin (1878) when Britain took over Cyprus and France took Morocco from the Ottomans, Italy had been given assurances that it would have a free hand to intervene in Libya. On 29 September 1912, in a 20-day war (the Italo-Turkish War), Italy invaded and captured the Turkish provinces of Tripolitania, Cyrenaica and Fezzan, setting up effective control there. Italy also took control of the Turkish Dodecanese islands of the Aegean including Rhodes, Kos and Samos.

It was a comparatively minor war but showed the increasing weakness of the Ottoman Empire. It also saw the first use in warfare of aeroplane

Pre-War

reconnaissance and the first bomb dropped by an aeroplane. Powered flight was a young technology having been pioneered barely 9 years before by the Wright brothers in 1903. Coincidentally, Wilbur Wright died in May 1912 so would not have seen this military innovation of the brothers' technology.

Despite Turkey's defeat, a young officer Mustafa Kemal distinguished himself at the battle of Tobruk. We shall meet him again under the name Kemal Atatürk.

Spurred on by the evidence of Ottoman weakness, and while the Italo-Turkish War was still in progress (October 1912), Bulgaria, Serbia and Montenegro allied to gain final independence from Turkey (the 1st Balkan War). The Ottoman Empire mobilised three armies against the Bulgarians, the Greeks and the Serbs. Montenegro declared war on 8 October moving towards Novi Pazar, a strip separating them from Serbia - which we first met in Part 2. The other allies joined in a week later. Bulgaria reached the outskirts of Istanbul and Gallipoli, and captured western Thrace and eastern Macedonia. Serbia took Skopje, Monastir, modern-day Albania and Kosovo to link with the forces of Montenegro. Greece attacked through Macedonia and captured Thessaloniki (Salonika), linking with the Serbs to the northwest and the Bulgarians in the east. The Ottoman fleet was twice defeated by the Greek Navy.

In January 1913, the Ottoman Empire was prepared to concede defeat but, after a successful internal coup by young army officers, decided to continue the war. However the new Balkan countries won and the war ended with the Treaty of London (1913). Turkey ceded all possessions in Europe to the Balkan allies west of a line from Enos on the Aegean Sea to Midia on the Black Sea, with the exception of Albania, while the Great Powers began to draw the lines of a new Albanian state. Turkish sovereignty over Crete was withdrawn and it was united with Greece. The future of the Aegean islands which Greece occupied was left to the Great Powers to adjudicate.

The Balkans was still in uproar. In the lead-up to the 1st Balkan War, Serbia had promised Bulgaria most of Macedonia, but then Serbia and Greece said they would keep a large part of it. The king of Bulgaria, now calling himself 'tsar' Ferdinand I, invaded his former allies, Serbia and Greece, in June 1913 without consulting his own government and without any official declaration of war (the 2nd Balkan War). Bulgaria attacked the Serbian army at the Bregalnica river and then the Greek army in Nigrita. The Serbian army resisted the sudden

Maps:1. Boundaries before the First Balkan War   2. After the Second Balkan War

night attack, while most of them did not even know who they were fighting, as Bulgarian camps were located next to Serbs and were considered allies. Montenegro's forces were just a few miles away and also rushed to the battle. The Bulgarian attack was halted.

The Greek army made a tactical retreat for two days while Thessaloniki was cleared of a Bulgarian regiment still there from the first war and then counter-attacked, defeating the Bulgarians at Kilkis-Lahanas (Kukush), destroying the town and expelling most of its Bulgarian population. The Greek army destroyed 161 Bulgarian villages and massacred thousands of inhabitants while the Bulgarians did the same to the Greeks at Nigrita, Serres, Demir Hisar and Doxato. The Greek army then occupied western Thrace and advanced north into Bulgaria towards the capital, Sofia.

But by 30 July the Greek army was outnumbered by Bulgarian counter-attacks and King Constantine of Greece realised that his army could no longer continue the war. He agreed to a Bulgarian request for armistice.

As it happened, Rumania had raised an army and declared war on Bulgaria on 10 July since Bulgaria had not made good its strategic promises to Rumania after the 1st Balkan War. The Rumanian forces had reached the outskirts of Sofia by the time Greece accepted the Bulgarian armistice proposal.

The Ottomans now decided to intervene and, finding no opposition, recovered eastern Thrace including Adrianople, regaining an area in Europe which was only slightly larger than the present-day European territory of the Republic of Turkey. The war was ended by the Treaty of Bucharest (1913).

Overall, not a lot was achieved on any side during the second war. But a lot of death, population displacement, fear and resentment was created in an area already inflamed and a key part of the international powder keg.

Part 10: The State of the World - January 1914

Britain: On the death of Edward VII, his son George V of the house of Saxe-Coburg and Gotha, ascended the British throne on 6 May 1910. In January 1914, the Prime Minister was Herbert Asquith and the Secretary of State for War was John Seely, 1st Baron Mottistone.

Irish Home Rule was high on the British political agenda with a Bill due to become law in 1914. The Curragh Mutiny of the Ulster Volunteers, occurred at the main British Army base in Kildare, Ireland (then still part of the United Kingdom) in protest against the idea of Home Rule. The Cabinet considered military action against the Volunteers and many officers threatened to resign rather than obey.

The Cabinet claimed the issue was a misunderstanding, but Seely and Sir John French, who was Chief of the Imperial General Staff (CIGS, Head of the Army), were forced to resign. Seely was replaced by Asquith himself, taking on a dual role, and General Sir Charles Douglas became CIGS.

Pre-War

The campaign for votes for women was an ever-present issue with both the Suffragists and the more radical Suffragettes much in the news. Suffragettes chained themselves to railings, set fire to post boxes and their contents, smashed windows and even set off bombs. Arrest led to hunger strikes and to force-feeding. One of their members, Emily Davison, died under the King's horse, Anmer, at the Epsom Derby on 4 June 1913 trying to pin a "Vote for Women" banner onto the horse as it galloped past.

Britain had the largest empire the world had ever known and it could truly be said "upon which the sun never set" as it occupied almost every time zone around the world. Much of the empire was based on trade and colonisation rather than military power. Although the Royal Navy was the most powerful force in the world, militarisation by other powers, especially Germany, was a growing concern.

France: Under President Raymond Poincaré and Prime Minister Gaston Doumergue, the Third Republic also had a major overseas empire particularly in Africa and southeast Asia. Her navy, based in Toulon, was able to concentrate its strength in the Mediterranean while Britain looked after French interests in the Channel under the terms of the Entente Cordiale. However, France's main concern was with her neighbour Germany. Still smarting under the terms of the treaty that ended the 1870 Franco-Prussian war, France saw every move by Germany as aimed against her.

Germany: The Second Reich under Kaiser Wilhelm II and Chancellor Theobald von Bethmann Hollweg saw Germany as being surrounded by ill-wishers with France to the west and Russia to the east already in alliance against Germany and Austro-Hungary. Germany was a land-based European power and was very aware that during the 18th and 19th centuries the British, French, Belgians, Dutch, Portuguese and Spanish had carved up a lot of the world between them, although Spain was on the decline and had lost most of her former colonies.

Germany came rather late to this land-grab, mainly because Germany had only just emerged, but it soon made its mark in German East Africa (formed 1880); German South West Africa; Togo; Kamerun (Cameroon); German New Guinea and German Samoa. But everyone had a finger in the pie of China and Germany gained some strategic territories there, especially Kiaochow (Jiaozhou) with its main city and port Tsingtau (Qingdao).

At the start of 1914, the German Ambassador to Britain was Prince Karl Max Fürst von Lichnowsky.

Austria-Hungary under Emperor Franz Joseph and Joint Foreign Minister Count Leopold Berchtold was firmly a European power with no overseas interests at all. With many different ethnic peoples within its borders, it had recently acquired Bosnia-Herzegovina from a declining Turkey and had ambitions even further in the Balkans.

Italy had been unified only recently under the campaigns of Victor Emmanuel and Garibaldi. France still had control over parts of the Italian peninsula, especially Rome, until the time of the Franco-Prussian war when Napoleon III was forced to recall his garrison from Rome to protect Paris (1871). Now under King Victor Emanuel III (crowned 1869) and Prime Minister Giovanni Giolitti, Italy had entered the Triple Alliance with Germany and Austria in 1882.

The Russian Empire: Tsar Nicholas II and his Prime Minister Vladimir Kokovtsov were still coming to terms with the Russian defeat in the Russo-Japanese war of 1905 when most of the Russian naval fleet was obliterated by the Japanese navy in the Tsushima Straits. At home the repercussions from the war were calling for change and revolution had already brought in a short-lived parliament (Duma). Under these circumstances, conflict with Austria in the Balkans was not what anyone in Russia would have wanted.

The Ottoman Empire (Turkey) had been in decline for some time and had lost Cyprus to Britain after 1878, the whole of North Africa to Spain, France, Italy and Britain (reading west to east), and all but a toe-hold in Europe following the Balkan Wars (1912-13). The Arab population of the empire was ready to revolt. No one saw Turkey as a military threat.

The United States had a general policy of isolationism, but that hadn't prevented them intervening in Cuba's War of Independence from Spain (1898) initially to assist Cuban aspirations but later attacking Spain's Pacific empire, leading to the Philippine Revolution and ultimately to the Philippine-American War. By 1914, President Woodrow Wilson and his Secretary of State William J Bryan were still of the isolationist persuasion and it would take a lot to get them involved in anything going on in Europe.

France had begun work on the Panama Canal in 1881 but, after the project collapsed, the United States took over in 1904. A decade later the canal was officially opened on 15 August 1914. This difficult engineering project greatly reduced the amount of time taken for ships to travel between the Atlantic and Pacific Oceans, and avoided the hazardous Cape Horn route around South America.

Alliances & Tensions: Two major military alliances were set up in Europe: the Triple Alliance of Germany, Austria-Hungary and Italy; countered by the Dual Alliance of France and Russia. Britain wasn't in a formal alliance with any of these but had an "understanding" or Entente with France and Russia and an alliance with Japan.

The two Balkan wars had already stuck a stick into the hornet's nest of the area. This was an area where Austria and Russia had territorial ambitions against a weakening Ottoman Empire … whether the local inhabitants wanted it or not. However, the locals were already at each others' throats.

Morocco had been a major point of tension in 1906 and 1911 but had calmed down in the period up to 1914 as the world powers had agreed who would rule Morocco … and it wasn't the Moroccans.

Britain and Germany were in an arms race, building bigger and more powerful battleships, larger field guns, more powerful explosives.

At the same time there were major population displacements in progress

Pre-War

including refugees from former Turkish lands in the Balkans and émigrés from pogroms, or riots resulting in expulsions, in Russia mainly against Jews but also other minority groups. But anti-Jewish riots also broke out elsewhere in the world. In the United Kingdom, in 1904, the Limerick Pogrom caused many Jews to leave the city. During the 1911 Tredegar Riot in Wales, Jewish homes and businesses were looted and burned over the period of a week, before the British army was called in by Home Secretary Winston Churchill, who described the riot as a "pogrom".

Part 11: Events January to May 1914

New Year's Day in the British Empire was marked by the merging of the Northern and Southern protectorates of Nigeria and the Lagos Colony to form Nigeria, although they remained divided for administration. Lagos and the South with a costal trading economy developed more rapidly than the north.

The "fledgling" aircraft technology was continuing to expand. Also on New Year's Day, the St Petersburg-Tampa Airboat Line in the United States started services between St Petersburg and Tampa, Florida. As such it was the first airline to provide regular scheduled commercial passenger services with heavier-than-air aircraft, using a Benoist XIV flying boat.

Advances in modern work practices saw the Ford Motor Company introducing an eight-hour working day on 5 January and a daily wage of $5.

The film industry had started and on 2 February Charlie Chaplin made his film début in the comedy short *Making a Living*. His character of The Tramp was introduced a few days later (7 February) in his second film *Kid Auto Races* at Venice. On 10 February the film *Hearts Adrift* was released with the name of the star, Mary Pickford, displayed above the title for the first time.

The early months of 1914 saw much ocean liner activity. On 26 February RMS Britannic was launched at the Harland & Wolff shipyards in Belfast. This ship was sister to the RMS Olympic and the ill-fated RMS Titanic which had sunk in 1912. On 29 May, RMS Empress of Ireland sank with the loss of 1,012 lives after a collision with a coal refuelling ship in the Gulf of St Lawrence, Canada. On a happier note, the following day saw the maiden voyage of RMS Aquitania.

The Balkans was still sizzling after the Balkan Wars. On 28 February, ethnic Greeks in Northern Epirus proclaimed the Autonomous Republic of Northern Epirus. The Great Powers under the Protocol of Corfu (17 May) provided for the provinces of Korçë and Gjirokastër, constituting Northern Epirus, to be granted autonomy under the nominal sovereignty of Albania. Only 2 months earlier, the recently independent Albania had received its new monarch, Prince William of Wied.

In Britain, the Suffragette movement was still very active. On 10 March, Mary Richardson used a meat chopper to damage Velázquez' painting *Rokeby*

Venus in the National Gallery in London.

Developments in medicine saw the Belgian surgeon Albert Hustin make the first successful non-direct blood transfusion on 27 March, using anticoagulants.

However perhaps the most important development of early 1914 occurred on the other side of the Atlantic. During the Mexican Revolution (1910-20), diplomatic relations between the USA and Mexico were strained. President Woodrow Wilson refused to recognise the presidency of Mexican General Victoriano Huerta. The instabilities caused by the revolution were threatening American lives and economic interests in Mexico. The Gulf of Mexico port of Tampico was besieged by Constitutionalist (Anti-government) forces while, at a local level, relations between U.S. forces and Huerta's federal garrison remained surprisingly friendly. On 9 April, Mexican authorities in Tampico mistakenly arrested eight US sailors legitimately moving fuel to the gunboat USS Dolphin in what became known as the Tampico Affair. The US naval commander demanded a formal apology and a 21-gun salute to the US flag. General Huerta ordered the release of the sailors within 24 hours and gave a written apology but refused to have the US flag raised on Mexican soil and to provide the 21-gun salute. President Wilson received Congress's permission to invade the area, but the US occupation of Veracruz had already begun. Wilson ordered an increase in US forces in Mexican waters.

In the subsequent fighting, 19 Americans were killed and 72 wounded with Mexican losses around 150-170 killed and 195-250 wounded. While some in the United States called for a full invasion of Mexico, Wilson limited American involvement to the occupation of Veracruz which lasted until November 1914 and which, in the meantime, became a primary cause of Huerta's resignation in August 1914 as his southern armies' supplies ran out. The Tampico incident had later repercussions, stemming from lingering US-Mexican resentments. But you will have to wait for the "Zimmermann Telegram" until Part 43!

Back in Britain, on 25 May, the House of Commons passed the Third Irish Home Rule Bill as the Government of Ireland Act 1914. Irish aspirations were to be thwarted however as the outbreak of war in August 1914 put its enactment on hold.

The Wiltshire Regiment consisted of two regular battalions (1st and 2nd), a reserve battalion (3rd), and a Territorial Force battalion. The 1st Battalion was stationed at Tidworth Camp on Salisbury Plain under the command of 7th Brigade in 3rd Division. The 2nd Battalion was in Gibraltar while the Thirds were a depot/training unit in Devizes. The Territorials were based on Trowbridge.

Men with Purton connections known to have been serving in 1914 prior to the outbreak of war include from the 1st Battalion: Edward Holder (enlisted 1903), Thomas Morgan (1909), and Henry Woodward (1902). In the 2nd Battalion were William George Morgan (1910) and William Titcombe (1907).

Part 12: June 1914: Assassination

Since 1900, how many sparks could have exploded Europe into a catastrophic continental war with global consequences? Tangier, Morocco in 1905?; Agadir in 1911?; the Balkan Wars in 1912-13? In a way, the way that it happened took much of the world by surprise.

Bosnia-Herzegovina had been placed under Austro-Hungarian control in 1878 under the terms of the Congress of Berlin, though officially it was still part of the Ottoman Empire. In 1908 Austria-Hungary, in a proclamation by Emperor Franz Joseph I, annexed the occupied region, causing unrest among local ethnic and religious groups - Muslims and Orthodox Serbs now saw themselves governed by a Catholic Empire. Next door, Serbia was seeing a resurgence of its own regional power after independence from Turkey (1867) and its successes in the Balkan Wars. It would never have seen itself as a military adversary to Austria, but Belgrade became a hothouse of political propaganda.

In particular, a secret military society calling itself "Unification or Death", but unofficially known as the "Black Hand", had been formed in 1901 by members of the army in Serbia. Its aim was to unite all South Slavic territories into a single country along the lines of the unification of Italy in 1870 and Germany in 1871.

Archduke Franz Ferdinand was the nephew of the Austrian Emperor and had been made heir to the throne following the suicide of his cousin Crown Prince Rudolf at Mayerling in 1889 - this incident was dramatised in the 1969 film with Omar Sharif in the title role. Franz Ferdinand was absolutist in his monarchist views and was doing little to help even the strained relations between the Austrian and Hungarian halves of the dual monarchy, calling all Hungarians "rabble", whether duke or peasant, and was little-loved throughout the Empire.

He and his wife the Duchess Sophie were sent by the Emperor on a state visit in 1914 to Sarajevo, the Bosnian capital, to show the flag and to encourage local support of the Habsburg dynasty. Franz Ferdinand was not a particularly wise choice of ambassador. It was also perhaps unfortunate that the Austrians chose 26 June as the date around which the whole trip revolved as it marked the anniversary of the Battle of Kosovo in 1389, a key date in the Serbian psyche as it reflected the humiliation of Serb defeat by the Turks, ending Serbia's independence as a nation. And here was another humiliation happening.

Not only was the date unwise, but the Archduke was seen as a high profile target. Serbs feared that when he eventually became Emperor he would continue and even heighten the persecution of ethnic Serbs living within the Empire. Black Hand had trained a small group of teenage insurgents to enter Bosnia and assassinate the Archduke. Was the Serbian government actively involved in the plot? That's an intriguing question ... but years later it was revealed that the leader of the Black Hand, Colonel Dragutin Dimitrijevic, was also the head of Serbian military intelligence.

On Sunday, 28 June 1914, as Franz Ferdinand and his party were driven by open-topped car through Sarajevo, the first of the Black Hand terrorists, nineteen-year-old Nedjelko Cabrinovic, threw a bomb at the Archduke's car. The chauffeur saw the bomb being thrown and accelerated to avoid it. It bounced off the back of the car and exploded in front of the car behind, whose occupants were seriously injured. To avoid capture and interrogation, Cabrinovic (supposedly) swallowed a cyanide capsule and jumped into the river, however he was hauled out and detained.

After a scheduled reception at the Governor's residence, the Archduke's entourage resumed its tour of Sarajevo just before 10.45 am, but with an added trip to the local hospital to visit those injured earlier in the morning. Because of the detour, the Archduke's chauffeur took a wrong turning and had to reverse and ended up driving within ten feet of another Black Hand agent, Gavrilo Princip. Princip fired two pistol shots straight into the car. One bullet hit Sophie, killing her instantly. The other hit Franz Ferdinand in the neck and he died within minutes. Princip also attempted suicide, but was captured.

On 29 June, the Head of the Austrian Legation at Belgrade informed Vienna that Serbia was complicit in the assassination in Sarajevo, and anti-Serb riots broke out in Sarajevo and elsewhere in Bosnia.

Back in Vienna, when the news arrived, there was little public reaction. The British-naturalised, Czech-born historian Zbyněk Zeman who specialised in Austria-Hungary and its successor states later wrote, "the event almost failed to make any impression whatsoever. On Sunday and Monday, June 28 and 29, the crowds in Vienna listened to music and drank wine, as if nothing had happened."

Meanwhile the Emperor's Chamberlain Prince Alfred of Montenuovo didn't like Franz Ferdinand either and determined to downgrade the importance of the funeral. Franz Ferdinand had been a champion of creating a navy, despite the indifference of an almost landlocked empire to sea power, so it was perhaps fitting that the bodies were transported to Trieste by the Austrian dreadnought battleship SMS *Viribus Unitis* (United Peoples - which they weren't) and then to Vienna by special train. Most foreign royalty had planned to attend, but Montenuovo announced that the deceased were only distantly related to the royal family and there would be no invitations. The funeral would be a private affair for the immediate imperial family. On top of that, the three children of the Archduke and Duchess were excluded from what few public ceremonies there were. Montenuovo also tried unsuccessfully to make the children foot the bill. On 4 July 1914, the Archduke and Duchess were interred at Artstetten Castle, because Montenuovo determined that Sophie could not be buried at the Imperial Crypt.

Kaiser Willhelm II of Germany had wanted to attend the funeral and convene an informal peace conference with other world leaders and thus prevent the slip into war. Although he saved face by announcing on 2 July that he would not attend, before he could be disinvited, the peace plan was made impossible and a last chance for peace was lost.

- - - - -

There were a few other events in June 1914 that should not go unnoticed as they had repercussions later on. On 23 June, after being closed for deepening works,

Pre-War

the Keil Kanal, now called the Kaiser-Wilhelm-Kanal was reopened by the Kaiser. The British Fleet visited under the command of Vice-Admiral Sir George Warrender and the Kaiser inspected the dreadnought HMS *King George V*.

Then on 29 June in Russia, Chionya Gusyeva attempted but failed to assassinate the monk Grigori Rasputin at his home town in Siberia. Rasputin had been seen as having too much power over the Russian Imperial Family and the Russian government in general.

On the same day, the 1914 International Exhibition was opened at the "White City" at Ashton Gate in Bristol. Its unfortunate timing saw the Exhibition close on 15 August and the site was turned into a military depot. I can't find any proof that the site eventually became the home of Bristol City's Ashton Gate Stadium ... I wonder if anyone can confirm or deny this.

Part 13: July (and a bit of August) 1914: The Road to War

Since the 1878 Congress of Berlin, military spending had escalated in most of the European Powers - Germany's by five times, and Britain, Russia, and France had tripled theirs. However spending in the Austrian Empire had not even doubled despite major advances and changes in armaments. The empire had lost ethnic Italian areas to the newly resurgent nationalism in Italy - Lombardy and Vencie. It also had many territories with a Slav population, and the emergent Serbia was seen as a threat to the empire's holding onto those provinces especially in the south. The Serbian successes and territorial gains at the expense of Turkey in the Second Balkan War of 1913, especially alarmed Vienna and Budapest. Count Alois Ährenthal (d.1912) when foreign minister had overseen the annexation of Bosnia and Herzegovina in 1908. He had assumed that any future war would be in the Balkan region and that assumption had pointed the empire's military and political policy in that direction.

- - - - -

On Sunday 28 June 1914, Archduke Franz Ferdinand, heir to the Austrian throne, had been assassinated in Sarajevo by Serbian nationalists. That same day the Prime Minister of the Hungarian half of the Empire, István Tisza, travelled to Vienna to meet the Minister of Foreign Affairs Count von Berchtold and the Army Commander Conrad von Hötzendorf. Von Berchtold and von Hötzendorf proposed an immediate invasion of Serbia. Tisza, also a social scientist, suggested that they should wait to find out if the Serbian government would confirm or deny its involvement in the assassination. Back home in Budapest, he wrote to Emperor Franz Joseph saying he could not support armed invasion because there was no proof of Serbian involvement. Tisza felt that war with the Serbs would bring an armed response from Russia and a more general European war - he used the term *Weltkrieg* (World War) in his letter, the first known instance of the term. As a Hungarian he was also concerned that, after a successful war against Serbia, Austria would seek to annexe Hungary, reducing its status from being a partner in the Empire and Dual Monarchy to that of a vassal state.

The Emperor was now 84 years old and against anything that smacked of change, including war which he saw as an unnecessary adventure. He was certainly too old to lead the army and had appointed Archduke Friedrich von Österreich-Teschen as Supreme Army Commander but left von Hötzendorf the power to take strategic decisions. And for some years, von Hötzendorf had wanted to confront the resurgent Serbian nation in a preventive war.

Austria's political leaders, including von Berchtold, backed by their ally Germany, decided (5 July) at Potsdam, outside Berlin, to attack Serbia before it could incite a revolt. However they recognised that world opinion would at least require them to take the interim step of an ultimatum. On 23 July, Austria presented Serbia with the "July Ultimatum" - a list of ten humiliating demands which they believed Serbia could never accept - and with a deadline for acceptance by the Serbian government by 5 pm on the Saturday evening, 25 July 1914 . After much argument and soul-searching, Serbia eventually accepted nine of the ten demands and partially accepted the remaining one. But Austria-Hungary still cut diplomatic ties with Serbia and began to mobilise its forces.

On 28 July, Austria-Hungary declared war on Serbia and started a gunnery bombardment of the Serbian capital, Belgrade, only about 50 miles from the empire's border.

The response from Russia must have been expected: that day Tsar Nicolas II ordered a partial mobilisation of forces followed by full mobilisation on 31 July. Germany was Austria's partner in the Triple Alliance and declared war on Russia on 1 August, in response to the Russian defence of Serbia, and mobilised its own forces. The same day, France, in alliance with Russia under the Dual Alliance, also mobilised against an expected attack on France by

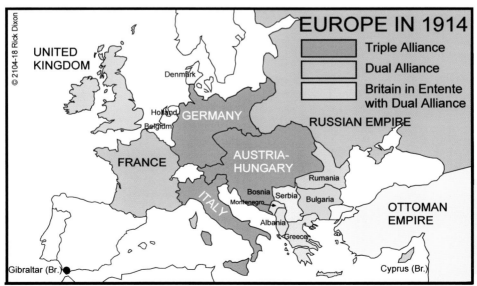

EUROPE IN 1914

Triple Alliance
Dual Alliance
Britain in Entente with Dual Alliance

© 2104-18 Rick Dixon

UNITED KINGDOM

Denmark

Holland

Belgium

GERMANY

RUSSIAN EMPIRE

FRANCE

AUSTRIA-HUNGARY

ITALY

Bosnia

Montenegro

Serbia

Rumania

Bulgaria

Albania

Greece

OTTOMAN EMPIRE

Gibraltar (Br.)

Cyprus (Br.)

Pre-War

Germany. And the New York Stock Exchange closed to await developments.

On 2 August, Germany invaded Luxembourg and occupied it in line with its strategic Schlieffen Plan for the conquest of France. Germany also issued an ultimatum to Belgium, with a 12-hour deadline, to allow free passage of German troops towards France.

Believing it would be granted that free passage though Belgium, Germany declared war on France early on 3 August.

- - - - -

Theory had it that Germany would occupy Paris in 39 days and see the capitulation of France within 42 days. Theory had it that all the dominoes that would fall, had fallen ... and that Britain wouldn't go to war over Belgium. Theory had it that, if the worst came to the worst, 'It will be all over by Christmas'. Theory isn't everything.

Part 14: War - August 1914

... But then theory isn't everything after all. On 3 August at 7 am (local time) Belgium refused Germany's ultimatum demanding free passage of its troops through to France, and the same day Britain sent a note to Germany confirming its commitment under the Treaty of London (1839) to protect Belgian sovereignty.

Still considering this a bluff by the British, German troops invaded Belgium at 8.02 am (local time) on 4 August.

4 August 1914, British Declaration of War: The United Kingdom therefore declared war on Germany for the violation of Belgian neutrality. Perhaps another element that Germany had not fully anticipated was that this meant that the entire British Empire was now at war with the German Empire. In the face of the situation, the United States declared its neutrality. As a historical aside, Mahindra Gandhi was on board ship from South Africa and by that time had reached the English Channel when he learned that war had been declared. He arrived in London later that day.

Next day, Montenegro declared war on Austria-Hungary in support of Serbia ... and Germany eventually got round to declaring war on Belgium which it had already invaded the day before. On 6 August, Austria-Hungary declared war on Russia.

The British Empire factor was seen by Germany when the Norddeutscher Lloyd steamer SS Pfalz was arrested trying to leave Melbourne with a shot across the bows, said to be the first Allied shot of the War. A German merchant ship commandeered by the Imperial German Navy as a minelayer, SS Königin Luise, was laying mines off the English east coast and was sunk by the light cruiser HMS Amphion, which was the first German naval loss of the war. The next day (6 August) Amphion hit one of Königin Luise's mines and sank with

150 British sailors killed, the first British casualties of the war, together with 18 of Königin Luise's crew who had been rescued after their ship's sinking and were being held on board Amphion. German Zeppelins dropped bombs on Liége in Belgium, killing 9 civilians.

The Belgian army may not have been a match for the Germans, but with support, they managed to hold up the German advance for much of August. Without their efforts, Britain and France would not have had time even to get to Belgium to do anything at all. However between 5 and 16 August, in the Battle of Liège, the German Army all but overran and defeated the Belgians, though on 12 August, at the Battle of Haelen, Belgian troops repulsed the Germans. But by 20 August German forces had occupied Brussels.

British Empire: In the empire's territories, on 7 August troops of the British Gold Coast Regiment (now Ghana) entered the German West African colony of Togoland and met a German-led police force at a factory in Nuatja, near Lomé. The Togo police opened fire on the patrol, and Trooper Alhaji Grunshi returned fire. He is thought to have been the first soldier in British service to have fired a shot in the war. Togoland surrendered to Britain and France on 26 August. Another first occurred on 9 August:the light cruiser HMS Birmingham rammed and sank a German submarine U-15 off Fair Isle, the first U-boat lost in action.

In Europe: Between 15 and 24 August, in the Battle of Cer, Serbian troops succeeded in defeating the Austro-Hungarian army, marking the first Entente victory of the war.

Much more serious was the German victory over the Russian Army at the Battle of Tannenberg (26-30 August). The German Eighth Army almost completely destroyed the Russian Second Army, whose commander Alexander Samsonov was also killed. In a series of follow-up battles, including the First Battle of the Masurian Lakes, the Russian First Army was also put out of action. Russia didn't recover enough to be a fighting force in the war until spring 1915. Tannenberg showed the tactical advantage of being able to move troops rapidly by train. One single German army could out-manoeuvre 2 Russian armies.

British Expeditionary Force: Troops of the British Expeditionary Force (BEF) had been mobilised and the 1st Battalion Wiltshire Regiment (still also known as the 1st Duke of Edinburgh's) set sail for Normandy landing at Rouen between 13 and 14 August 1914. Among these from Purton were: Charles James Kibblewhite, Ernest Henry Kibblewhite; Albert Tom King; Thomas Morgan; and Walter Edmond Titcombe. The Battalion moved with 7th Infantry Brigade of the 3rd Division to Belgium, where they fought at Mons in the Battle of Ciply (23 August) under General Smith-Dorrien's II Corps of the BEF.

Charles James Kibblewhite *(pictured)* was killed in action* aged 29 on 24 August 1914, the first Purton man to be killed in the war. Born in Purton in 1885, Charles was the son of William and Thirza Kibblewhite of Gorse Hill. Charles has no known grave and is remembered on the La Fertesous-Jouarre Memorial. France.

1914

Mons was the first major action for the BEF. It managed to hold the German advance temporarily but led to the month-long Great Retreat to the Marne. During the retreat, the Wiltshires later fought at Le Cateau (26-27 August) where British, French and Belgian forces made a successful tactical retreat from the German advance. Further east down the battle line at St Quentin, French forces managed to hold back a German advance. All these battles became known collectively as the Battle for the Frontier.

The next sailing of the 1st Wiltshires brought Purtonian Edward Holder, landing at St Nazaire on 31 August 1914. He joined the battalion at Vailly-sur-Aisne and would later have joined the others at the Battle of the Aisne (7-10 September 1914).

The 2nd Battalion of the Wiltshire Regiment had been in Gibraltar, but was now returning to England and landed at Southampton on 3 September.

Around the world:

Britain was in alliance with Japan and on 23 August Japan declared war on Germany. The short term advantage for Britain was that German ships were denied use of re-coaling stations in the Pacific.

Despite the war, Sir Ernest Shackleton's Imperial Trans-Antarctic Expedition set sail on the Endurance from England on 8 August in an attempt to cross Antarctica.

On 28 August at the Battle of Heligoland Bight, British cruisers under Admiral Beatty sank 3 German cruisers.

* Charles Kibblewhite's name does not appear on the Purton War Memorial. Bob Lloyd in his CD book Purton & The Great War (2014) writes: "Names found on a Memorial are as likely to be because *that person* lived in the area or *had family* who lived there and wished the name to be remembered. A good example for this would be Ernest Harrison; his father was the Vicar at St Mary's, Purton from 1917. He is listed on the Memorial in Purton and also on the War Memorial in Aston Abbotts near Aylesbury where he was married and his wife's family lived. My further research has concentrated both on further research into the dead but more towards those who served and survived the Great War." *[My bold-italics, Rick Dixon]*

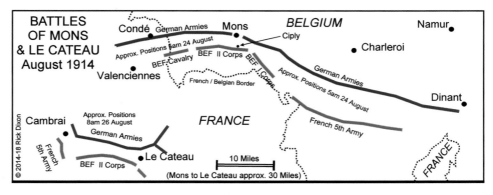

BATTLES OF MONS & LE CATEAU August 1914

Condé · German Armies · Mons · BELGIUM · Namur · Ciply · Charleroi
Approx. Positions 5am 24 August · BEF II Corps · BEF I Corps
BEF Cavalry · Valenciennes · French / Belgian Border · German Armies · Approx. Positions 5am 24 August · Dinant
Cambrai · Approx. Positions 8am 26 August · German Armies · FRANCE · French 5th Army
French 5th Army · BEF II Corps · Le Cateau · 10 Miles · FRANCE
(Mons to Le Cateau approx. 30 Miles)

© 2014-18 Rick Dixon

My Family's War

My Great Great Aunt and Uncle

- A First World War British Soldier
photo courtesy of Tracey Rapson, member of Purton Artists

Used on the the August 2014 cover of Purton Magazine

Part 15:   September 1914

Following the August battles at Mons and Le Cateau, the German armies quickly approached the River Marne northeast of Paris. The allied victory at 1st Battle of the Marne (3-9 Sept), caused the Germans to retreat to the line of the River Aisne and they fortified the high ground north of the river. Of a total of 2 million fighting men on both sides, half a million were killed at the Marne. It was the most concentrated slaughter of the whole war.

The Battle of the Aisne was fought between 7-10 September 1914, with subsidiary actions to 28 September. **Henry Philip Drury**, of Purton (born Greenhill, 1885) serving with the 1st Battalion Wiltshire Regiment had arrived in France on 31 August 1914. He joined his Battalion at Vailly on 19 September.

At the Battle of Aisne Heights half a mile east of Vailly, 20 September, 1st Wilts were with II Corps of the BEF 2nd Division. Drury was killed in action on 22 September 1914, aged 29. He had enlisted before the war in 1903. Along with others, he was buried close to where he fell but in an unmarked grave. Henry is remembered on the La Ferte-Sous-Jouarre Memorial.

The actions at the Aisne continued until 28 September, but quickly became a side issue. Both sides attempted to use the fighting on the Aisne to pin their opponents in place, while their remaining mobile armies took part in the Race to the Sea, where each attempted to find an opening to outflank their enemy. By the time the Race to the Sea and the first battle of Ypres came to an end, the Western Front had taken shape - a 475 mile long line of fortifications running from the North Sea to the Swiss border.

BATTLES OF THE MARNE & THE AISNE September 1914

Although a stalemate had arisen, the German army bombarded Rheims destroying much of the cathedral and the city on 21 September.

During the Marne offensive, on 8 September, Private Thomas Highgate became the first British soldier to be executed for desertion during the War.

Left: La Ferté-sous-Jouarre Memorial to the Missing. The Memorial commemorates 3,740 officers and men of the British Expeditionary Force (BEF) who fell at the battles of Mons, Le Cateau, the Marne and the Aisne between the end of August and early October 1914 who have no known graves.

12 September is an important date: The Schlieffen Plan for the German war strategy timed the occupation of Paris for Day 39. Germany invaded Belgium early on 4 August so they should have been in Paris by 12 September. Instead they had been turned back at the Marne and the plan was stalled.

On 3 September, the 2nd Battalion Wiltshire Regiment landed at Southampton having been recalled from Gibraltar. They moved to Lyndhurst where they were placed under the command of 21st Brigade in 7th Division.

At sea, on 5 September the British scout cruiser HMS Pathfinder was sunk by a German submarine (U-21) in the Firth of Forth off Edinburgh, the first ship ever to be sunk by a self-propelled torpedo fired from a submarine. Then on 22 September, U-9 torpedoed three Royal Navy armoured cruisers in the North Sea, HMS Aboukir, Cressy and Hogue, with the death of more than 1,400 men.

In Africa, South African troops opened hostilities in German South-West Africa (modern-day Namibia) with an assault on the Ramansdrift police station on 13 September and later, on 21 September, British Imperial police forces captured Schuckmannsburg in the Caprivi Strip of German South-West Africa.

Elsewhere round the world: on 1 September the name of the city of Saint Petersburg in Russia was changed to Petrograd. The same day, the last surviving passenger pigeon "Martha" died at Cincinnati Zoo. On 3 September, Pope Benedict XV succeeded Pope Pius X as the 258th pope.

The poem "For the Fallen" by Laurence Binyon *(pictured)* was first published in The Times on 21 September, after the Battles of the Marne and the Aisne: it's fourth verse (of 7) is the most known:

> *They shall grow not old, as we that are left grow old:*
> *Age shall not weary them, nor the years condemn.*
> *At the going down of the sun and in the morning,*
> *We will remember them.*

- - - - -

The following men with Purton associations served at Aisne with the 1st Wilts:

Date Arrived France

13 Aug	Thomas Morgan	Edward Holder
	Daniel George Bull	Arriving in France on 21 September
14 Aug	Albert Greenaway	and serving at Neuve-Chapelle:
	Ernest Henry Kibblewhite	William A Coward
	Albert Tom King	Henry Reginald Jefferies
	James Pound	Albert John King
	Walter Edmond Titcombe	
22 Aug	Walter Reginald Beacham	
31 Aug	Henry, Philip Drury	

1914

Purton men serving with other regiments were:

Active Service Date
24 Jul   Charles Ernest Strange, Royal Marines.

4 Aug	Harold Rogers Ward, Wiltshire Yeomanry, Labour Corps.
11 Aug	Mervyn Painter, Army Service Corps
10 Aug	George Henry Charles Mills, Army Service Corps.
15 Aug	Wilfred Eggleton Cook, 2nd Battalion Manchester Regiment.
16 Aug	Charles C Lander, Army Service Corps.
18 Aug	Francis Charles Titcombe, Royal Engineers.
22 Aug	William G Selwood, 1/ Hants Regiment.
11 Sep	Mervyn Stronge Richardson, 2nd Battalion Royal Welch Fusiliers.
18 Sep	Edward Ernest Francis Albert Parsons, Royal Dublin Fusiliers.
24 Sep	John Painter (emigrated 1911), 9th Battalion Australian Imperial Force.

My Family's War

George Smith: The Flying Cabinet Maker

A lot of things have been written about the First World War - but not about my grandfather, a Mr George Smith of Sherston in Wiltshire.

In his younger years he was apprenticed to a cabinet maker, but as WW1 loomed he became a carpenter repairing the wooden-framed aircraft for the Royal Flying Corp (RFC). Later he became a pilot instructor of these very flimsy aircraft.

As the photos show, training was rudimentary and not always successful. The photos are genuine from my grandfathers' own collection.

He was invalided out of the RFC, with a bad heart, and went on to have six children, one of whom was my mother. He died in his eighties during the 1970s.

CHRIS COMPTON

Part 16: October 1914

Germany's "Race to the Sea", after their stalled advance on Paris, attempted to get round the Belgian, British and French front lines to seize an alternative route westwards. Even by late August, the German army had reached Antwerp at the head of the River Scheldt estuary (about 45 miles from the North Sea coast) and held it under siege for much of September.

The 2nd Battalion of the Wiltshire Regiment completed its transfer from Gibraltar, via Lyndhurst and landed at Zeebrugge on 7 October as part of 1st Brigade of 7th Division, ordered to defend Antwerp. However, by the time they arrived, the city was already falling and the Antwerp garrison surrendered on 9 October. The 7th was redeployed to hold bridges and other strategic points to help the westward evacuation of 33,000 soldiers of the Antwerp garrison (around one third of the total Belgian army) who escaped north to neutral Holland, to be interned for the rest of the war. A million civilian refugees left for Britain, Holland and France - most later returned but many remained in Holland after 1918. Once the Belgians had passed through, the 7th was moved west, where the infantry entrenched in front of Ypres, the first British troops to get there.

After actions in early October, the 1st Battle of Ypres was fought between 19 October and 22 November with heavy losses for the 7th Division while they held back the German advance. On 24 October, while the 2nd Wilts were at Reutel, a village some 6 miles east of Ypres, a German attack led to the capture of 8 Purton men of the Battalion: James Clarke, Arthur Cook, Raymond Dixon, Herbert Fisher, Edwin Iles, William Morgan, Edwin Painter and William Titcombe. They were held as Prisoners of War for the next 4 years: Herbert Fisher died of pneumonia in 1918 while still a POW.

Henry Reginald Jefferies *(pictured)* was the son of Albert and Charlotte Jefferies, of Clarden Lane, born in 1892. He served with the 1st Wilts, arriving in France in September, and joined the Battalion with reinforcements at La Couture. On 23 October they moved to Neuve-Chapelle. Just after midnight the following day shelling of the Battalion's trenches and the nearby village continued until 7 pm. Shell fire blew in many of the trenches with the soldiers in them buried as a result. Henry Jefferies was killed in action that day and has no  known grave though he was reportedly buried in a trench south of Neuve-Chapelle church. He is remembered on the Le Touret Memorial.

Further north, the Belgian army held the German advance at the Battle of the Yser (16 - 31 October) with heavy losses.

Another Purton man, Victor Howard Phelps had joined the Royal Navy in 1913. On 21 October 1914 he joined the company of the super-dreadnought battleship HMS Audacious (23,400 tons). On 27 October Audacious hit a mine off Tory Island, north-west of Ireland. The light cruiser HMS Liverpool, part of the accompanying fleet, stood by and the White Star liner Olympic, elder sister of the ill-fated Titanic, arrived on the scene. The crew of Audacious were taken off by 7.15 pm with the ship visibly sinking. Audacious floated upside down until 9 pm, when three explosions threw wreckage 800 yards to hit and kill a petty officer on Liverpool ... the only casualty in the sinking. The loss of Audacious was only officially announced in The Times 4 years later on 14 November 1918, three days after the end of the war.

Arriving in France in October 1914 with the Wiltshire Regiment would have been the following men with Purton associations:

1914

1st **Wilts** Thomas Painter	Raymond Philip	Edwin Lewis Iles*
2nd **Wilts** *(those starred taken POW, 24 October)*	Baker Dixon*	William George
	James Linsell	Morgan*
James Clark*	William Titcombe*	Edwin C Painter
Arthur Nelson Cook*	Herbert Fisher*	

11th Hussars   Alan Wortley Barrington-Foote

Other Locations

To India: William James Hedges 1/4 Wilts, 14th Machine Gun Corps
Royal Navy: Victor Howard Phelps

- - - - -

The War at Sea

SS Rohilla had been converted into a naval hospital ship. On 30 October, the ship ran aground on a reef off Whitby, Yorkshire, Lifeboats from Whitby, Upgang, Redcar, Tynemouth and Scarborough recovered crew and medical staff over the next three days and 146 of the 229 on board, including the Captain and all the nurses, survived. The Gold Medal of the Royal National Lifeboat Institution was presented to Major H. E. Burton and Coxswain Robert Smith of the Tynemouth lifeboat and to Coxswain Thomas Langlands of the Whitby boat.

Elsewhere round the world:

On 3 October, 25,000 Canadian troops embarked on an escorted transport convoy, all arriving safely in England on 14 October. They were mobilised to the Western Front in 1915.

On 28 October in the naval Battle of the Malacca Straits (Penang), Malaya, the German cruiser Emden sank a Russian cruiser Zhemchug, and a French destroyer Mousquet, in harbour before escaping. The same day the assassins of Archduke Franz Ferdinand at Sarajevo, were sentenced to death, except Gavrilo Princip who was under 20 at the time and received twenty years imprisonment.

On 29 October, Turkey declared war on Russia and Turkish warships shelled the Russian Black Sea ports; Russia, France, and Britain declared war on Turkey separately between 1 and 5 November. On 31 October, at the Battle of the Vistula River, Russia defeated German and Austro-Hungarian forces around Warsaw.

In October 1914, Ivor Novello published *Keep the Home Fires Burning* in response to the battles of August and September including Mons, the Marne and the Aisne. There are many other songs associated with the Great War, but many of them pre-dated it. *Goodbye Dolly I must leave you*, (Paul Barnes & Will D. Cobb) for example was written in America at the time of the Spanish-American War (1898). It featured the line "See - the boys in blue are marching and I can no longer stay", because of the American blue uniforms of that time. It was changed to "See - the soldier boys are marching" for the British audience and was popularised in the Music Halls during the Boer War (1901-02). *Boiled Beef and Carrots* (Charles Collins & Fred Murray) dates from 1909, while *It's a Long Way to Tipperary* (Jack Judge) was first performed in 1912.

My Family's War

Edward, Ernest and Sidney Holder

Mac (Malcolm) Holder of Victoria, Australia, and formerly of Purton, writes:
Edward* Holder was my dad's brother. Dad [Ernest[†] Holder] also served as a Petty Officer in the Royal Navy and there was another brother Sidney[‡].

All three came home: Edward lost an eye and had severe gout, the result of trench warfare. Sidney was badly shell shocked and spent the rest of his life in a care home in London.

Dad was lucky; he was on the New York run and came back unscathed.

- - - - -

Notes by Rick Dixon, from Bob Lloyd's research:

* Edward Holder had joined the army in 1903, aged 18. On the outbreak of war he was remobilised from the Army reserve and arrived in France with the 1st Battalion Wiltshire Regiment, 600 HSE Labour Corps, on 31 August 1914, joining the Battalion at Vailly. He later transferred to the 13th Battalion Hertfordshire and Bedfordshire Regiment.

[†] Ernest Holder enlisted on 23 November 1916 and was posted to 4 August 1917 to HMS Cornwall, a Monmouth-class armoured cruiser. Cornwall was on convoy escort duties from 1917 to the end of the war.

[‡] Sidney Holder's name is listed in the Memorial book in St Mary's Church where his regiment is given as Royal Engineers.

My Family's War

Bonny

Dick Scott writes: The photo is of Bonny, my aunt's pony and trap standing outside Pry Farm. The photo was sent to me by my cousin Diana Bush née King. Written on the back is "Bonny sent to war 1914 - nearly broke our hearts". Bonny was Diana's mother, Mrs Flo King's (née Scott)

1914

pony which she drove daily to Miss Fentemen's school in Bath Road, Old Town until Bonny was requisitioned by the army for the War effort.

Part 17: November 1914

The **1st Battle of Ypres** continued. It was fought around an arc to the east of the city, still held by the Allies and part of the front line from the North Sea to the Swiss border. A series of German attacks known as Fabeck's offensive ran from 29 October to 14 November but, fortunately, German radio traffic was intercepted and with aerial reconnaissance gave the Allies some advance warning of the German intentions.

I find it difficult to imagine things like this without any sense of context. Accepting that Ypres was and is much smaller than, say Swindon, superimposing maps of the two towns, the entire bulge round Ypres would stretch from Blunsdon in the north, out east towards South Marston and Wanborough with Chiseldon being our local equivalent of Messines in the south. Not great distances are they? … a circuit of some 10 miles. I've put equivalent place names below to help the idea of distances, but these are very approximate.

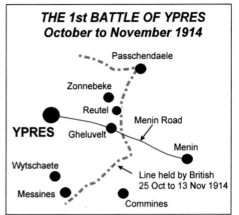

THE 1st BATTLE OF YPRES
October to November 1914

The German offensive was centred on the Gheluvelt crossroads on the Menin road which formed the boundary between the British 1st and 7th Divisions. Each division's flank was held by a Guards Division: to the left of 7th Division by the 1st Grenadier Guards and the 1st Coldstream Guards held the right of 1st Division. These had been reinforced with companies of the 1st Black Watch and a platoon of the 1st Gloucesters.

The German artillery attack began early on 29 October against the Black Watch and Coldstream units. The British machine gunners weapons jammed … and the cartridges for rifles were too large! The Germans broke through and captured most of the Black Watch and Coldstreams. British artillery continued to fire on enemy guns rather than German infantry which didn't help. In gaining the Gheluvelt crossroads, the Germans had a staging point for attacking Ypres.

The continued German push fell on the exhausted British 7th Division on the Menin road and Messines sector. German infantry advanced under cover of morning mist, but failed to break through. Hastily constructed wire fences stalled the German advance. When the mist cleared, the German infantry was exposed

Approximate equivalent place name positions: WW1 name; (modern reformed spelling); Wiltshire equivalent based on distance from Swindon:

Commines Canal	Ogbourne St George	Messines	Chiseldon
Ghulevelt (Geluveld)	Bishopstone	Wytschaete (Wijtschate)	Coate Water
Givency-la-Bassée	Market Lavington	Ypres	Swindon
Menin road	Wanborough	Zonnebeke	South Marston
Menin town	Lambourn, Berks		

and suffered heavy losses.

On 30 October the Germans broke into Messines after nearly five hours of fighting, and the British forces there retreated. A British counterattack advanced to the Messines road but suffered heavy losses in trying to reach Messines town. But the most serious German attack was aimed at Gheluvelt. It was the last significant ridge for British observation positions east of Ypres. After huge losses on both sides, the British pulled out of Gheluvelt to form a new line a third of a mile west. Eventually the German advance was broken due to officer casualties to British rifle fire.

Frustrated at Gheluvelt, General von Fabeck tried to break the Wytschaete-Messines line at the southern base of the bulge around Ypres. Wytschaete fell and German infantry secured the ridge. Wytschaete was recaptured by the British 12th Lancers, but the 1st Lincolns and Northumberland Fusiliers lost about 30 percent of their strength in an unsuccessful attempt to recapture the ridge.

To safeguard their retreat, the British shelled Messines to hold the Germans back. RFC aircraft attacked German ground forces and harassed advancing columns. Wytschaete was held but only with the help of reinforcements from the French 32nd Division. The Germans suffered heavy casualties attacking the 32nd. It was here that a young Lance Corporal (Gefreiter) named Adolf Hitler won the Iron Cross 2nd Class for rescuing a man under fire.

By the morning of 1 November, the Germans had secured the line and both towns. But the ridges to the west of the Wytschaete-Messines line were reoccupied and held by the 32nd Division. The British were exhausted and most divisions had been reduced to a shadow of their former selves. The 7th had only 2,380 men left, and was withdrawn from the line and replaced by 8th Division newly arrived from Britain. The Germans had also suffered high losses, and needed to pause, regroup, reinforce. The front fell quiet. Action was limited to raids by both sides and heavy shelling of Ypres by German artillery.

On 11 November, the Germans began their final attempt to break through the British lines around Ypres in what became known as the battle of Nonne Bosschen (Nun's Copse) mounted by twelve and a half divisions along a nine-mile front, stretching from Messines to Reutel.

The British and German armies were exhausted but the main German threat came from two fresh divisions with 10,000 men attacking eleven tired British battalions, reduced in strength to around 4,000 men after three months of fighting, along the line of the Menin road. The German attack was preceded by one of the heaviest artillery bombardments of the war to date, lasting some 2½ hours. The advancing German troops were protected by morning mist, but were turned back by accurate British fire. The most successful German attack was made by their 1st Guards Brigade, advancing towards the British 1st (Guards) Brigade, under Brigadier General Charles FitzClarence who had around 800 men, and were outnumbered three to one by the Germans, who overran the British front line, in one of the few bayonet attacks of the war. Strong resistance and accurate British artillery fire isolated the German Guards, preventing reinforcements from reaching them.

1914

The Germans retreated into Nonne Bosschen woods, to be driven out again by the 2nd Oxfordshire Light Infantry. FitzClarence was organising a counterattack to recover the line lost earlier, but was shot and killed before the attack could begin. The counterattack was abandoned.

This was the last major German offensive of the 1st Battle of Ypres. Allied defences, heavy snowfall and hard frost ended large-scale fighting. Field Marshal Roberts came over to visit from Britain on 11 November, caught a chill, and died of pneumonia on 14 November. In a reorganisation the following day, the BEF's I Corps was relieved by two French corps and France took over defence of the line from Zonnebeke to the Ypres-Comines canal. The new British line ran 21 miles from Wytschaete to the La Bassée Canal at Givenchy. The Belgians held 15 miles and the French defended some 430 miles. The German withdrawal was detected on 20 November.

The German attempt for a final war victory failed through uncoordinated assaults, without retaining reserves. Continually attacking supposed weak spots merely exhausted their infantry. German intelligence always believed the small numbers of enemy infantry were outposts and overestimated the strength of Allied forces. After Ypres, Chief of the German General Staff Erich von Falkenhayn was convinced that Germany would never have another opportunity to win the war. In a meeting on 18 November that could have saved millions of lives, he recommended a diplomatic solution to end the war but Chancellor Bethmann-Hollweg, Field Marshal Paul von Hindenburg and General Erich Ludendorff disagreed.

The battle was the greatest crisis yet for commanders and their staffs still struggling to come to terms with the power of modern weaponry and adapting as quickly as possible to the new conditions of trench warfare. It showed the superiority of defence over offence - the Allied success had been defensive, not offensive. This was an impasse that would last until the late summer and autumn of 1918.

Recent estimates of the 1st Battle of Ypres are of between 50,000 and 85,000 French, 21,600 Belgian, 55,400 British and 134,300 German casualties.

The War at Sea

On 1 November, at the Battle of Coronel off the Pacific coast of central Chile, a Royal Navy squadron commanded by Rear-Admiral Sir Christopher Cradock was defeated by superior German forces led by Vice-Admiral Graf von Spee. This was the first British naval defeat of the war, resulting in the loss of HMS Good Hope and HMS Monmouth, with no survivors from either: 1,600 British officers and men were killed.

In the Siege of Tsingtao, the Japanese and British together seized Jiaozhou Bay in China on 7 November. This had been the base of the German East Asia Naval Squadron. Then on 9 November, while the main force of the East Asia Squadron retreated, the German cruiser Emden, which had remained to harass merchant shipping, was sunk by the Australian cruiser HMAS Sydney at the Battle of the Cocos Islands (800 miles south west of Java).

Elsewhere

On 5 November, Britain and France declared war on Turkey and Britain annexed Cyprus, which it had been administering under Ottoman leave since 1878. *(See Part 3.)*

U.S. troops withdrew from Veracruz in Mexico on 23 November. They had been occupying the city since April 1914. *(See Part 11.)*

And on 24 November, Benito Mussolini was expelled from the Italian Socialist Party due to his opposition to the party's stance on neutrality.

Purtonians

Fred Selwood of Purton arrived in France on 11 November 1914 with the 1st Battalion Wiltshire Regiment.

George F Gretton (born Adelaide, Australia, later of Diana Lodge, Purton) arrived in France as a Captain of the Indian Army in the 20th Deccan Horse.

Part 18: December 1914

All was "comparatively" quiet on the northern sectors of the Western Front. Apart from a few skirmishes, all sides were licking their wounds after heavy losses in October and November.

However further south on 17 December a French offensive under the command of Marshal Pétain commenced near Arras (1st Battle of Artois). Pétain's forces were struggling and requested a British offensive to push the German line further north. The BEF's commander, General French, planned six simultaneous attacks with most of the forces from the Indian Corps. They had only arrived in France a few weeks before and had suffered heavy losses at Ypres. Many of those surviving Ypres were exhausted and suffering from the winter conditions compounded by a lack of warm clothing and adequate food. Taking part in this with the 20th Deccan Horse was Major George Gretton, originally from Australia but who later settled at Diana Lodge in Purton.

On 19 December in freezing rain the Lahore Division took the first two German lines while coming under heavy machine gun fire. Further north, the Garhwal Brigade and the Ghurkhas took 300 metres of the opposing line at Festubert. The Germans regrouped and counter-attacked that same morning. On 20 December the German artillery shelled the Indian troops and a series of mines exploded under the British lines killing many.

British losses at Artois were high, especially among the Indian units. In addition to battle wounds, many suffered frostbite and trench foot. The British faced heavy losses (4,000 for the BEF compared with 2,000 for the German Army) with no strategic gain. The Indian soldiers, ill-prepared for the conditions, were close to mutiny and the British general staff began to withdraw them from the Western Front.

1914

Artois had been the first offensive on the Western Front by either side after Ypres in November, but failed to break the frontline stalemate.

There was an unofficial and temporary Christmas truce between British and German soldiers on much of the Western Front particularly around Ypres, and French troops in other sectors. Apart from tales of carol singing and football matches in no-man's-land, the truce allowed both sides to recover and bury the bodies of the many soldiers who had died between the trench lines and in water-filled shell craters. It began on Christmas Eve and ran until New Year's Day in several places, before both sides recommenced sniping at each other.

On 16 December, German battleships had bombarded Hartlepool, Scarborough and Whitby on the Yorkshire coast. Then on Christmas Eve there was the first German air raid on Dover. Most of the hand launched bombs fell ineffectively in the sea, but it was a shock that anything like that was possible. On Christmas Day, British aircraft were launched from warships, together with submarine support, to attack the German port of Cuxhaven. Little damage was caused.

Eastern Fronts

In the east, on 6 December, German troops overran Łódź, in modern day Poland, pushing Russia back. By the 15th, the Russians were in retreat toward Moscow. Then on 17 December, Austrian troops defeated the Russians at Limanowa in southern Poland.

In the south, Austro-Hungarian forces occupied Belgrade, Serbia's capital, on 2 December, but the Serbs retook it on 15 December. By 19 December, the Serbs had won a decisive victory over Austria-Hungary in the Battle of Kolubara.

Italy meanwhile had proclaimed its neutrality on 5 December.

More was going on at sea. The German naval squadron of Maximilian von Spee, consisting of 2 armoured cruisers, (Scharnhorst and Gneisenau), 3 light cruisers and 3 auxiliaries had sunk HMS Good Hope and HMS Monmouth at Coronel. The squadron was intercepted at the Falkland Islands where all but one light cruiser (SMS Dresden) and an auxiliary were sunk on 8 December. Apart from the 2 escaping ships, there were only 215 rescued German survivors, with about 2,000 killed. There was little damage to the British squadron.

On 18 December, Egypt, already under British administration from the Ottoman Empire, was annexed by Britain as a protectorate. Turkey had only just entered the war on the side of the Central Powers. But with its ally Austria struggling to its west against the Serbs, it now had Britain holding strategic points of its empire to the south (Egypt) and in the Levant (Cyprus). Making life more difficult, the Turks were pushed back by Russia (28 December) after fighting in Armenia for several weeks in their north-east. On 17 December the Turkish authorities expelled the Jews living in Tel Aviv sending them without warning to Egypt via the port of Jaffa. Some were expelled so quickly, they didn't have time to let their families know.

By now, plans were afoot in Britain to take decisive action to surround Turkey by action closer to the capital, Istanbul, by targeting the straits locking the Black Sea from the Aegean and Mediterranean, which would allow the Russian southern fleets to participate more widely. Gallipoli seemed like a good landing point.

And Australian and New Zealand troops arrived in Cairo on 23 December.

The following men from Purton arrived in France in December 1914:

Arthur Kenneth Richardson, 1st Battalion Royal Welch Fusiliers
William Shailes, 1st Battalion Wiltshire Regiment
Samuel Edward Lawrence Freegard, 2/4th Battalion Wiltshire Regiment

Other News

On 19 December, Mohandas Gandhi and his wife left England by sea for India. While on board he began to learn Bengali.

On 26 December, the US Government protested at British interference with American merchant ships at sea. However, the same day Germany announced that they would treat food as contraband subject to seizure, stifling the US protest.

My Family's War

Chris Compton wrote about his grandfather, George Smith, who lived in Sherston, near Malmesbury, and became a pilot instructor. Chris has provided us with another true anecdote:

The Pickled Thumb

When the pilots had finished their training they were sent to France to fly over the battlefields. They flew with a gunner who sat behind the pilot. The pilot's job was to survey the battlefields, return to base, and give a full report of the enemies strengths and weaknesses, so that a military advantage could be gained by the British.

A new pilot and gunner were sent out to the Somme, the gunner was shooting at the German lines, when a field gun shell hit the gunner, evaporating him, leaving only his thumb in the grip of the gun.

The aeroplane managed to struggle home whereupon my grandfather pickled the thumb and kept it in a jar at his home until the day he died.

I always wanted that thumb as it was a "friend" I had known all my life. Not frightening or gory, just sad, and with its story well worth keeping, but it was not to be. After Grandfather's funeral the house was burgled and all his silver … and the thumb were stolen and the question is "where is the thumb now?" I should love to know.

1914

My Family's War

Captain Mervyn Stronge Richardson

(pictured) of Purton House, wrote many letters home. These are a selection from December 1914:

6 December 1914: We have had an awful time since we got back into the trenches. It rained all the first night, and most of the next day, and we are up to our necks in water and mud, as we are beside a river which is rising, and in consequence is flooding the trenches, which are very low indeed. Last night the parapets were falling in, and men had to be kept shoving them up with planks. We have not a single dossing place that the rain does not get through, so that you got almost as wet as you slept as when you were outside.

I have been struggling with the bottoms of the trenches to get them clean, paving them with bricks, instead of having liquid mud in, and water over one's boots. None of us have had dry feet since we came in. This life soon picks out the weaklings.

Yesterday one of our Company wanted some earth for something, and he saw a mound of it, and started digging, and came across fourteen dead Germans fully equipped, and later on a man was enlarging his shelter in the trench, and he came across another man. These trenches were German, [taken] by our troops and converted [to our use].

16 December 1914: I crept up to the German trenches the other night, and could hear them talking, and walking about. The German trenches are only about 100 yards off ours.

31 December 1914: I will tell you of the extraordinary day we spent on Christmas Day. On Christmas Eve we had a sing-song with the men [of 'A' Company] in the trenches. We put up a sheet of canvas, with a large "Merry Christmas" and a portrait of the Kaiser painted on it, on the parapet. The next morning there was a thick fog, and when it lifted about 12 o'clock, the Germans (Saxons) who were only about 150 yards in front of us saw it, they began to shout across, and beckoning to our men to come half way and exchange gifts. They then came out of their trenches, and gave our men cigars and cigarettes, and 2 barrels of beer, in exchange for tins of bully beef. The situation was so absurd, that another officer of ours and myself went out, and met seven of their officers, and arranged that we should keep our men in their respective trenches, and that we should have an armistice until the next morning, when we would lower our Christmas card, and hostilities would continue. One of them presented me with the packet of cigarettes I sent you, and we gave them a plum pudding, and then we shook hands with them, and saluted each other, and returned to our respective trenches. Not a shot was fired all day, and the next morning we pulled our card down, and they put one up with "thank you" on it.

- - - - -

The Christmas truce Mervyn witnessed was to the north-east of Armentières with 'A' Company 2nd Battalion Royal Welch Fusiliers when he was confronted with seven Saxon officers. Reference was also found to him compiling a poem of the event later published in the Times or Morning Post. 'A' Company was in the frontline trenches at Frelinghein opposite the brewery that was in German hands. The German soldiers opposite were Machine Gun Company troops of the 6th Jäger Battalion attached to the 134th Infantry Regiment. In her book *Remembrance Wakes* his mother, Ethel Richardson, recorded that nineteen years after the event she still had the packet of cigarettes given to Mervyn by the German.

The above is taken from 'Purton & The Great War' by Bob Lloyd.

Part 19: January 1915

It is simplistic to say there was little activity on the Western Front. Armies or platoons still attacked and counter-attacked, and men were still dying. However nothing occurred that could be given a name such as the "Battle of This or That Place". The weather was dreadful and both sides were trying to come to terms with what had happened in the 5 months since the war had begun.

Early in January, a hospital unit was set up some sixty miles behind the front line by British civilian volunteers with the help of the Anglo-French Hospital Committee of the British Red Cross Society. The Hôpital Temporaire d'Arc-en-Barrois *(pictured)* was created in a local château for the aid of wounded French soldiers. With 110 beds it was run by the French army's Service de Santé (Health Service). The first military casualties arrived on 27 January 1915 from the Argonne Forest battlefront. In February 1915 the total number of beds was increased to 180 and the hospital ran essential services including an operating theatre, anaesthesia, radiography and dentistry, with a pharmacy and clinical laboratory. It was financially supported internationally.

Many well-known writers, poets, artists and illustrators served there as volunteers: Kathleen Scott (widow of the Antarctic explorer Robert Falcon Scott) as an ambulance coordinator; the painter and physician Henry Tonks (anaesthetist and ward physician); future Poet Laureate John Masefield (volunteer orderly - *pictured)*; poet Laurence Binyon (author of For the Fallen *"They shall not grow old as we who are left grow old ...")* as a hospital orderly. The English Impressionist painter, Wilfrid de Glehn and his American-born wife, artist Jane Emmet de Glehn served there - Wilfrid as a hospital orderly, military interpreter and ambulance driver; Jane supervising laundry and tea service and sketching soldiers' portraits for the benefit of a limb prosthetics fund.

Major offensives were ongoing on the Eastern Front despite the freezing weather of central Poland. On 31 January, Germany faced Russia at the Battle of Bolimov and used large-scale battlefield poison gas for the first time. The German army fired 18,000 artillery shells containing liquid xylyl bromide tear gas (also known as methyl-benzyl bromide or T-stoff) against the Russian Army. T-stoff is a colourless liquid with a melting point of 21°C - below that (and in the Polish winter) it is a solid. The attack depended on the heat generated by the explosive shells volatising the T-stoff to create an aerosol. But the winter weather was so cold that the chemical reverted to powder in the air, and was blown back towards the German lines or fell harmlessly to ground.

The War at Sea
Britain's main actions that month were at sea. On New Year's Day, HMS Formidable was sunk off Lyme Regis by a German U-boat with the loss of 547 crew. Then on 24 January the British Grand Fleet defeated the German High Seas Fleet at the Battle of Dogger Bank. Britain was able to decode German radio traffic and knew where and when the German fleet would be, so the German squadron was taken by surprise and fled for home. During a chase lasting several hours, the Royal Navy slowly caught up with the Germans and engaged them with long-range gunfire. The British disabled the armoured cruiser SMS Blücher, but the Germans put the British flagship HMS Lion out of action with heavy damage. Due to a signalling mix-up, the remaining British ships broke off pursuit to sink Blücher and the rest of the German squadron escaped, returning safely to harbour, though some had heavy damage requiring extended repairs.

The Air War
There was also action from the air when, on 19 January, 2 German Zeppelins dropped bombs for the first time on Great Yarmouth and King's Lynn in Norfolk, killing more than 20. Zeppelin L3 *(pictured)* was the one that attacked Great Yarmouth.

Ottoman Front

In the war in the Levant, a large force of the Ottoman Army attacked the Suez Canal on 26 January. Formerly Ottoman, Egypt was held by Britain as a Protectorate and the canal was a strategically important transport artery to the British Empire to the south and east. Two Ottoman companies under the command of the German General Kreß von Kressenstein succeeded in crossing the canal on 3 February. Strong British defence by 30,000 men of the Imperial Service Cavalry Brigade and the Bikaner Camel Corps supported by Egyptian Army units and Indian mountain artillery forced the remaining Ottoman units to abandon the attack. The Ottoman companies that had crossed the canal withdrew later that same evening.

Japan

Japan was allied to Britain and was a major player in denying ports to Germany in the sea war in the east. But Japan had its own territorial ambitions in China. On 18 January, Japan placed an ultimatum before the weak Republic of China government, known as the Twenty-One Demands. Japan sought to extend its control over Manchuria and the Chinese economy, including recognition of Japan's seizure of the German treaty ports in China. Japanese demands for new powers would have made China little more than a puppet state. British and US disapproval forced Japan to back down and Japan lost a great deal of prestige and trust in Britain and the US. The Japanese watered down their demands and agreed a treaty with China in May.

Other News

Technological advances were continuing apace: on 5 January, Joseph E. Carberry set an altitude record for a fixed-wing aircraft (with a passenger!) of 11,690 feet, this only some 13 years after the very first powered flight. On 19 January Georges Claude patented the neon tube lighting system for use in advertising. Then on the 25th, the first coast-to-coast long-distance telephone call was made in the United States by Alexander Graham Bell, between New York and San Francisco.

Nature also had a role to play. On 13 January, the Avezzano earthquake near the city of L'Aquila in Italy registered 6.8 on the Richter scale and killed 29,000 people. We can compare this with the British losses at Ypres (7,960 dead, and 17,900 missing, 29,600 wounded). Despite improved building techniques, the recent 6 April 2009 earthquake at L'Aquila (6.3 magnitude) damaged perhaps 10,000 buildings and 308 were killed.

- - - - -

In January 1915, the following Purton men were mobilised and arrived in Fance with the 1st Battalion Wiltshire Regiment at Locre, Belgium:

    Nelson (d. 20 May 1915)
    Frank Sutton (d. 30 March 1917)

Neither man survived the war and their stories will be told later.

My Family's War

Reginald Stevens

Bob Stevens writes:

The soldier in the picture is my father at the age of 17½, Reginald John Stevens - a sapper in the Royal Engineers. Unfortunately the exact date of the photograph is unknown. Reg was born on 29 January 1897. He told me that, when he enrolled for service, he was obliged to lie about his age in order to be accepted. Therefore it must have been in 1914 or just before his 18th birthday in January 1915.

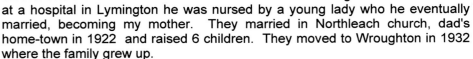

He suffered 2 wounds at different times; shrapnel in his side and a bullet in the shoulder. He survived but lost a brother and a brother-in-law in the war. Whilst convalescing at a hospital in Lymington he was nursed by a young lady who he eventually married, becoming my mother. They married in Northleach church, dad's home-town in 1922 and raised 6 children. They moved to Wroughton in 1932 where the family grew up.

Dad had the 3 WW1 medals, Pip, Squeak & Wilfred, which are now with my son in Exeter. The information on my Dad's 1914 'Mons' Star is as follows:-
R.J. STEVENS, SPR: 65097, R. E.

The Military Service number above suggests a fairly early entry. (Service Numbers in 1958 were upwards of 4000000.)

Of interest to his family and grandchildren is that his name is displayed on the Roll of Honour (as wounded) in Northleach Church together with two other Stevens's, one his brother Arthur, who gave their lives in WW1.

Eccentricity or Experience: I remember that early in the Second World War my father dug an Underground Shelter in the garden at Wroughton. It had a corrugated steel roof, duck boards and seating and was covered in turf. It has taken me 70 years plus to recognise that he was not eccentric but merely reacting to his WW1 experience. It was only filled in when replaced by two Anderson shelters later in WW2. The whistle *(pictured)* is a souvenir of his service, as also was a bayonet, (in Exeter). Ugh!

BOB STEVENS (Son)

Part 20: February 1915

Turkish Front

We've already noted that the war on the Western Front had come to a stalemate. The Allies were rethinking their strategies. Might an offensive through the Balkans work, or even a landing on Germany's Baltic coast? Anything could be better than the costly attacks in France and Belgium.

Early in 1915 the Russians found themselves threatened by the Turks at Sarikamish in the Caucasus and appealed for a diversion to give them some relief. However by 4 January the Russians had defeated the Turks in temperatures around -30°C; more than 30,000 Turks froze to death. Britain decided to mount a naval bombardment to take the Gallipoli Peninsula on the western shore of the Dardanelles, capture Constantinople, and link up with the Russians. If they could take Turkey out of the war, they might persuade the Balkan states to join the Allies.

In political support to this, on 15 February the Allied governments suggested to Greece that she and other Balkan states should intervene in support of Serbia. Greece was promised military support at the port of Salonika (Thessaloniki). The aim of this was to drive a military wedge between Turkey and Austria-Hungary.

British warships began the bombardment of the outer forts of the Dardanelles on 19 February, but bad weather caused delays and little damage was done. Three Royal Navy battleships were sunk and three others damaged; the attack was stopped. Two Royal Marines battalions (29th Division) landed at the Aegean island of Lemnos on 23 February to prepare landing parties to demolish the Turkish guns. On 25 February, the navy resumed bombardment of the outer forts with more success and, the following day, the Marines landed at the forts at Kumkale on the mainland and at Sedd-el-Bahr (Seddülbahir) on Gallipoli, putting many of the Turkish guns out of action. A promising start it would seem … On the 20th, the Australian and New Zealand troops, still in Egypt, were ordered to prepare to move to Gallipoli and would land there in March.

Western Front

Meanwhile, on the Western Front, the 1st Canadian Division crossed from England into France on 9 February including Captain Prower, formerly of Purton. To the south, French forces were trying to drive the Germans back into the Champagne region, but gained only a few hundred yards at the cost of 50,000 casualties. During this, on 26 February at Malancourt in the Argonne, German troops used flame-throwers against French troops for the first time.

On 24 February, the first British Territorial Division left England for France (46th North Midland).

The War at Sea

At sea, there were several new and important developments starting on 1 February when the Admiralty stopped neutral fishing vessels using British ports. Then on the 6th the British liner RMS Lusitania sailing home from New York

RMS Lusitania in 1907

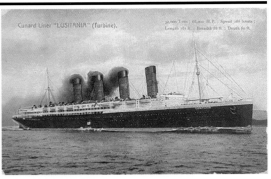

arrived into Liverpool safely ... but flying the US flag instead of the Red Ensign. The next day the Foreign Office tried to justify the use of a "neutral" flag but, by the 10th, US President Wilson had protested the use of US flags on British merchant ships to deceive the Germans.

The next day, the SS Dacia sailed from America for Bremen in Germany with a cargo of cotton. Having crossed the Atlantic it was intercepted and seized by French naval forces on 27 February.

Germany, however, had decided that the waters around the British Isles were a war zone. On 4 February they announced a submarine blockade of Britain would begin on 18 February. On the 19th, the Norwegian ship Belridge was torpedoed by a German submarine, without warning, but did safely reach port. The German Government claimed that the Belridge was attacked in error.

Britain responded by completing a net across the Irish Sea, on 22 February, between Scotland and Ireland, denying the North Channel as a passage for submarines. That day, Germany began its unrestricted submarine war and the day after sank the US ships Carib and Evelyn and torpedoed the Norwegian Regin.

The Air War
In the air war, on 17 February, 2 German Zeppelins were blown off course by strong winds in the North Sea and were destroyed on landing in Denmark. These were the same L3 and L4 that had bombed Norfolk in January.

Eastern Front
On the Eastern Front, the Russians suffered heavy losses at the 2nd Battle of the Masurian Lakes between 7 and 21 February (also known as the Winter Battle). Of strategic importance, Memel in East Prussia (now called Klaipėda in Lithuania) was reoccupied by German forces on 17 February and on 21 February the 20th Russian Army corps surrendered. In the aftermath of the Masurian Lakes, after the Battle of Przasnysz (22-27 February) some 20,000 Russian troops were taken captive while allowing the main Russian armies time to retreat and regroup. At the same time Austro-Hungarian forces were attacking Russian Poland (Galicia) and retook Czernowitz (Bukovina) on the 17th and Stanislau on the 19th.

Other Sectors
On the Political front, the British, French and Russian governments agreed on 5 February to pool their financial resources for prosecuting the war. On the 16th, Britain extended the prohibition of Trading with the Enemy to include territories in British, enemy, or friendly occupation.

Britain and Belgium had concluded an agreement on 3 February delimiting the Uganda-Congo border so that British colonial troops could protect the Congo and seek out German insurgent forces without prior consultation.

Also in February, the Bulgarian Government negotiated a loan of £3 million from Germany. On 6 August they went on to negotiate a fresh loan for 400 million francs with Austro-German banks. And by then, although neutral, their fate was sealed with the Central Powers whether they liked it or not.

In the East, there was a problem in Singapore. On 27 January, the commander of the Indian 5th Light Infantry announced they would transfer to Hong Kong for garrison duties, replacing another Indian regiment. However, rumours circulated among the Indian troops (sepoys) that they might instead be sent to Europe, or to Turkey to fight against their fellow Muslims. Three Indian officers and other ring-leaders amongst the sepoys rebelled when they were ordered to board HMS Nile. The mutiny (15 February) lasted seven days and resulted in the deaths of 47 British soldiers and local civilians, before it was finally quashed.

On the southern Ottoman Front on 2 February Turkish advance-guards, having crossed the Sinai desert, again attacked the on the Suez Canal: they engaged British outposts the next day but withdrew on the 4th. Also on 2 February, the British Aden protectorate was invaded by Turkish forces.

In South Africa, many Afrikaaners were against the proposal for Union of South Africa forces to invade German South West Africa. Units under Lt-Col Maritz at Northern Cape rebelled and commandos were formed in the Orange Free State (OFS) and Transvaal. The Maritz Rebellion ended on 4 February with the surrender of the remaining rebels. This cleared the way for South African units, on 22 February, to advance from Swakopmund on the German South West African coast towards the capital Windhoek.

On the 16th, Oyem in the German Kamerun was occupied by French forces.

In February 1915, the following Purton men were mobilised to France:
John Mervyn Prower, 8th Canadian Battalion.
Mervyn Thomas Webb, "A" Battery, 186th Brigade, Royal Field Artillery.

Part 21: March 1915

Spanbroekmolen - 12 March

James Pound enlisted in peacetime in 1906 at the age of 17 years, 11 months. He was born in Purton the son of Charles and Elizabeth Pound and his occupation was given as agricultural labourer. He had arrived in France in August 1914 with the 1st Battalion Wiltshire Regiment, was wounded in action on 31 October 1914 and transferred to the UK on 9 November 1914 with gunshot wounds to the right groin and left finger. On 10 February 1915 he rejoined the 1st Battalion at Locre (Loker), Belgium, part of a replacement draft of 34 men.

On 12 March 1915, the 1st Battalion was at Kemmel, Belgium, about 6 miles southwest of Ypres. James Pound's company left billets at Loker at 2.45 am and marched 2½ miles via Kemmel to a section in front of Spanbroekmolen, near Wijtschate on the Messines-Ypres road arriving at dawn (5.30 am) and occupied trenches with the Worcestershire Regiment to their right. Mist delayed an artillery bombardment but by 2.30 pm it was clear enough for the artillery bombardment to begin and continue till 4.10 pm with field guns firing shrapnel to cut the enemy wire, and high explosives to beat down the German trenches. At 4.10 the infantry assault was launched but failed to reach its objectives and they withdrew under heavy fire at 7 pm.

The Wiltshires returned to billets at Loker having lost 32 killed, 48 wounded and 12 missing. James Pound was among those killed, aged 26. He has no known grave but is remembered on the Menin Gate at Ypres (Panel 53). Wiltshire Regiment records in Salisbury list a grave for James: "Spanbroek Molen. 2500 yards E of Lindenhoek near Kemmel. Not marked." A number of men who died on this date, and were recorded as buried at the same location, can be found in the Commonwealth War Graves Commission cemetery at La Laiterie. This cemetery was used at the end of the war to concentrate many burials from around the Kemmel area. There are 180 burial plots that are not identified; simply a Soldier of the Great War. James could possibly lie under one of these stones.*

*[*Information on James Pound and Spanbroekmolen extracted from Purton & The Great War by Bob Lloyd with permission.]*

The Battle of Neuve-Chapelle - 11-13 March

Spanbroekmolen was an ancillary attack within the Battle of Neuve-Chapelle. More troops had arrived from Britain and relieved French forces in Flanders, forming a continuous 35-mile British line from just north of Ypres south to Givenchy-lès-la-Bassée. The BEF launched an offensive at Neuve-Chapelle, 20 miles south of Ypres (and 14 miles south of Spanbroekmolen), to break through the German lines and rush on to the Aubers Ridge and possibly Lille. The French Tenth Army's involvement was reduced to heavy artillery support due to lack of troops that had not been relieved from British sectors.

Neuve-Chapelle was the first deliberate British offensive of the war and showed the new method of offence on the Western Front. The First Army prepared the attack with great attention to detail and achieved tactical surprise and a break-through. After the first planned attack, unexpected delays slowed operations, communication failures hindered the command structure as the telephone system broke down. The German defenders were reinforced and dug a new line behind the British break-in.

Elsewhere on the Western Front

On 7 March the Royal Flying Corps made their first tactical bombing raids in support of ground troops in Menin and Courtai.

In March 1915, the following Purton men were mobilised to France:
Edwin Frank Brown, 7th Battalion Middlesex Regiment
George Edward Butcher, 2nd Battalion Wiltshire Regiment.
John Davies, 4th Battalion Gloucestershire Regiment

Arthur James Gunter, Wiltshire Regiment.
Denis Law, 3rd Battalion Wiltshire Regiment, Labour Corps.
Percy Charles Matthews, 2nd Battalion Wiltshire Regiment.
Albert James Parsons, 1st Battalion King's Royal Rifle Corps.
Ernest Ponting, Royal Field Artillery.

In the Turkish Sector

Things were hotting up out east. On 4 March the French government decided to send an Expeditionary Force to the Dardanelles. And on the 5th the Greek government offered naval and military forces for operations there. Britain also commenced a naval bombardment of Smyrna (Izmir) lasting from 5 - 9 March.

Britain had landed 2 battalions of the Royal Marines on the Turkish island of Lemnos on 23 February to plan an assault at the Dardanelles to destroy the Turkish gun batteries. On 7 March, Greece requested an explanation of the Lemnos landings which Britain explained on 9 March to be a military necessity, and on 20 March, Britain guaranteed that Lemnos would be given to Greece after the war.

General Sir Ian Hamilton was appointed on 12 March to command the military operations at Gallipoli and took command on 17 March. Meanwhile on 13 March the Mediterranean Expeditionary Force sailed from Egypt.

An allied naval attack in the Dardanelles was repelled on 18 March by the Turkish shore batteries and the British battleships HMS Irresistible and HMS Ocean and the French battleship Bouvet were all sunk by Turkish mines.

Also on 18 March General Sir John Nixon was appointed to command the British and Indian forces in Mesopotamia. The German General, Liman von Sanders was appointed to command Turkish forces at Gallipoli on 25 March.

Between March and May 1915, the Russian Navy's Black Sea Fleet began seaplane carrier raids against the Bosphorus and the Ottoman Empire's European Black Sea coast. This was the first time that battleships played a subsidiary role to plane carrying ships.

On the political front, on 4 March, the Russian government laid claim to Constantinople to which Britain and France agreed on 14 March. Eyeing up future territory, France lodged a claim with Britain for control of Syria and Cilicia (south-western Turkey) on 17 March.

At Sea, Britain began a blockade of German East Africa on 1 March and on 11 March announced a blockade of all German ports. Off the coast of Chile, the Royal Navy cornered the German light cruiser SMS Dresden at the Chilean Robinson Crusoe Island (Más a Tierra). This, the last surviving ship of the German East Asia Squadron, was left with no option but to scuttle on 14 March. On 28 March a British passenger ship, RMS Falaba was sunk by a German submarine in the middle of the St George's Channel between Wales and Ireland. In response, Britain declared a complete embargo on international trade with Germany to which the Americans objected. Following a short political crisis, Britain and America agreed that the US would only export rubber to Britain.

My Family's War

Roger Moreton

Libbie Sheppard has provided us with the following letters from her Grandpa, Roger Morton (b. 1893), who wrote frequently to a friend named Russell Smith, who kept them so we still have access to them. Roger had joined up in September 1914 and was obviously frustrated at not being at the front as we can see from this snapshot of March 1915, when he would have been about 22, and at the rank of sergeant:

Birkenhead February 1915
I am not gazetted to the battalion, it is only a reserve one, really I am in the 1st Cheshires and I am only gazetted here for duties till there is a vacancy for me in the 1st, which is out at the front now.

Birkenhead 3rd March 1915
I had a nice slack week-end at 168, sat and talked and smoked all Saturday and Sunday. I'm working pretty hard, averaging 8 hours per day, and some days more, teaching these blessed recruits how to wield a gun. How long I'm going to be here I don't know but I wish with all my heart to go out as unless one does go, there is no promotion after it. I have at last had my photo taken, I hope it will be a good one. You say something about tea for lady friends, tea for lady friends indeed! I don't think a lady has been to this place since the days of Eve and goodness only knows when there will be another here.

Lingdale House, Birkenhead 10th March 1915
The above address is my new billet, I've been moved to another Co'y and am in an empty house. (I mean empty from a civilian point of view.) We have about 20 men here and four of us sleep and eat in one room, so we pig it a bit as you might expect. We don't mess till 8 and finish about 9, so I go to bed as soon as I can. The work with this company is not as strenuous as the other, but it's rather more boring as it's nearly all musketry and that is the most boring thing going.

Birkenhead 17th March 1915
I've just had a pretty hard day, been on the range from 8.30 am till 4.30 pm with an hour for lunch, putting men through a musketry course - then from 4.45 to 6 pm shooting, myself, with a revolver, then I boxed, and now I'm trying to scribe to you. Thank goodness one of our men has gone out to the front so there are only three of us in the room now. Nine of our fellows went out last week so I expect my turn will not be long in coming. I certainly think I shall get out, we haven't nearly finished with the 'Boches' yet, in fact I think we have the dickens of a job before us. I'm going to the theatre with Alice tomorrow - 'The Cinema Star' - I don't know what it will be like. I'm having a pretty good time considering we're at war, and I hope to go out and fight anytime now.

You will be pleased to know that Roger survived the war.

Part 22: April 1915

Two major campaigns started this month:

On the Western Front the **2nd Battle of Ypres** commenced on 22 April. During this battle the Germans used poison gas for the first time in large scale on that front.

An example of many that illustrates the horrors of poison gas is that which occurred at the Battle of 's Gravenstafel, a hamlet about 4 miles north-east of Ypres, German troops had carried 5,730 gas cylinders, weighing 41 kg each, to the front by hand. A total of 171 tonnes of chlorine gas was released over a 4-mile front. The cylinders were opened by hand, relying on the prevailing winds to carry the gas towards the allied lines, but because of vagaries of the wind, many German soldiers were injured or killed in the process.

The French Territorial and colonial Moroccan and Algerian troops in the path of the gas cloud suffered 6,000 casualties, many of whom died within ten minutes, primarily from asphyxiation and tissue damage in the lungs, and many more were blinded. Chlorine is denser than air, so it quickly filled the trenches, forcing the troops to climb out into heavy enemy fire.

The 4-mile gap it created in the front line was a surprise to the German army who had underestimated its effect and had too few reserves to take advantage of it. Canadian Expeditionary Force troops were able to defend the flank of the break-in by urinating into cloths and putting them to their faces, to counter the effects of the gas. Casualties were especially heavy for the 13th Battalion CEF, which was enveloped on three sides and over-extended by the demands of securing its left once the Algerian Division had broken.

In April 1915, the following Purton men were mobilised to France:
Thomas Henry Embury, 2nd Battalion Wiltshire Regiment.
Leonard Cecil Ovens, Middlesex Regiment.
Albert Edwin Tuck, West Riding Regiment.

A few days later, after unsuccessful naval bombardments, 25 April saw the start of the **Gallipoli Campaign** (lasting until January 1916). The Australian and New Zealand Army Corps, newly arrived via Cairo, landed at Anzac Cove while British and French troops landed at Cape Helles. The intention was take the Gallipoli peninsula, speed on to Istanbul and take Turkey out of the war.

Purtonian, Geoffrey Charlton Paine Rumming, Royal Naval Air Service, was sent to Gallipoli with No 3 Armoured Car Squadron, on board the SS River Clyde during the landings on V beach. The landing did not go as planned and there were many wounded soldiers in the water requiring assistance. Petty Officer (PO) Peering seeing this called for help and was assisted by numerous 13 platoon, D Company, Anson Battalion members as well as Chief Petty Officer (CPO) Rumming. They joined Sub Lt Arthur Tisdall in carrying out numerous journeys to rescue soldiers in the water and stranded on rocks. He later recalled; "There were four men in the boat, Sub Lt Tisdall, a black bearded PO, a seaman and myself. We got 3 wounded in the boat on the first trip and

4 in the second trip. Beyond getting a few bullet holes in the boat above the waterline, the first trip was quite successful. On the second trip Sub Lt Tisdall and myself clambered over a spit of rock to get to the men lying higher up.

"We got shot at and lay down for a time. As we were lifting the last wounded man into the boat I got hit again in the back. We had taken the boat a little further ashore, and when we went to push off again found her grounded. When we did eventually succeed in getting off, Lt Tisdall and myself were unable to climb into the boat and so we hung onto the side as the other 2 men, keeping as low as possible, rowed back to the River Clyde".

On this trip back Tisdall and another man were wounded. The small party had tried for over an hour to recover as many men as possible from under the Turkish machine guns. One of the witnesses to this action was Lt Cmdr Wedgwood, Rumming's CO who was a close friend of Winston Churchill, recommending CPO Rumming and another CPO (Russell) for the Victoria Cross.

This was not awarded but they were awarded the Conspicuous Gallantry Medal instead. Sub Lt Tisdall was awarded the VC; he was later killed in action on 6 May.

Although the allied forces eventually completed their landing the Ottoman defenders stopped the Allied advance halfway between the Helles headland and Krithia village, having inflicted 3,000 casualties. With more Ottoman reinforcements arriving, the fighting at Helles and Anzac, became a battle of attrition.

Italy: On 26 April, Italy signed the Treaty of London agreeing to leave the Triple Alliance with Germany and Austria-Hungary and join with the Triple Entente of Britain, France and Russia.

Part 23: May 1915

Western Front

On 3 May, a Canadian soldier John McCrae, wrote the poem "In Flanders Fields". He was a field surgeon in the Canadian artillery and in charge of a field hospital during the 2nd Battle of Ypres. His friend and former student, Lt. Alexis Helmer, was killed in the battle, and his burial inspired the poem.

On 9 May, the Allied spring offensive began. French forces attacked in Artois, captured the Lorette heights and advanced on Vimy Ridge. The British attacked further north in support of the French at Aubers Ridge to prevent German troops being moved south beyond the La Bassée canal. No ground was won and no tactical advantage gained -- a total disaster for the British with 11,000 dead or wounded.

The British attack was repeated further south on 15 May when the BEF attacked at the Battle of Festubert (15-25 May). A 60-hour bombardment by 433 guns firing about 100,000 shells preceded the attack, but made little impact on the German Sixth Army's front line defences. The initial advance made some progress in good weather. The attack was renewed on 16 May but by 19 May the

British 2nd and 7th divisions (which included the 1st Wilts) had to be withdrawn due to heavy losses.

Nelson Caldwell, born in Purton in 1894, and the son of John and Mary Caldwell, The Turnpike, Rockley Road, Marlborough, had arrived in France on 19 January 1915 as part of a draft of 128 men joining the 1st Battalion Wiltshire Regiment at Locre (Loker). Between Nelson's arrival date and his death, the 1st Battalion was in the trenches at Locre, Kemmel, La Clyte, Dickebush, Vermezeel and Elzenwalle. He died, aged 21, on 20 May 1915 of wounds received at Festubert.   Nelson is buried in Elzenwalle Brasserie Cemetery *(pictured)*, Flanders, Belgium.

On 18 May the Canadian Division and 51st (Highland) Division renewed the advance but made little progress against German artillery fire. The Allied forces entrenched themselves at the new front line while the Germans reinforced theirs. From 20-25 May the attack was resumed and Festubert was captured. The offensive had resulted in a 3km (2 miles) advance.

On 9 May the first British New Army division sailed for service in France.

In May 1915, the following Purton men were mobilised to France:
Charles Lockey, 3rd (Reserve) Battalion Duke of Cornwall Light Infantry.
Ernest Reuben Hewer, Royal Field Artillery.
Thomas Norman Hale, Royal Field Artillery.
Arthur Edgar Ovens, Royal Field Artillery.

Italy
On 13 May, both the Italian Prime Minister and the Foreign Minister resigned in the light of political moves away from the Central Powers towards the Allies. The new government ordered mobilisation on 23 May and declared war on Austria-Hungary.   Next day, Italy formally joined the Allies and crossed the Austrian frontier at midnight 24-25 May. Germany immediately cut off diplomatic relations and war was declared between Germany and Italy on 27 May.

The Italian fleet started operations in the Adriatic and the Italian Government announced a blockade of the Austro-Hungarian Adriatic coast. A British naval battle squadron had formed at Malta and joined the Italian Adriatic fleet on 27 May.

Valona (Vlorë) in Albania was formally occupied by Italian forces on 29 May.

Gallipoli Campaign
On 5 May, Ottoman forces began shelling Anzac Cove from a new position behind their lines while, on the 6th, Allied forces tried for the second time to capture the strategic village of Krithia on the peninsula. Little ground was taken after two days of costly fighting and the objective remained out of reach. On 19 May the Ottomans made their third attack on Anzac Cove but were repelled by the Australian and New Zealand Army Corps.

Naval losses were also increasing. Between 13 and 27 May, HMS Goliath

was sunk by a Turkish destroyer (750 dead) and a German submarine (U21) sank HMS Triumph (78 dead) and HMS Majestic (49 dead).

On 15 May Admiral of the Fleet John Arbuthnot "Jacky" Fisher resigned as First Sea Lord, in frustration over Winston Churchill's Gallipoli campaign. Churchill, himself, resigned as First Lord of the Admiralty on 27 May. Fisher was replaced by Sir Henry Jackson and Churchill by Arthur Balfour on 28 May.

Eastern Fronts
In the east, the Austrians and Germans began their spring offensives against Russia in the Baltic provinces and Galicia.

Russo-Turkish Front
The Battle of Dilman, North Persia, on 15 May was a total victory for the Russians against an Ottoman force of predominantly Kurdish troops. On 19 May, Van, in Turkish Armenia, was taken by Russian forces and the Armenian garrison relieved. A Russian Expeditionary Force to West Persia landed at Enzeli on 21 May. Russian forces captured Urmia in North Persia on 24 May.

Africa
South African forces occupied Windhoek in German South West Africa on 13 May, while in East Africa British forces secured control of Lake Nyasa on 30 May. In West Africa, the Siege of Garua in German Kamerun began on 31 May, with French and British forces surrounding the fort.

Politics
On 17 May, Prime Minister Herbert Asquith reorganised his Liberal government as a coalition of all parties with effect from 25 May.

Meanwhile on 7 May, the British Foreign Minister (Sir Edward Grey) gave Serbia a conditional guarantee that Bosnia and Herzegovina (Austrian) would be ceded to Serbia after the war.

On 24 May, the Entente Governments declared that they would hold Turkish Ministers personally responsible for the Armenian massacres earlier in the year.

China agreed to the Twenty-One Demands of the Japanese on 25 May, and signed agreements regarding Shantung, South Manchuria and Inner Mongolia.

The Lusitania
On 1 May, the American 5,189 ton oil tanker SS "Gulflight" was torpedoed without warning west of the Scilly Isles. She was damaged but reached port. This was the first United States ship attacked by German submarine.

Then on 7 May, the British ocean liner RMS Lusitania, homebound for Liverpool, was torpedoed and sunk by the German U-boat U-20 off the Old Head of Kinsale, Ireland, killing 1,198 civilians, many of them American, en route from New York to Liverpool. This created a US-German diplomatic crisis. In a speech on 9 May, President Wilson defined United States policy in regard to the "Lusitania Outrage" in which he said, "There is such a thing as a man being too proud to fight. There is such a thing as a nation being so right that it does not need to convince others by force that it is right". Britain was

An artist's impression of the sinking

alarmed at the lack of threat in this speech, having expected America to declare war immediately.

Wilson sent a subdued note to the Germans protesting about submarine warfare against commercial shipping. An evasive German reply was received with indignation. The pacifist Secretary of State Bryan resigned in the face of potential war, and was replaced by Robert Lansing.

Elsewhere at sea, on 27 May, the British Minelayer HMS "Princess Irene", a commandeered and converted liner, blew up while being loaded with mines and was destroyed by an internal explosion in Sheerness harbour.

Other News
At Quintinshill, Scotland, on 22 May a troop train bound for Liverpool collided with a local train. A north-bound express then hit the wreckage and a fire set off by the trains' gas coach lighting engulfed two goods trains on adjacent tracks. 226 were killed, mostly troops of the Royal Scots bound for Gallipoli - the highest number of fatalities in a rail accident in the United Kingdom.

31 May saw the first German airship raid on London.

Part 24: June 1915

The Second Battle of Artois continued. The British 7th Division including the 2nd Wilts moved into the Givenchy sector *(Givenchy-Lès-la-Bassée)* shortly after their costly involvement in the Aubers Ridge and Festubert assaults. It proved to be a very difficult line to hold, being subject to constant mining, sniping and trench mortar activity. A decision was taken to make a large-scale attack on the German front between a point east of Givenchy to just south of Rue d'Ouvert, to capture some key points.

Percy Charles Matthews, was only 17 years old when he enlisted, the son of John and Agnes Matthews, Linden Villa, Purton. He had arrived in France in March 1915 and joined the 2nd Battalion Wiltshire Regiment at Estaires. On 15 June, the Battalion was in the trenches at Givenchy. During the day their trenches were shelled and those platoons suffered a few casualties. At 6 pm the battalion broke out of their trenches to attack and were subjected to heavy frontal and enfilade fire. The attack was subsequently cancelled and the Wiltshires withdrew, handing over their position to the Bedfordshire Regiment. During the action the Germans used incendiary bullets, and also sniped the wounded in front of their trenches.

Percy was reported missing in action on 15 June 1915 aged 17 years, 9 months old. His parents were later told that he had been killed in action, the youngest recorded Purton casualty of the war. Percy has no known grave and is remembered on the Le Touret Memorial *(pictured)*, Pas De Calais, France. He is remembered on the Purton War Memorial and in the Memorials in St Mary's Church.

The Artois offensive ended on 18 June. It is an irony that the Battle of Waterloo was fought exactly 100 years previously on 18 June 1815, some 83 miles to the east, in territory held in 1915 by the Germans.

On 7 June the German Zeppelin LZ37 was destroyed in the air near Ghent in Belgium by Lt Warneford of the Royal Naval Air Service. This was the first shooting down of an airship by an aeroplane.

On 2 June, Britain announced a blockade of the coast of Asia Minor and 2 days later British forces made a third attempt to capture the strategic village of Krithia at Gallipoli. The next major attack by British forces was on 28 June in the Gully Ravine area.

On the Southern Front, on 3 June San Marino declared war on Austria-Hungary. The River Isonzo (Soča) area was important to the Italians as it was the only pass between Italy and Austria on which they could mount an attack and divided Italy from one of its major goals, Trieste. The Italians captured Monfalcone (now in Slovenia) on 9 June and then mounted a major offensive on 29 June, the first of 12 battles in the Izonzo area.

On the Russian Front, on 3 June, joint Austrian and German forces recaptured Przemysl, a crucial city in southeastern Poland, and the entire Russian front began to collapse.

In Western Africa, on 10 June, British and French troops captured Garua, effectively conquering the German colony of Kamerun. They completed the victory by capturing Naugundere on the 28th.

To the south, on 19 June, South African forces began an advance on Otavifontein, in German South West Africa (Namibia). An anti-British revolt in South Africa was ended on 21 June with the arrest of General De Law.

In Mesopotamia, the 6th (Poona) Division captured Amara on 3 June. And on 27 June a joint British and Indian force began an advance up river on the Euphrates.

Following the sinking of the Lusitania in May, William Jennings Bryan resigned as US Secretary of State on 9 June, the same day as President Wilson sent a second Lusitania note to Germany demanding reparations and prevention of 'the recurrence of anything so obviously subversive of the principles of warfare'. America refused to recognise the war zone that Germany has proclaimed around the British Isles.

During June 1915, the following men with Purton connections mobilised:

To Gallipoli:
    Arthur Robert Bunce, 5th Battalion Wiltshire Regiment.
    Frederick Keen, 5th Battalion Wiltshire Regiment.
    Harry Robert Thomas Matthews, 6th Battalion Wiltshire Regiment.

To France:
    John Charles Arthur Evans, Royal Field Artillery.
    Alfred J Mussell, Wiltshire Regiment *(Battalion unknown)*.
    Bertram Plummer, 4th Battalion Royal Irish Regiment.
    Leslie Victor Selby, Royal Field Artillery.

Part 25: July 1915

Tom Martin *(pictured)* was born in Purton in 1886 and enlisted in England in 1911 with the 21st (Empress of India's) Lancers. He was stationed in Cairo at the outbreak of war, and later moved to the frontier station at Risalpur with the rank of Lance Corporal. (The most famous engagement of the 21st had been at the Battle of Omdurman, Sudan in 1898, where Winston Churchill, then an officer of the 4th Hussars, rode with the unit.)

Risalpur today is a city in Nowshera District, in modern day Pakistan, some 45 km from Peshawar. It is located in a depression some 1014 feet above sea level. The famous Khyber Pass lies 90 km to the north.

Tom died of sunstroke on 30 July 1915. He was buried in Nowshera Military Cemetery, India, and is remembered on the Delhi Memorial (India Gate) - *pictured*. Of the 13,300 Commonwealth servicemen commemorated by name on the memorial, just over 1,000 lie in cemeteries to the west of the River Indus, where maintenance was not possible, Nowshera being one such place. Tom is listed on Swindon's Roll of Honour.

Tom's Brother Dan also served with the 21st Lancers; he survived the War and later emigrated to Canada.

The following men with Purton connections were mobilised:
Gallipoli:
    Alfred W Matthews, 5th (Service) Battalion Wiltshire Regiment
    Herbert Stanley Woolford, Wiltshire Regiment
    Bertie William Curtis, 5th Battalion Wiltshire Regiment.
    Arthur Ockwell, 5th Battalion Wiltshire Regiment.

Sidney Rowland Smith, 5th Battalion Wiltshire Regiment.
Albert Canning, 1/7th Battalion Manchester Regiment

France:
Edward John Bunce, 6th Battalion Wiltshire Regiment
Louis Walter Gough, Royal Field Artillery, Royal Horse Artillery

Egypt:
Edwin E Saunders, 54th Brigade, Ammunition Column Royal Field Artillery

In Britain the Munitions of War Act became law creating the Ministry of Munitions (2 July) and the National Registration Act came into force on 15 July.

On the **Eastern Front** a series of battles on the Russian borders with Germany and Austria-Hungary resulted in the Russian "Great Retreat" as their forces pulled back from Poland (which was part of Russia), taking machinery and equipment with them.

The Hooge Mine
Towards the tail end of the 2nd Battle of Ypres, the Belgian village of Hooge in the Ypres salient was completely destroyed. Both sides had exploded mines beneath the front line trenches there however the largest crater was created by a mine detonated at Hooge by the 175th Tunnelling Company of the Royal Engineers on 19 July 1915. The explosion created a crater that had a lip 15 feet above ground level, 120 feet wide and 20 feet deep. It has since been filled in, but several other large mine craters in the course of the fighting can still be seen.

In Africa, Union of South Africa forces under General Botha took the surrender of German South-West Africa with assistance from Canada, Britain, Portugal and Portuguese Angola. South Africa occupied South-West Africa until March 1990 when it became independent as Namibia.

In the **Ottoman theatre**, on 5 July Turkish forces took control of Lahej in South Arabia (modern-day Yemen) where Saudi Arabia is fighting Yemeni factions at the time of writing. And Anglo-Indian forces captured Nasiriyah in Mesopotamia (modern Iraq) on 25 July. A few days later, on 29 July, British and Russian forces co-operated to form the East Persia Cordon to prevent Turkish and German infiltration from Persia into Afghanistan and therefore protect British India just to the east.

On 14 July, Hussein bin Ali, Sharif of Mecca in the Hejaz, opened direct negotiations with British Government for co-operation against the Turks. This set the scene for the eventual posting of T.E. Lawrence to the Hejaz in October 1916.

The **Central Powers** (Germany, Austria-Hungary and Turkey) signed a Treaty of Alliance with Bulgaria on 17 July. Albania would be ceded to Bulgaria in return for Bulgarian participation in the war. Bulgaria declared war on Serbia in October 1915.

On 28 July 1915, Pope Benedict XV published an appeal for peace, commemorating the first anniversary of the outbreak of the war, asking warring sides to lay down their weapons and begin negotiations. His appeal went unheard as the conflict grew and worsened. Benedict later focused his efforts on humanitarian assistance and above all on helping the victims of the greatest atrocity of the war: the Armenian Genocide in which the Ottoman authorities massacred some 1.5 million people between April 1915 and 1918.

Part 26: August 1915

August 1915 was a bad month for Purton.

Ernest Henry Kibblewhite (aged 27 and son of William and Elizabeth E Kibblewhite, Station Road, Purton), **Arthur Robert Bunce** (aged 21 and son of John Robert and Mary Ann Bunce, Pavenhill, Purton) and **Sidney Rowland Smith** (aged 18 and son of James and Charlotte Smith, The Common), were all serving with 5th Battalion Wiltshire Regiment. They were killed in action on 10 August 1915, when the battalion was decimated by a Turkish attack at Chunuk Bair on the Gallipoli peninsula. None have a known grave. They are remembered on the Helles Memorial Panel 156 to 158. The Memorial at Helles bears more than 21,000 names. Sidney was reported missing in action, and later presumed to have been killed.

A few days later **George Arthur Paginton** (aged 28 and son of George and Louisa Paginton, of Pavenhill) was killed in action on 16 August 1915. George was attached from the 6th Wilts to the 7th (Service) Battalion Royal Dublin Fusiliers. The Turks launched an early morning attack in large numbers. The battalion was withdrawn to reserve at 1000 hrs. During the action the Dubliners lost 11 officers and 137 other ranks. George has no known grave and is remembered on Panels 190 to 196 on the Helles Memorial.

Frederick John Mills was born in Purton the son of Samuel and Ann A Mills, of Wootton Bassett Road, Purton, but had emigrated to Australia in 1911 or 1912. He joined the 18th Battalion, Australian Imperial Force, with the rank of Bugler and landed at ANZAC Cove on 18 August 1915. An eyewitness

The Helles Memorial

The Lone Pine Memorial

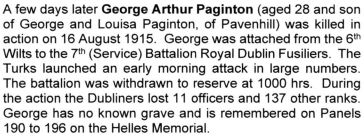

Above, top to bottom:
Arthur Bunce
Sidney Smith
George Paginton
Frederick Mills

(no picture of Ernest Kibblewhite is available)

report says, "Bugler Mills was in a charge against Hill 60 on Sunday morning 22 August 1915. He came on a Turkish machine gun in the charge and endeavoured to use it on the Turks. Whilst doing this he was wounded in the wrist. Shortly afterwards he was shot through the heart." His body was never recovered so he has no known grave. He is remembered on the Lone Pine Memorial at Gallipoli which commemorates more than 4,900 Australian and New Zealand servicemen who died in the Anzac area whose graves are not known.

All 5 men are remembered on the Purton War Memorial and in the Memorials in St Mary's Church.

In August 1915, the following men with Purton connections were mobilised:

To France:
George King, Royal Engineers, Labour Corps.
Ernest Jessie Matthews, B Sub Section, "A" Battery 61 Howitzer Brigade Guards.

To Gallipoli:
Arthur Paginton, 7th Battalion Royal Dublin Fusiliers *(see above).*
Frederick John Mills, 18th Battalion Australian Infantry Force *(see above).*

To the Royal Navy:
Herbert Ernest Martin, Royal Navy.

Western Front
1 August is regarded as the start of the 'Fokker Scourge' with the German Fokker 'Eindecker' (single deck or wing) monoplane dominant over the Western Front. It was the first type of aircraft to have a 'synchronization gear' which allowed a machine gun to fire through the spinning propeller without striking the blades. This gave an important advantage over other fighter aircraft where the pilot could only guess where his guns were pointing. By late 1915 the Germans achieved air superiority, making it difficult and dangerous for Allied planes to acquire aerial reconnaissance. This began the era of the 'Air Aces'.

At Home on 16 August, Lowca and Harrington, near Whitehaven (Cumbria), were shelled by a German submarine.

Gallipoli Sector
On 1 August, Constantinople harbour was raided by British submarines but without significant result.

Meanwhile on the Gallipoli peninsular, an attempt was made on 6 August to break out from Anzac Cove to create a third bridgehead to link up with Anzac forces and then capture nearby heights. This involved a major Allied landing at Suvla Bay on the northern shore with a diversionary attack at Sari Bair:

The next day saw the assault against Russell's Top. 232 Australians died in the battle.

Eastern Front
The Russian retreat of July 1915 was followed by a large land grab in Russian Poland by the German forces. On 5 August, Warsaw fell, followed by Novo-

Georgievsk and Osovets, and Kovno in Lithuania. Brest-Litovsk fell to the Germans on the 25th and Byelostok the next day.

Germany had started a naval attack on Riga, Estonia, on 8 August. On 19 August the British submarine E-1 torpedoed the German battle cruiser Moltke in the Gulf of Riga, and E-13 was attacked by German warships while aground in Danish waters. The German naval attack on Riga continued until 21 August.

Further south, Ivangorod was taken by Austro-German forces on 5 August.

Lusitania follow-up
On 19 August, the White Star liner SS Arabic was torpedoed by the German submarine U-27 and sunk with two Americans among the 44 killed. The U.S. threatened a diplomatic break unless Germany repudiated the action. The German ambassador passed back a note, saying that "liners will not be sunk by our submarines". Wilson had not stopped the submarine campaign, but he won agreement that unarmed merchant ships would not be sunk without warning and, most importantly for him, he had kept the U.S. out of the war.

HMS Baralong, a British special service ship, had responded to Arabic's distress calls and, though unable to save Arabic, picked up survivors and destroyed U-27 while it was attacking the British steamer Nicosian, which was carrying munitions and mules.

In the same area, 21 August saw the first authenticated case of a German submarine firing on a ship's survivors in lifeboats after the sinking of SS Rue, off Lands End.

Meanwhile, Wilson requested and received funds from Congress for 500,000 troops plus a five-year Navy plan for major construction of battleships, cruisers, destroyers and submarines.

Part 27: September 1915

Battle of Loos 25-28 September
This, the largest British battle of 1915 on the Western Front, was part of the attempt by the Allies to break through the German defences in Artois and Champagne and end the war in the trenches. Despite an opening artillery bombardment the British guns had not broken through the German barbed wire In many places. In the following advance over open fields (25 September), British losses to German machine guns and artillery were heavy. The British also used poison gas (chlorine) for the first time in the lead up to the attack, releasing about 140 tons of it with mixed success.

William Booker, son of Thomas and Eliza Booker of Moonsleaze, Braydon, Purton, was serving with the 10th Battalion Gloucester Regiment.

On that first day of the Loos offensive, the 10th Battalion were part of the first wave in their sector attacking the Bois-Carré feature and Hulloch beyond. Gas clouds, uncut barbed wire and murderous German machine gun fire took a terrible toll. The Battalion took 459 casualties on the first day of the Battle, just over 60 men made it to the German trench system at Bois-Carré. William was killed in action during this attack, aged 23.

Loos was the first set piece battle that Kitchener's "New Armies" had been trained for. Few of those involved apart from some of the officers and NCOs had seen enemy fire until they crossed the parapets. The Battalion had

scarcely arrived in the frontline trenches before they were sent across no-man's land and into the German strongholds and machine gun emplacements amongst the French mining villages and slag heaps.

A lull fell on 28 September, with the British retreating to their starting positions, having lost over 20,000 casualties, including three major-generals.

William has no known grave and is remembered on the Loos Memorial *(top right)*, panel 60 - 64, and on the War Memorial in Lydiard Millicent *(lower right)*.

In September 1915, the following men with Purton connections were mobilised:

To France:
    Cecil George Hull, 9th Battalion Gloucestershire Regiment
    Reginald Charles Iles, Royal Engineers
    Robert Mills, 7th Battalion Wiltshire Regiment
    Leslie James Smith, Berkshire Regiment

To Gallipoli:
    William John Edmonds, 5th Battalion Wiltshire Regiment
    Mervyn Kempster, West Somerset Yeomanry

To the Royal Navy:
    Percy John Barnes, Royal Navy (HMS Liverpool)

Technology

The first prototype tank was constructed in Britain during August and September 1915 and nicknamed Little Willie. The prototype that would become the Mark I tank was demonstrated to the British Army in February 1916. The word "tank" was used at the time to disguise the function of these ambiguous machines.

Eastern Front

On 5 September, Tsar Nicholas took over personal command of the Russian armies in the face of steady German advances. This did not prevent the German forces capturing Vilna in Russian Poland (Vilnius, now capital of Lithuania) on 18 September.

Lusitania follow-up

On 1 September, the German government accepted United States demands for limitation of submarine activity.

My Family's War
Lilian Monks, the Munitionette

A family story from Rick Dixon

It was only in 1999 that I was even aware that Gran Lomas, born Lilian Monks, had been a Munitionette - a woman working in artillery munitions. The whole family, at least as I knew it, lived in Glossop, Derbyshire, where I was born in 1950. Grandad as a teenager had emigrated with his father and family from Tideswell, Derbyshire, to Lloydminster, Canada in 1907. (Lloyd for short.) Grandad came back to England during the Great War to work in munitions. He and Lilian (Gran) married during or after the war. They moved back to Canada where my Mum was born in Saskatchewan in 1924. That much I knew. And as a child in the 1950s-60s little was said, and I didn't know to ask about the Great War years.

When Dad died in 1999, we took Mum to Canada, visiting the cousins who still lived in Lloyd. They showed us old family photos including the one in this article: Gran as a young lady, wearing overalls and a mob cap at a munitions factory together with 3 co-workers - she's 2nd from the left. What I have pieced together is still a 'work in progress'.

But which munitions factory? Still thinking "Glossop" I thought first of the Royal Ordnance Factory at Risley in Cheshire, but soon discovered Risley was a WW2 establishment. The only R.O.F. that fitted the bill for the Great War was Leeds. Now Leeds isn't too far by train from Glossop, but Mr and Mrs Monks would never have allowed their daughter Lilian, at such a tender age of say 25

1915

(as she would have been in 1916), to have gone unescorted to such a distant location. That suggested the Monks side of the family actually lived in Leeds.

Gran never suffered from any of the chemical poisoning from trinitrotoluene (TNT) and sulphuric acid that coloured other workers yellow so was probably working on finishing of shells rather than stuffing them or in chemical manufacture. Grandad worked as a lathe operator perhaps in finishing which could be how they met.

Grandad would have been 31 in 1916 ... I remember him always called Gran "kid"! The first actual date I can put in here is that they married in 1917 and uncle Frank was born in England in 1918, and auntie Mabel in 1920. In 1921 or 1922 they moved back to Lloyd to the log cabin farmstead that great-grandad had established. Mum was born in a blizzard there in November 1924. It was actually at Big Gulley Lake some 14 km from Lloyd itself and the snows had already started by late September that year. The midwife didn't get through until May the following spring!

Gran couldn't cope with the -40°C winters and +40°C summers ... with the attendant flies ... so they moved back to Derbyshire in 1928. Not all the Lomas family had gone to Canada in 1907, and those that remained had moved the 13 miles north from Tideswell to Glossop in the meantime. So that was where Gran and Grandad decided to settle. Grandad was employed again in lathe working and I remember something being said about him working on the very first dies for making contact lenses.

If it hadn't been for the Great War none of this would have happened and I wouldn't be here to tell the tale. But I am going to have to do an awful lot more digging in records and archives. What a shame I didn't know to ask them when they were alive.

Part 28: October 1915

Edith Cavell

To many, the most memorable event of October 1915 was the execution of British nurse Edith Cavell. When Brussels fell to the German invasion in November 1914, she began sheltering wounded British and French soldiers, and Belgian and French civilians of military age, hiding them from the Germans and providing them with false papers. They were then helped out of occupied Belgium to Britain via neutral Holland. In doing this, Cavell was helping soldiers to escape to a country at war with Germany, i.e. Britain, and was therefore violating German military law: "Conducting soldiers to the enemy". For that the penalty was death. She was arrested on 3 August 1915 and charged with harbouring Allied soldiers.

The Geneva Convention (1906 version) stated that protection of medical personnel was forfeit if they had used their position as cover for any belligerent action.

Cavell was one of 27 put on trial. Five were condemned to death, though 3 were later reprieved. Cavell and Phillipe Baucq (an architect in his thirties) were executed by firing squad on 12 October 1915. The German legal position did not prevent international outrage.

The night before her execution, she told the Reverend Stirling Gahan, an Anglican chaplain who had been allowed to see her, "Patriotism is not enough. I must have no hatred or bitterness towards anyone." These words are inscribed on her statue in St Martin's Place, near Trafalgar Square in London.

The Fall of Serbia
At the time of the Great War, Bulgaria owned the Aegean coastline between the Greek island of Thasos and the border with European Turkey. When Bulgaria signed a treaty with Germany on 12 September 1915, Greece was alarmed. On 2 October, the Greek Prime Minister, Venizelos, without parliamentary approval asked Britain and France to land troops at Salonika (modern Thessaloniki) as soon as possible. Allied troops began arriving off Salonika the following day, landing on 5 October. King Constantine and the Greek government protested and announced a policy of armed neutrality. Venizelos resigned.

Austria captured Belgrade, the Serbian capital, on 9 October and Serbia, foreseeing an attack from the east by Bulgaria, asked Greece for help under the terms of the 1912 Serbo-Greek Treaty. Greece declined. Bulgaria entered the war when its forces invaded Serbia on 14 October. An advance by British and French forces from Salonika into Serbian Macedonia only managed to slow the fall of Serbia and allow many of the Serbian army time to escape to Albania, and onward to Corfu. Britain and Montenegro declared war on Bulgaria on 15 October and Britain began a naval blockade of the Aegean coast.

On 16 October Britain offered the island of Cyprus to Greece on the condition that Greece entered the war on the Allied side. The Greek Government rejected the offer and remained neutral.

Gallipoli
In October 1915, the following men with Purton connections were mobilised to Gallipoli: Ernest John Godwin, Australian Imperial Force
          Arthur Frederick Purnell, 6th Battalion Wiltshire Regiment

The actions at the Dardanelles had stalled and as summer turned to autumn, severe south-westerly storms lashed the Gallipoli peninsula (8 October). Considerable damage was done at Anzac Cove, particularly to the water supply.

A War Office memorandum had been issued to hospital ships warning against defeatism and saying that medical staff must maintain a hearty tone of optimism to raise the confidence and courage of the fighting men in their charge.

However, talk was of an evacuation but General Sir Ian Hamilton suggested that half the total force might be lost in the process. The Cabinet's Dardanelles Committee dismissed Hamilton as commander of the Mediterranean Expeditionary Force, appointing General Sir Charles Monro in his place.

The decision was taken to wind down actions at Gallipoli and the final meeting of the Dardanelles Committee was held on 30 October. The next day, Monro advised Lord Kitchener there should be a complete withdrawal from Gallipoli. He estimated that evacuation could lead to a casualty rate of 30-40 percent of the force and an equal amount of war material.

On 21 October, Vera Deakin, daughter of former Australian Prime Minister Alfred Deakin, established the Australian Red Cross Missing and Wounded Enquiry Bureau in Cairo. And perhaps the youngest Australian soldier to die at Gallipoli was Private James Martin, 21st Battalion (Victoria) from enteric fever, aged 14, on 23 October.

In the Air and on Sea
On 13 October, the most severe airship raid on London and the English east coast resulted in 200 casualties. And on 23 October, the German armoured cruiser SMS Prinz Adalbert was torpedoed in the Baltic by the British submarine E8; only three men were rescued from a crew of 675.

My Family's War

My thanks to Jan Walker who has provided us with this story:

Purton Remount Depot

My Grandfather, Frank Shailes, was born at Clardon in Purton in approximately 1890 and I believe worked in the paintshop at the Great Western factory until his retirement. There was, however, a time when he was a very young man when he helped at the Remount Depot at Manor Hill in Purton. His name does not appear on any list of permanent staff but his brother Donald does. It is possible that he went along with his brother to help with the horses on an informal basis. This theory is rather contradicted by the fact that he accompanied the horses to the docks at Felixstowe and I remember my father taking him on a trip to the East Coast so he could relive some memories of that time.

As a young child the details of the trip rather went over my head but there was considerable excitement at the time as it was a long trip for an Austin A30 or A40 which was the family car at that time.

It was only when Bob Lloyd began his research into Purton's World War One history that I recalled this story and now wish that I had asked more questions of my grandfather.

In the tradition of village lads having nicknames, my Grandad was known as 'Bumper'. I have no idea why!

Part 29: November 1915

In November 1915, the following men with Purton connections were mobilised:

To France:
Edward George Mills, "K" Battery Royal Horse Artillery
Joseph New, Army Ordnance Corps

To Gallipoli:
Percy Edward Dash, 5th Battalion Wiltshire Regiment
Frederick Henry Litten, 5th Battalion Wiltshire Regiment

Service in UK:
George Titcombe, 8th Battalion Wiltshire Regiment

Serbia

The fall of Serbia was complete by the end of November 1915. Despite the British Prime Minister, Herbert Asquith, declaring the independence of Serbia to be an essential object of the war, little could be done to prevent the fall.

Following a series of losses, the Serbian Government, which had already abandoned Belgrade, now left Nish for Prizren on 3 November. Nish fell to Bulgarian forces on the 5th.

Austria and Bulgarian forces pushed further in from both sides and the Serbian Government was forced to leave Prizren for Scutari on the 23rd. The Serbian King Peter I fled to Albania on the 24th.

On 25 November, the Serbian Army was ordered to retreat, and they began their retreat through Albania on the 30th with the Austrians in pursuit. Due to appalling weather and poor roads, the retreat wasn't finally completed until 10 February 1916.

French and British forces also withdrew back to Greece.

Austro-Hungarian and Bulgarian soldiers committed many atrocities against the Serbs.

Austro-Hungarian soldiers executing Serb civilians)

As well as executions of prisoners of war, civilian populations were subjected to mass murder and rape; villages and towns were burned and looted.

Gallipoli

On 4 November, Lord Kitchener sailed for Gallipoli to see the situation for himself. Arriving on the 10th he inspected positions at Helles, Anzac Cove and Suvla. On 22 November, he advised the British Government that Gallipoli should be evacuated. This would involve taking off more than 93,000 troops, 200 guns and more than 5,000 animals as well as vast quantities of stores and ammunition.

On 15 November, Winston Churchill, one of the main architects of the Gallipoli campaign, resigned from the British Government and went to serve with the British army in France as a Major with the 2nd Battalion, Grenadier Guards.

On 27 November, very poor weather led to 15,000 troops being evacuated from Anzac Cove for frostbite, trench foot and exposure.

Mesopotamia

In Mesopotamia (approximately modern Iraq) there were mixed outcomes for the Allies. On 2 November, Kasvin (West Persia) was occupied by a Russian force. Representatives of the Central Powers left Teheran on 15 November as Russian forces advanced.

On the 10th, the Indian Corps began to leave France for service in Mesopotamia, but while they were still in transit, on 11 November, a British and Indian advance on Baghdad began, carried out by 6th (Poona) Division. The Turks halted the advance at the Battle of Ctesiphon on the Tigris River between 22 and 25 November and the defeated 6th (Poona) Division began a retreat to Kut-al-Amara on the 25th.

On 24 November, Field Marshal von der Goltz of Germany took command of Turkish forces in Mesopotamia.

At Sea

The "unseen war" continued. On 7 November, a German cruiser SMS Undine was sunk by the British submarine E19. The same day, an Italian liner SS Ancona was torpedoed and sunk without warning by an Austrian submarine, with over 200 lives lost. Then on the 17th, the British hospital ship Anglia was sunk by a mine off Dover.

Two new British maritime regulations came into force on 10 November. The Ship Licensing Committee was formed and prohibited voyages between foreign ports except under licence. The Requisitioning (Carriage of Foodstuffs) Committee was also formed and authorised the military requisitioning of merchant ships for carriage of foodstuffs.

Pact of London

On 30 November, in order to bolster the Allies position, the formal signature of the Pact, by Great Britain, France, Russia, Japan and Italy, ensured that each declared it will not make a separate peace with the Central Powers.

Other News

On November, Albert Einstein presented his "field equations" to the Prussian Academy of Science. These equations specify how the geometry of space and time is influenced by whatever matter and radiation are present, and form the core of Einstein's general theory of relativity.

The first meeting of the Women's Institute was held on 16 September 1915 on Anglesey, North Wales. The WI was first established in Stoney Creek, Ontario, Canada, to educate rural women and to encourage countrywomen to get involved in growing and preserving food. When it started in Britain these skills helped to increase the supply of food. Education and the sharing of skills have always been at the heart of the organisation, and this remains true today.

Part 30: December 1915

In December 1915, the following men with Purton connections were mobilised:

To France:
Richard Beasant, "C" Battery, 88th Brigade, Royal Field Artillery
John Reginald Lane, 6th Battalion Wiltshire Regiment
Frederick Walter Sutton, 6th Battalion Wiltshire Regiment
Bertie Woodward, Royal Wiltshire Yeomanry

To Gallipoli:
Charles Reginald Edmonds, 5th Battalion Wiltshire Regiment. *(3 Dec 1915)*

To Egypt:
Elliott Leonard Woolford, Royal Army Medical Corps

Western Front

Albert Parsons of Purton *(pictured)* was born in 1894, the son of Lilly Susan Parsons, Station Road, Purton. He had been in France with 1st Battalion, King's Royal Rifle Corps since March 1915. On 13 November his group was moved from Bethune to Fosse Cottages in preparation for taking over the Front Line just north of Hohenzollern Redoubt. They were moved again on 30 November to billets in Beuvry, holding the same line and alternating A and C Companies into Z1 trenches, and B and D Companies to

billets every three days. On 24 December a mine exploded near Hohenzollern but, although there was much enemy shelling, there were no casualties.

Albert died of wounds received in the trenches, aged 21, on 27 December 1915. He is buried in Bethune Town Cemetery *(left)*, Pas de Calais, France. His headstone inscription reads "Peace perfect peace, the strife is over the battle done".

Reorganisation & Conscription

The British and French High Commands were changed drastically in December. General Joseph Joffre became Commander-in-Chief of the French Armies on 3 December, with General Castelnau appointed as his Chief of Staff on the 9th. The French President, Raymond Poincaré, had appointed Aristide Briand as Prime Minister back in October 1915, and Briand formed a "war government" on 9 December.

On the British side, Field Marshal Sir John French resigned as Commander-in-Chief of the British armies in France and Flanders on 15 December. General Sir Douglas Haig was appointed as his replacement. Lieut-Gen. Sir A.J. Murray was replaced as Chief of the Imperial General Staff by Lieut-Gen. Sir William Robertson and Lieut-Gen L. E. Kiggell became Chief of the General Staff.

Recognising that volunteer enlistments were not keeping pace with casualties, compulsory military service was brought in on 28 December. Single men would be conscripted before married men.

Gallipoli

Hardly had 18-year-old Charles Edmonds arrived at Gallipoli, than the rules were changed. On 8 December the allied forces at Anzac Cove and Suvla Bay were ordered to evacuate; by 20 December the evacuation was complete. Then on 28 December the British and Indian force at Cape Helles was ordered to evacuate, with the remainder of the Gallipoli Peninsula forces ordered out on the 28th. The last units of the Indian Expeditionary Force left, bound for Egypt, on New Year's Eve.

What had seemed back in April 1915 to be an easy stroll into Istanbul, had resulted in no strategic gain for the loss of:

Ottoman Empire:	174,800 casualties	(56,600 deaths)
United Kingdom:	120,200 casualties	(34,100 deaths)
France:	27,200 casualties	(9,800 deaths)
Australia:	28,200 casualties	(8,700 deaths)
New Zealand:	7,500 casualties	(1,600 deaths)
India:	4,800 casualties	(1,400 deaths)
Canada:	142 casualties	(49 deaths)

(Figures rounded)

Serbia

All was over bar the retreat. Austro-Hungarian forces continued their push into Montenegro. As the Bulgarians and Austrians closed in to wipe out final resistance, French troops withdrew back to Salonika, and the Serbian Government and military headquarters were set up at Scutari in Albania (Shkodër)

After fighting at Kosturino in modern-day North (FYR) Macedonia, British forces began their retreat back to Greece on 7 December.

The neutral Greeks weren't helping the allied withdrawals, so on 6 December the British Government tried to put economic pressure on Greece by making the wartime "export restrictions" apply to that country and the French General Sarrail demanded full withdrawal of Greek troops from Salonika. The Greek Government refused to withdraw from its own territory.

By 13 December, Britain partially relaxed its economic pressure and the last Allied forces in Macedonia withdrew into Greek territory on the 15th.

The Bulgarian and Greek General Staffs concluded an agreement establishing a temporary neutral zone along the Greek frontier. However on 30 December the Consuls of the Central Power nations were arrested in Salonika and deported.

At Sea

On 17 December the German light cruiser SMS Bremen was sunk after hitting Russian mines in the Baltic. Most of her crew of 290 men were lost.

HMHS Britannic departed from Liverpool on her maiden voyage as a hospital ship on 23 December. Then on 30 December the armoured cruiser HMS Natal blew up in Cromarty Firth as result of series of internal explosions, possibly due to faulty cordite. Around 405 were killed.

In the Air
Powered flight, from being a flimsy, whimsical invention in 1903, made headway with the first all-metal aircraft, a Junkers J-1, which had its test flight in Germany in December 1915. This aircraft became known as the "Tin Donkey".

Other News
On 8 December, John McCrae's poem *In Flanders Fields* appeared anonymously in "Punch" magazine.

In the US, the government demanded that Germany withdraw its military (von Papen) and naval (Karl Boy-Ed) attachés from the Embassy in Washington for alleged complicity in the planning of acts of sabotage. They were recalled to Germany on 10 December.

Also on 10 December, the 1 millionth Ford car rolled off the assembly line at the River Rouge Plant in Detroit.

Part 31: January 1916

On 31 January 1916, Albert Henry Ricks was mobilised to France with the 14th Battalion (West of England) Gloucester Regiment. Mercifully no Purton men were hurt that month. Compulsory conscription had been introduced in a Parliamentary Bill at the end of December 1915, passed as the Military Service Act on 24 January. However this would take some time to have an effect on mobilisation as there was a notice period after letters were issued and then basic training had to be completed before raw recruits could be sent abroad.

The winter weather was too bad for either side to consider offensives on the Western Front, although there were sporadic incidents including German troops taking Fort Vaux at Verdun on 7 January. Paris was bombed by Zeppelins on 29 January for what turned out to be the last time.

Gallipoli had now been abandoned with the final units of the rearguard of the Newfoundland Regiment evacuated on 9 January 1916. 508 mules which could not be embarked were killed so as not to fall into Turkish hands, and 1,590 vehicles were left behind with destroyed wheels.

South-Eastern Europe
On 5 January, following the fall of Serbia, Austria-Hungary commenced its offensive against Montenegro, capturing the strategic Mount Lovchen on the 10th. By 12 January an armistice was arranged between Montenegro and Austria, but Austrian advances continued, taking Cetinje on the 13th. On 20 January, talks broke down and the armistice ceased. Antivari was occupied by Austria on 22 January, and Podgoritza the following day. Montenegro surrendered on 25 January.

In next-door Albania, Austria occupied Scutari on 23 January and San Giovanni di Medua (modern day Shëngjin) 2 days later.

Earlier in the month, on 10 January, the British and French governments informed Greece that they would be occupying Corfu in order to move the Serbian army there; France occupied Corfu the following day and, despite Greek protests, the Serbs began to land on 15 January.

Mesopotamia & Persia

The 6th (Poona) Division had been besieged at Kut-al-Amara (modern day Iraq) since December and British forces began attempts to relieve the division. A force set out on 4 January and confronted the Ottoman armies at Sheikh Sa'ad on the 6th. The Ottomans defeated the British force between 13 and 14 January at the Battle of Wadi, then again on 21 January at Hanna. The first attempt to relieve Kut had failed.

On 13 January, Ottoman Turkish forces occupied Kermanshah in western Persia.

On the Allied side the only success was from the Russians who captured Keupri-Keui (Turkish Armenia) for the second time on 17 January.

At Sea

HMS King Edward VII, the flagship of the 3rd Battle Squadron of the Grand Fleet steamed out of Scapa Flow and struck a mine that had been laid by the German auxiliary cruiser SMS Möwe off Cape Wrath, north of Scotland, and the engine rooms quickly flooded. In the evacuation procedure on to other ships, miraculously only one life was lost, as a man fell between the battleship and one of the rescue vessels.

Around the World

On New Year's Day, British forces captured Yaunde in German Kamerun and the German colony surrendered to Britain and France on 28 January.

On 12 January, Britain proclaimed the Gilbert & Ellice Islands in the Pacific as a colony; they had formerly been a protectorate. Today they are 2 independent countries: Kiribati and Tuvalu.

Stamp from Rick Dixon collection.

Medical advances

On New Year's Day, The British Royal Army Medical Corps carried out the first successful blood transfusion using blood that had been stored and cooled.

Other News

The Girl Guides formed their Dutch branch in neutral Netherlands on 31 January.

My Family's War

Childhood Memories, *by Rick Dixon*

On 11 December 1915, an army padre, the Reverend Philip "Tubby" Clayton, opened an abandoned house at Rue de l'Hôpital 43, in Poperingen, Belgium. The address has since been renamed Gasthuisstraat in its Flemish name. He formed a new club there welcoming all British soldiers. It became a rare place where soldiers could meet and relax regardless of rank, an Every-Man's Club. A notice was hung by the front door bearing the message: "All rank abandon, ye who enter here."

This was Talbot House and became known as Toc H, toc being the army telephone alphabet name for "T", just as ack was for A, hence Ack-Ack anti-aircraft guns. In the current NATO alphabet, T is Tango.

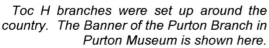

At school in the 1960s, I would often see older teachers wearing a little enamel lapel badge shaped like an ancient Roman oil lamp - similar to the one shown. I never knew why until one afternoon whoever was supposed to be teaching us, whatever subject it might have been, was not available. An old padre attached to the school's teaching staff took the lesson and soon had us all enthralled and horrified simultaneously.

More as a discussion group than a lesson, and very avant-garde for the time, he told us about the formation of Toc H, just behind the front line and a safe haven for anyone to "chill-out" as you would say today, with no rank being more important than another.

My abiding memory is of him telling us that, as a non-combatant padre, he was dealing all the time with wounded soldiers in the trenches. He said, "What do you do, what can you possibly do, faced with a man half of whose face has been blown away by an exploding shell, when all you have is a pitifully small field-dressing?"

It still makes me cry to think about it. Such as when typing this note.

I looked out for those little lapel badges ever after. Their wearers were the men who were just "old teachers" but had in fact been heroes in the trenches, gaining just a little bit of respite courtesy of Tubby Clayton.

Toc H branches were set up around the country. The Banner of the Purton Branch in Purton Museum is shown here.

Part 32: February 1916

The following Purton men were mobilised:

In February 1916, Harold William Matthews (aged 18), Wiltshire Yeomanry, was transferred for munitions work.

Leonard Waite Mussell (aged 17) was assigned to No. 7 Stationary Hospital at Boulogne with the Royal Army Medical Corps. In his career before the army, he had been a pharmacy dispensing assistant. He was the son of Alfred Charles and Annie Mussell, of Hill View, Purton.

Western Front

On 21 February, the German armies commenced a major offensive at Verdun in the French Sector of the Western Front. This turned out to be the longest battle in the war, lasting until December 1916. On the first day, Germany bombarded French positions for 9 hours and then occupied the first line of French trenches. The Germans captured Fort Douaumont on the 25th and that same day Marshall Pétain was put in charge of the defence of Verdun. The German 1st offensive ended on the 26th.

At Sea

A joint German-Austrian communiqué advised the United States on 10 February that all defensively armed merchant ships would be considered as belligerents from 1 March onwards. A clarification on 21 February said they would be classed as cruisers.

The US rejected the right of Germany and Austria-Hungary to sink armed merchant ships in a reply of 16 February. Perhaps in a placatory move, the German ambassador in Washington responded that Germany would pay an indemnity for American lives lost on the Lusitania in 1915.

However on the 29th, a German note informed the United States that Germany would not postpone the extended submarine campaign.

In the Air

On 28 February, a new British air squadron was formed to bomb German industrial centres. Much of this was in response to continuing German Zeppelin raids on Britain, though British fighter planes were getting better at shooting the airships down by this time.

Africa

On 17 February, the last German garrison in the German colony of Kamerun surrendered to British forces. The German troops were moved across the border for internment in Spanish Rio Muni (now Equatorial Guinea). The last German post, Mora, surrendered the following day.

On the other side of the continent, Lieutenant-General Smuts succeeded Tighe in command of British forces in East Africa.

America

The United States wanted the war over sooner rather than later. In the House-Grey Memorandum, drafted on 22 February by the US and Britain, was the statement: 'Should the Allies accept [the American idea of a conference to end the war] and should Germany refuse it, the United States would "probably" enter the war against Germany'. But we need to wait another year to see American intervention ... and it perhaps came from an unexpected direction.

Italy
Italian forces had not made much progress against Austria-Hungary along the Isonzo river valley, now partly in Italy - upstream as far as Gorizia - but flowing out of modern Slovenia, where the river is called the Soča. On 15 February the 5th Battle of the Isonzo began, and there were to be 11 of them altogether between 1915 and 1917, or 12 if the battle of Caporetto is counted in. This was a stalemate war with neither side achieving much but at high cost:

The total casualties of these battles were enormous. Half of the entire Italian war casualty total - some 300,000 out of 600,000 - was suffered along the Soča (Isonzo). Austro-Hungarian losses, weren't as high at around 200,000 but still a large proportion of their war total of around 1.2 million casualties.

More than 30,000 casualties were ethnic Slovenes, majority of them being drafted into the Austro-Hungarian Army. Slovene civil inhabitants from the Gorizia and Gradisca region also suffered in many thousands when resettled in refugee camps but were treated as state enemies by Italians. Several thousands died of malnutrition in Italian refugee camps.

Elsewhere round the word
On 3 February the Parliament buildings at the Canadian capital, Ottowa, burnt down. Reconstruction was quick, opened for parliament on 26 February 1920, although the Centre Block wasn't completed until 1922. The Peace Tower was finished by 1927.

Part 33: March 1916

Mervyn Stronge Richardson was born on 21 June 1894 at Killynether Castle, Newtownards, Co Down, youngest son of Capt. Arthur Percy Richardson and Ethel Mary Richardson, by 1914 of Purton House. A member of the Officer Training Corps (OTC) at Radley College, he attended the Royal Military College and was commissioned as a lieutenant on 15 August 1914 to the Royal Welch Fusiliers (RWF), initially with the 2nd Battalion. In September 1914, aged 20, he took a draft of 182 men over from the battalion barracks in Wrexham to join the battalion on 25 September just north of Paris, accompanied by his servant. This was the time of the "Race to the Sea" when the German forces tried to outflank the British and French and secure the Belgian Channel ports. (See Part 15).

By March 1916, now a captain and attached to the 1st Battalion RWF, Mervyn was in trenches at Fricourt, 2½ miles east of Albert on the Somme in France. A few months later the 1st Battle of the Somme would start around this area

following an allied conference at Chantilly on 12 March between Belgium, France, Great Britain, Italy, Japan, Portugal, Russia, and Serbia to discuss the summer offensives.

But on 18 March, enemy artillery and trench mortars were active. Around midnight Mervyn was on a night working party, inspecting and repairing barbed wire defences, when he and L/Cpl Chamberlain were hit by a 5-inch howitzer shell. Both died the following morning. Much of his story is related by his friend and fellow officer, the writer and poet Robert Graves.

Mervyn is buried, aged 21, near Maple Redoubt beside two friends in Point 110 New Military Cemetery, Fricourt. The Cemetery is named Point 110 after the elevation marked on the trench map. His headstone inscription reads "I have fought a good fight. I have finished my course. Leander", a quote from 2 Timothy 4:7 and a reference to his having been "Captain of the boats, Radley College, Leander Club". Mervyn is also remembered on the War Memorial in Newtownards in N Ireland and other places.

The following men with Purton connections were mobilised in March 1916:

To France:
Leonard Dunsford, 2nd Canadian Pioneer Battalion. (Eldest Son of Arthur and Blanche Maud Mary Dunsford, Holly Lodge, Purton.)
Harry Titcombe, Royal Field Artillery.

To Egypt:
Arthur Martin, Royal Field Artillery.
Arthur Anthony Brown, 271st Brigade, Royal Field Artillery.

At Sea
At the beginning of March, Germany began its extended submarine campaign against allied shipping.

On the 15th a neutral Dutch merchant ship Tubantia was torpedoed and sunk by a German submarine in the North Sea.

But on 24 March, the French ferry SS Sussex was torpedoed by SM UB-29 in the English Channel with at least 50 killed, including many American nationals and the composer Enrique Granados. By 4 May, Germany pledged to the United States a suspension of the intensified submarine warfare policy.

In America
Newton D. Baker was appointed Secretary for War in the US on 6 March. Hardly had he got his feet under the desk when, on 8-9 March, in the Mexican Revolution, Pancho Villa led about 500 Mexican raiders in an attack against Columbus, New Mexico, killing 12 US soldiers. A garrison of the U.S. 13th Cavalry Regiment drove them back. A week later on 15 March, President Woodrow Wilson sent 12,000 United States troops over the US-Mexico border to pursue Villa and the next day the US 7th and 10th Cavalry regiments, under

General John J. Pershing, joined the hunt for Villa in Mexico with a further 15,000 men. US forces remained in Mexico for 10 months.

About the same time, the US invaded Cuba for the 3rd time, in order to end the corrupt Menocal regime there.

Portugal

On 9 March, Germany declared war on Portugal and Austria-Hungary followed on the 15th. This followed a British request for Portugal to intern 36 German and Austro-Hungarian ships in Lisbon. By August 1916, the Portuguese Expeditionary Corps (Corpo Expedicionário Português, CEP), had been established with 30,000 soldiers, later reaching 55,000 infantry soldiers, plus 1,000 artillerymen, to be sent to France, to man 12 km of battlefront. As it happened, only the first two divisions reached France, as the American entry into the war cut the number of transport ships available. Meanwhile Portugal strengthened its forces in its African colonies. Mozambique had been under attack from German colonial forces, and Germany had stirred up native unrest in the south of Angola.

China

On 22 March, following a rebellion by Yunnan province against autocratic rule (the National Protection War) and followed by Guizhou and Guangxi, the temporary Emperor of China, Yuan Shikai, abdicated the throne. The Republic of China was restored.

Part 34: April 1916

Mesopotamia

The British garrison at Kut-al-Amara, in Basra province of Mesopotamia (now Iraq), had been besieged by a Turkish army since the beginning of the year. Several attempts to relieve the garrison had failed before British forces on the River Tigris tried again to break the Turkish lines. On 1 April the British Relief Force attacked at Fallahiyeh, Sannaiyat and Bait Aissa.

On 5 April, the Force seized Hanna and Fallahiyeh, and the first attack on Sannaiyat began on 6 April, with a second on 9 April.

Percy Edward Dash was born in Purton in 1897 and, at the time he enlisted, his parents Francis and Ellen Dash were living in Clifton Street, Swindon.. When he enlisted in May 1915 he declared his age as unknown but he was in fact only 17 years old. With the 5th Battalion Wiltshire Regiment, he had survived Gallipoli. The 5th Wilts were evacuated to Egypt then redeployed in February 1916 to Basra province. On 9 April 1916, the Battalion was in contact with the Turks at Sannaiyat. 5/Wilts advanced in darkness at 4.20 am. They lost their direction after machine gun, sniper fire and star shells, and dug in about 650 yards from the Turks. Many wounded crawled back or were collected. Those collecting the wounded displayed conspicuous gallantry and some were recommended for the DCM.

Percy, by then 18, was among those killed in 5/Wilts (2 officers, 21 other ranks). He is buried in Amara War Cemetery, Iraq *(pictured)*, and is listed on the War Memorial in Ashton Keynes. Fred Selwood, also of Purton, was wounded during this action.

The memorial wall at Amara War Cemetery, Iraq

The Relief Force took Bait Aissa on 9 April but were overwhelmed by Turkish forces on 18 April and withdrew. A third British attack on Sannaiyat was repulsed by the Turks on 22 April.

On 23 April, a naval relief attempt was made up the navigable River Tigris but HMS Julnar, manned by volunteers, failed to break the Kut blockade and was grounded on the 24th with the crew captured by the Turks. Posthumous VCs were awarded to the 2 officers killed.

The Siege of Kut ended on 29 April when General Charles Townshend surrendered the British and Indian garrison to the Ottoman Empire. Not only a major blow to British prestige, it was a death warrant for the men. The Turks led them on a death march to Anatolia in May. 30,000 British and Indian troops had been killed or wounded during the siege and in the relief attempts. Of the captured garrison of 13,000 men, 70% of the British and 50% of the Indian troops died of disease or at the hands of their Ottoman guards. The Relief Force withdrew.

Amara War Cemetery contains 4,621 burials of the First World War, more than 3,000 of which were brought into the cemetery after the Armistice. In 1933, all of the headstones were removed from this cemetery when it was discovered that salts in the soil were causing them to deteriorate. Instead a screen wall was erected with the names of those buried in the cemetery engraved upon it *(pictured)*.

Purton men mobilised in April 1916
To France: Arthur James Tidmarsh: Army Service Corps (Motor Transport driver, 2nd New Army)

Ireland
The Government of Ireland Act 1914 ("The Home Rule Act") had been passed in Westminster in early summer 1914 and was due for Royal Assent in September 1914. The outbreak of war in August that year had resulted in Assent being postponed and the Act was never implemented, to the fury of the nationalist cause in Ireland.

Rebellion in Ireland was in Germany's interest if it diverted British efforts from the Western Front. So while nationalists were trying to organise an Uprising, Germany was willing to help with the supply of arms.

On 9 April, SS Libau set out from Germany with a cargo of 20,000 rifles and ammunition to assist Irish republicans in staging what would become the 1916 Rising aimed at overthrowing British rule in Ireland. The ship's captain, Karl Spindler, changed the name of the vessel to the Aud to avoid British detection. A few days later, on the 12th, the Irish nationalist activist, Ulster Protestant and poet Sir Roger Casement boarded submarine U-19 at Wilhelmshaven, Germany, bound for a rendezvous with the Aud at Tralee. Casement landed from the submarine at Tralee Bay on the 20th but, suffering from a recurrence of malaria, was discovered close by at McKenna's Fort the next day and was arrested by the Royal Irish Constabulary.

A team from the Volunteers didn't arrive in time to unload the Aud's rifles. The ship was intercepted by the Royal Navy on 21 April and the captain forced to sail towards Cork Harbour. Spindler scuttled the Aud on the 22nd near Daunt Rock, off Cork, to prevent the cargo of rifles falling into British hands.

Meanwhile, on 19 April, Alderman Kelly read the "Castle Order" to a meeting of Dublin Corporation. This forged document supposedly from the British authorities at Dublin Castle, suggested that the British government would make mass arrests of Irish Volunteers to prevent "trouble".

Eventually realising the Castle Order was a fraud to force his hand, and without the cargo of rifles or German Army support, the Chief of Staff of the Irish Volunteers Eóin MacNeill issued an order in Dublin, on 22 April, to postpone the Rising from Easter Sunday by 24 hours. The rebellion broke out in Dublin on Easter Monday, 24 April 1916. Members of the Irish Republican Brotherhood proclaimed an Irish Republic and the Irish Volunteers and Irish Citizen Army occupied the General Post Office and other buildings in Dublin. The British government proclaimed martial law in Dublin on the 27th and renewed their assault on the Irish Volunteer position in Mount Street with artillery shells causing fires and massive damage to buildings.

The republicans abandoned the post office on the 29th and surrendered to the British Army unconditionally, marking the end of the Easter Rising*.

The Uplees Explosion
On 2 April 1916, some empty sacks caught fire at a munitions factory of the Explosives Loading Company in Uplees, near Faversham in Kent and about 60 miles southeast of London. The sack fire spread and ignited 15 tons of TNT and 150 tons of ammonium nitrate, killing 116, including the entire works fire brigade. The victims of what was the worst ever disaster in the British explosives industry were buried in a mass grave at Faversham Cemetery.

France
1 April is nominally considered the date when German aircraft lost their mastery of the air on the Western front. Battles continued up and down the front with the Germans taking, then losing Bois de Caillette, Verdun; a major German

* Easter Sunday on 27 March 2016 is early; the earliest it could be in any year is 22 March. Meanwhile a hundred years later, Easter Sunday 1916 (25 April) was almost as late as it could possibly be (23 April).

offensive against the village of Le Mort Homme also near Verdun failed to capture it; and attacks from Fort Douaumont, the largest and highest fort on the ring of 19 large defensive forts protecting the city of Verdun. (Douaumont had been taken in February by a small German force.)

Then on 27 April, further north, the Germans launched one of the most heavily concentrated gas attacks of the war at Hulluch, near Loos in France. The 47th Brigade, 16th (Irish) Division was decimated in the attack, among a British list of 1,260 gas casualties and 338 killed. However, due to changing wind direction and leaky gas containers, the Germans are estimated to have lost up to 1,500 gas casualties in the operation.

Politics
On 6 April, the German parliament ratified unrestricted submarine warfare. US Secretary of State Robert Lansing warned Germany that the USA might break diplomatic relations unless torpedo attacks on unarmed ships stopped.

On the 26th, an agreement was signed in Berlin for repatriation of sick and wounded British and German POWs to Switzerland. This was also signed in London on 13 May.

On 29 April, the "Havre Declaration" was signed by France, Great Britain, Italy, Japan and Russia guaranteeing the integrity of Belgian Congo.

On a happier note, on 8 April, Norway approved active and passive female suffrage - active being the right to vote, and passive the right to run for office.

Charles Robert Ogburn was born in Purton in 1879 but, by the time he enlisted, he was the husband of Alice Jane Ogburn, Rugby. We was serving with the Oxfordshire and Buckinghamshire Light Infantry when he died aged 37 on 26 April 1916. He is buried at Portsdown (Christ Church) Military Cemetery, Hampshire. No other details are available. His next of kin was given as his wife Alice Jane Ogburn in Rugby.

Part 35: May 1916

Ireland
On 1 May, the leaders of the Dublin rising in Ireland surrendered to the British forces. The British army was cheered by the majority of the population of Dublin for the success in putting down the Rising. However, the actions by the British in the weeks following completely turned public opinion.

Courts martial were held from 2 May, and 90 people were sentenced to death. Fifteen were executed at Kilmainham Gaol by firing squad over the next 2 weeks. Not all of those executed were leaders. The most prominent leader to escape execution was Eamon de Valera, later to become President of the Irish Republic. 1,480 were interned in England.

Those executed became martyrs, and hatred of Britain grew. Sir Roger Casement was tried in London for high treason and hanged at Pentonville Prison on 3 August.

The Battle of Jutland

Germany's High Seas Fleet under the command of Vice-Admiral Scheer had been contained in Wilhelmshaven by a British blockade for most of the war to date. The German navy wasn't strong enough to engage the entire Royal Navy's Grand Fleet in open water. So, Germany devised a plan to lure out and destroy a part of the Grand Fleet. Success might break the British blockade of Germany's ports and allow their merchant ships to operate.

On 30 May, Scheer ordered a fast scouting group of five battlecruisers under Vice-Admiral Franz Hipper to lure Vice-Admiral Sir David Beatty's battlecruiser squadrons into the path of the main German fleet. Hipper stationed submarines beforehand on the likely routes of the British ships. However, the British learned from signal intercepts that a major fleet operation was likely so, on 30 May, Admiral Sir John Jellicoe's Grand Fleet sailed to rendezvous with Beatty, passing over the locations of the German submarine lines before they were prepared.

Beatty met the German force off the north coast of Denmark (Jutland) much earlier than Hipper had expected but, in a running battle, Hipper drew Beatty's force towards Scheer's main German Fleet. Although Beatty turned back towards Jellicoe's Grand Fleet, he lost 2 battlecruisers from a force of 6 battlecruisers and 4 battleships, against the 5 ships of Hipper's group. The Germans gave chase but were in turn drawn towards Jellicoe's Grand Fleet.

By 6.30 pm, the setting sun back-lit the German forces. Between then and about 8.30 pm, the two fleets fired at each other twice. There were a total of 250 ships between them. 14 British and 11 German ships were sunk, with great loss of life. The British had hoped to keep the Germans at sea and continue the battle the next day, but overnight the Germans broke through the rearguard of the Grand Fleet and returned to port on 1 June.

Both sides claimed victory. The Royal Navy lost more ships and twice as many sailors as the German fleet, but Scheer's plan of destroying a substantial portion of the British fleet also failed. Germany's ships, though in port, continued to cause the British to concentrate their battleships in the North Sea to contain them. By the end of 1916, Germany turned to unrestricted submarine warfare and the destruction of Allied and neutral shipping, further alarming the United States of America who believed they had negotiated an end to submarine warfare on 4 May.

The Battle of Jutland, known in Germany as the Battle of Skagerrak (Skagerrakschlacht) was the largest naval battle of the war and the only full-scale clash of battleships. The combined death toll of both sides was around 6,600 men.

Purton men mobilised in May 1916

To France:
Francis John Burgess, 1st Battalion, Wiltshire Regiment.

Robert Stanley Grimes, 29th Battalion Canadian Infantry (British Columbia Regiment).
Stanley Frederick Haines, Machine Gun Corps.
Albert James Parsons Salter, Royal Marine Light Infantry.

to India:
Reginald Edward Bye, 3rd Wessex Brigade, Royal Field Artillery.

France

Vimy Ridge, 8km northeast of Arras and about 7km in length, provides an unobstructed view for tens of kilometres in all directions and was therefore strategically important. The British operating in that sector discovered that German sappers had dug a tunnel network under the ridge to attack French positions by setting off underground explosives (mines) beneath the French trenches. German artillery and trench mortar fire intensified in early May 1916 to deter British counter-tunnelling. On 21 May, German infantry attacked British lines to force them from the ridge. The Germans halted their advance and entrenched their positions. The Canadian Corps relieved the British forces stationed along the western slopes of Vimy Ridge in October 1916. Of this, more in a later Part.

Other News

On 21 May, Daylight Saving Time was introduced in Britain. And on the 25th, Universal Conscription was started.

My Family's War

Rick Dixon writes:

Great Aunts

I have an early memory from my childhood in the late 1950s, in Glossop, Derbyshire. At the time, Mum, Dad, my sister and I lived in east London but visited grandparents in Glossop, by train, twice a year. On each visit we would call in on relatives there including several great-aunts … Edith, Ella, and more, they all seemed to begin with 'E'.

Dad had been compiling a family tree by questioning his own grandparents, my great-grandparents, and he showed me the tree. It showed so many elderly maiden great-aunts and I asked why they had never married.

His answer was that most of the marriageable men of that generation had been killed in the Great War. The Somme was one of the major events that caused this.

The huge male population reduction in Britain at that time is often referred to as the Loss of a Generation.

Part 36: June 1916

Purton men mobilised in June 1916 - *To France:*
William John Tuck, 1st Battalion Wiltshire Regiment.
James Richard Webb, Royal Berkshire Regiment, Labour Corps.

Salonika

Lieut.-General Sir George Milne had been appointed as General Officer Commanding British Forces, Salonika (Thessaloniki) in May 1916. With the Serbian government in exile also based in Salonika and faced with Greek government objections to the allies' presence there, the Allies proclaimed martial law in Salonika on 4 June.

Herbert Shopland was born in Purton in 1877 and the husband of Alice Mary Shopland and son of James and Laura Shopland. By the time the War started, he was living in Great Yarmouth, which was where he enlisted. He served in the Royal Army Medical Corps attached to the 28th General Hospital at Salonika in Greece. No details are available of his death on 18 June 1916. He was buried in the Salonika (Lembet Road) Military Cemetery and also remembered on the War Memorial in Great Yarmouth.

Lord Kitchener

On 5 June, British Minister for War, Lord Kitchener, and his staff were aboard HMS Hampshire on a diplomatic mission to Russia. The Hampshire hit a mine off the Orkneys, Scotland, and sank. Of the 655 crewmen and 7 passengers aboard, only 12 crewmen on life rafts managed to reach the shore alive.

Western Front

Battles were being fought in both the Ypres and Verdun sectors of the Western front. The Germans made their 1st attack on Fort Vaux, Verdun, with ground being lost and retaken in quick succession. For example, Fort Thiaumont at Verdun changed hands 16 times.

A new horror was unleased when phosgene gas was used for the first time at Verdun by the Germans on 22 June.

The Battle of the Somme was initiated on 24 June when the Allies opened up an artillery barrage along a 25-mile front against German trenches on the Somme, in advance of the start of the campaign on 1 July.

Eastern Front

On 4 June, Russia commenced a massive offensive under General Aleksei Brusilov against Austria-Hungary forces in Carpathia breaking through the Austro-Hungarian lines. Continuing until 20 September, the Brusilov offensive nearly knocked Austria-Hungary out of the war.

Arab Revolt

On 5 June, Hussein bin Ali, the Sharif of Mecca, with British support led by T.E. Lawrence (Lawrence of Arabia), declared the Arab Revolt against the Ottoman Empire. The Sharif's intention was to create a single unified Arab state spanning from Aleppo in Syria to Aden on the Indian Ocean.

On 6 June, an Arab attack on Medina was repulsed by the Turkish garrison but Hussein proclaimed the independence of the Hejaz on 7 June and Arab forces captured Jedda on the 9th. The next day, the Turkish garrison of Mecca surrendered to Hussein's forces.

America

The US war with Mexico continued. On 17 June, US troops under General Pershing marched into Mexico but his expeditionary force was beaten by Mexican troops on the 21st when President Carranza, ordered them to oppose the Americans at Carrazil. 18 American soldiers were killed or wounded.

My Family's War

My thanks to Chris Compton who has provided another family tale:

The World War One Crocodile

My Grandfather, a Mr Smith, was a pilot instructor during WW1 and, at his home in Sherston, he and his family kept chickens to supplement their income. Now we have set the background to our story, I will explain about the crocodile.

Granddad was somewhere hot, Egypt? with his aeroplane. In his leisure time he would dig up some croc. eggs, not allowed these days, and put them next to the boat engine during his journey home to Blighty, keeping them moist and turning them regularly.

When he returned home he placed them in the chicken incubator - where they hatched out. They had a great time feasting on the day-old chicks, so only one croc. was allowed to survive, and it grew to 2ft 6ins long, (you clever people can convert it to metric). It was then killed, stuffed and mounted in a glass case.

I still have that same crocodile and case in the roof and I have owned it for 60 years or more.

My brother and I always called it a crocodile, but it could be a Gorral. Perhaps someone can tell me what it is.

Similar pictures on the Internet, suggest it might be a gharial, from India. Any other thoughts?   Picture: Rick Dixon

Part 37: July 1916

Purton men mobilised in July 1916
To France:
> Edward Frank Curtis, 6th Battalion Wiltshire Regiment - see below.
> John Huntley, Royal Artillery.

Battle of the Somme
We're now about half-way in the Great War Project and it can't be a more relevant time to look at the horrors of war.

The 1st Battle of the Somme (1 July to 18 November 1916) was the bloodiest battle of the entire Great War. It caused over one million four hundred thousand casualties on both sides of which some 480,000 British were killed or wounded. On the first day alone, British Empire casualties were 57,470 of whom 19,240 were killed - the greatest ever losses of the British Army, before or since.

It is therefore not surprising that hardly a town or village in the UK got away unscathed. Purton was no exception.

The Somme is a major river in northwest France and the battle area was about 25 miles from Amiens in Picardy. It had been seen by the Allied command as a strategic point to make a breakthrough in the German trench lines and advance back into Belgium. Over a full week, in the preparation for the battle, Allied guns had fired over 1,700,000 shells at the German trenches, supply roads and barbed wire defences. And the allies had air supremacy: 386 fighter planes against the Germans' 129. So the Allied Command believed that the Germans would have been knocked out and the British troops could just walk in over no-mans-land and take the area. The reality was far from this.

The German defences had included deep bunkers which were almost immune from the bombardment. Also when, after a week of shelling, the shelling just stopped, it wasn't very difficult for the local commanders to realise they were about to be attacked.

In addition to the bombardment, British sappers had tunnelled under the German trench systems and exploded mines on 1 July. The mine at La-Boiselle (near Albert, Picardy) might have been effective but the Germans intercepted a British phone message detailing the time and date of the attack. The Germans moved and resited the machine guns at that position. 5,100 British troops were killed as they advanced towards those guns.

On 2 July, British troops advanced across 460m of no man's land at La-Boiselle in the afternoon and bombed into the German redoubt, then carried on to trenches beyond and consolidated a line about 910m wide. As a deception, the attack was preceded by a bombardment on nearby Ovillers at dawn under cover of a smoke screen. As a result the German artillery fired on Ovillers and not La-Boisselle, where a frontal attack was made by the 6th Wiltshires and the 9th Royal Welch Fusiliers. The attackers got across no man's land and captured the German front line trench with few casualties while the 9th Cheshires attacked on the right. Although the German resistance increased, British forces bombed their underground shelters. The British infantry occupied the west end of the village by dusk and dug in.

Though the 6th Wiltshire's losses were comparatively light, 2 Purton men were killed. **Harry Robert Thomas Matthews** (living with his grandparents George and Sarah at Purton Stoke) was killed in action on 2 July 1916. **Edward Frank Curtis**, son of James and Sophia Curtis of Station Road, Purton, was wounded somewhere between 2 and 4 July, and died of wounds 6 July 1916.

The Leipzig Salient (near Thiepval, Picardy) was a defensive position on the German front line which bulged forward around a quarry which had been fortified and enclosed by a major trench system (Hindenburg Trench). On 1 July, the Leipzig Salient was attacked by the 1/17th Highland Light Infantry who took the position but failed to advance further.

On 5 July, the British 25th Division attacked on a 460m front at the Leipzig Salient. The 1st Wiltshires gained a foothold on the Hindenburg Trench, surviving a major counter-attack. But on 7 July the Germans attacked the Leipzig Redoubt from the front and both flanks. The attack was defeated by the 1st Wiltshires and was then followed by German bombing attacks until 5.30 am. An attack by two companies of the 1st Wiltshire captured the German front line.

During this action, 2 more Purton men of the 1st Wiltshires were killed. **William John Tuck** (son of John and Emma Tuck, The Row, Purton) was killed in action 7 July. **Henry James Gibbs** (husband of Nellie Gibbs and son of Henry and Emily Gibbs of Greenhill, Purton) was reported missing in action on 7 July, and confirmed to have died on 8 July 1916.

Harry, William and Henry have no known grave and are remembered on the Thiepval Memorial. Edward is buried in a joint grave at Heilly Station Cemetery, Mericourt-l'Abbé.

In an attempt to divert German attention from the Somme, British and Australian forces attacked German positions at the Battle of Fromelles, to the north of the Somme. Between 19 and 20 July, this battle was responsible for one of the greatest losses of Australian lives in a single day. Casualties were 5,533 Australian killed or wounded and 1,547 British. The losses amounted to about 90% of the Australian force and 50% of the British. As horrifying as these figures sound, the Australian losses were even higher at the Battle of Bullecourt in 1917.

David Lloyd George
Lord Kitchener had been killed at sea in June. On 7 July, David Lloyd George was appointed Secretary of State for War as his successor.

United States
The USA was carrying on with its so-called Banana Wars in North America. On 29 July, US marines landed in Haiti, in response to the assassination of Haiti's dictator President Vilbrun Guillaume Sam by a mob following executions of his opposition, and growing instability. The Americans didn't leave until 1934.

However German provocations against the US continued too. On 30 July, German agents carried out a sabotage attack on an ammunition depot at Black Tom, New Jersey, killing at least 7.

Part 38: August 1916

Purton men mobilised in August 1916
To France:
    Randle Charles Barrington-Foote, Royal Field Artillery.
    John Richard Alison, Hampshire Yeomanry Carabiniers.
    Harry Sutton, Royal Berkshire Regiment, Labour Corps.

To Army Remount Depot:
    Charles Morse, Army Service Corps (Remount).

Mesopotamia
The 5th Battalion Wiltshire Regiment was on a route march towards Amara. There were high levels of sickness in the battalion and **Daniel George Bull**, of Upper Square, Purton, died on 31 August 1916. He is buried at Basra War Cemetery. Formerly employed by the GWR Company in Swindon in the locomotive and carriage department, he is listed on Swindon's Roll of Honour.

Ireland
The Irish revolutionary Roger Casement was executed by hanging on 3 August at Pentonville Jail in London. In 1965 Casement's remains were repatriated to the Republic of Ireland.

Battle of the Somme
The Somme campaign, still in its 2nd phase (commenced in July), continued with the Battle of Delville Wood (14 July - 15 September) which secured the British right flank. It also saw the first action by the South African 1st Infantry Brigade.
    The Battle of Pozières Ridge (23 July - 7 August) saw success for the 1st Australian Division, among others, as the Reserve Army took the plateau north and east of Pozières village, overlooking the village of Thiepval fortified by the Germans. Meanwhile, the Battle of Verdun to the south dragged on to a costly French victory as German troops were withdrawn north to bolster forces on the Somme. The 1st Battle of Verdun ended on 30 August 1916.

Munitions Explosion
On 21 August, a large explosion at the Low Moor Chemical Company munitions factory, Bradford, killed 38 and injured over 100 people. The factory produced picric acid and had been used for munitions work since the Boer War. It had expanded to cope with the new demand.

Rumania
During August, the Kingdom of Rumania entered the war on the side of the Allies.
    On the 25th Russian forces crossed the River Danube into Dobrudja (the Black Sea coastal province of Rumania), to assist the Rumanians who then had the wherewithal to declare war on Austria-Hungary on 27 August and mobilise their forces. The following day, Rumanian forces crossed into Austro-Hungarian Transylvania, and Germany declared war on Rumania, for attacking its ally. By the 29th, Rumanian forces had occupied Brasov in Transylvania. Rumania cut off diplomatic relations with its southern neighbour, Bulgaria (also

in the Central Powers alliance), and Turkey declared war on Rumania.

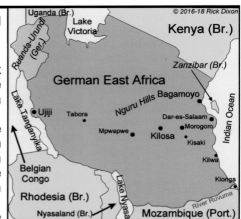

East Africa

German East Africa was under attack on all sides. (The colony became Tanganyika after the war and Tanzania upon independence in 1964.)

Although Belgium was part of the main front line in Europe for the duration of the war and its government was in exile, the Belgian Congo still had active forces. Belgian troops occupied Ujiji, on Lake Tanganyika on 3 August.

On 5 August, the main body of the British forces in Kenya began an advance through the Nguru Hills, and during the next 3 weeks captured the towns of Mpwapwa, Kilosa, Iringa and Morogoro in the central region, and Bagamoyo, the colonial capital (75km north of Dar-es-Salaam).

Italy

On 6 August, the Italian army initiated the 6th Battle of the Isonzo, against Austria, along the River Isonzo which today marks part of the border between Italy and Slovenia. Italy captured Gorizia on 9 August.

Italy declared war on Germany on 28 August, having previously been in alliance with Germany up until the outbreak of war in 1914. Italy had previously said that it could not fight alongside Germany, if Germany was at war with Britain.

Other News

Happier news was that Robert Baden-Powell published The Wolf Cub's Handbook in Britain during August. This established the junior section of the Scouting movement, the Wolf Cubs (modern-day Cub Scouts).

Part 39: September 1916

Purton men mobilised in August 1916

To France:
> Frederick Leach, Royal Flying Corps. (*mobilised July 1916*)
> William George Garlick, 28th Battalion, Australian Imperial Force (Ypres)
> Richard Stanley Selwood, 52nd Battalion, Australian Imperial Force (Ypres)
> *(William and Richard had both emigrated from Purton to Australia before the war and had enlisted from there.)*

To Egypt:
> William Nelson Gore, Royal Army Service Corps

Battle of the Somme

British attacks at Delville Wood and Pozières had started in August. On

3 September a further attack was made against the German second defensive system at Guillemont. By 6 September all three of these battles came to a conclusion with British and Australian victories. A further British victory at Ginchy on the 9th secured the sector.

The British advanced again on 15 September, over a front between Flers and Courcelette. This was the first time that tanks ("Little Willies") had been used in action in large numbers. Also, troops from the Canadian and New Zealand Divisions saw action at the Somme for the first time.
Cecil John Mildenhall *(pictured)* was born in Purton in 1889, the son of son of Lot and Elizabeth Mildenhall and had emigrated to Canada in 1913. Cecil was serving with the 4th Canadian Mounted Rifles Battalion on the Somme front having arrived from the Ypres Salient on 8 September. He was admitted to hospital at Wimereux. with gunshot wounds to his left thigh and foot. Cecil died of wounds aged 27 on 16 September 1916 and is buried at Wimereux Communal Cemetery, Pas-de-Calais. He is remembered on Swindon's Roll of Honour. CWGC records a family address in Swindon.

Another innovation was the introduction of air co-operation with tanks by the Royal Flying Corps. The Battle of Flers-Courcelette ended on 22 September and was shortly followed by British attacks on Morval and Thiepval, taking both by the 28th.

In September, the German armies on the Somme suffered about 130,000 casualties, their most costly month on the Somme. Combined with the losses at Verdun and on the Eastern Front, the German Empire was brought closer to military collapse than at any time before the end of the War.

Air War - in England
There were 2 major Zeppelin air raids over the south and east of England in September 1916. On the 2nd, the greatest number of airships in a simultaneous attack, 14 in all, raided London and other parts of England. Leefe Robinson, a British pilot, became the first to shoot down a German airship over Britain - the SL11 brought down at Cuffley, near Potters Bar (between London and Hertford) and just north of today's M25.

The night of 13-14 September saw a raid on the east coast and London with 170 serious casualties, most of them civilian. Airship L32 was shot down by aeroplane at Billericay, Essex, and L33 was brought down by anti-aircraft fire at Little Wigborough, near Colchester.

Air War - in France
Frederick Leach, aged 26, husband of Mrs Caroline Elizabeth Leach (née Young) of Pavenhill, Purton, had been sent to France with the Royal Flying Corps (RFC) No. 7 Kite Balloon Section. The Section was based at Barly, some 15km north of the Somme sector and attached to the British Third Army. Kite-balloons were used for observing enemy lines and activity. The stable basket underneath made it more suitable for reconnaissance photography than any aircraft of the day. But the balloons were filled with flammable hydrogen and usually lasted

about a fortnight before they were damaged or destroyed by enemy gunfire or aircraft. As a result, they were usually sited some distance from the front line.

German aircraft attacked these and other targets, while the aircraft of the RFC engaged to protect the balloons and shoot down the German planes, as well as their other observation and attack roles.

On 17 September, Manfred Albrecht Freiherr von Richthofen ("The Red Baron") won his first aerial combat near Cambrai, France, about 40km east of both Barly and Thiepval. He was 24 years old at the time. He is considered the ace-of-aces of the war, being officially credited with 80 air combat victories.

At the same time, allied aircraft were carrying out raids behind the German lines. On 24 September, 2 French airmen, Captain de Beauchamp and Lt Daucourt, flew 500 miles over German territory in daylight and dropped 12 bombs on the Krupp munitions works at Essen. They returned safely despite being fired on by the 250 anti-aircraft guns that protected the works. Although the bombs caused little damage, the sortie had shown the range and capabilities of the aircraft of the day.

Rumania

Seeing itself supported on its northern border by the Russian Empire, Rumania had entered the war on the Allied side in August. On 1 September, its southern neighbour Bulgaria, and no friend since the Balkan Wars of 1912-13, declared war on Rumania. However, things still seemed to be going well for Rumania as its forces took Sibiu, in Austro-Hungarian Transylvania.

But on 2 September, German and Bulgarian forces invaded Rumania's coastal province of Dobrudja, capturing Tutrakan on the 6th and Silistra on the 10th.

On its western front Rumania occupied Orsova (Hungary) on 8 September. But Sibiu was retaken by Austria-Hungary after a three-day battle on the 29th.

The Greek National Schism

Greece was in a perilous position. Not formally at war, it was being used extensively, and against its will, by the Allies. With Austro-German occupation of both Serbia and Albania to its west, and with Bulgaria to the north and east, Turkey further east and the open seas to the south, Greece was of immense strategic importance to the Allies.

On 2 September, all German ships in Piraeus, the port of Athens, were seized by the Allies.

Back in May 1916, Rupel, a strategic military fort by the Bulgarian border, was surrendered by the royalist government to German and Bulgarian forces. Germany confirmed that the integrity of Greece would be respected, but they couldn't control the Bulgarian forces, which moved the Greek population out and occupied Kavala nearby on 4 September.

In August 1916, during a rally in Athens, the former prime minister Eleftherios Venizelos had publicly announced his total disagreement with the Crown's policies.

There were now effectively two political groups in Greece. On one side were the Venizelists, actively campaigning with Venizelos for Greece to join the war on the allied side. On the other side, the Royalists, including the government, followed King Constantine who favoured the Central Powers but wanted to stay neutral at all costs.

On the 11th, the Greek Prime Minister Alexandros Zaimis resigned to be replaced on 16 September by Nikolaos Kalogeropoulos.

Again against the will of the Greek government, on 20 September the Allies set up an Albanian government in exile under Essad Pasha in Salonika (Thessaloniki). Greece was not under its own control.

Venizelos left Athens on 25 September and, on the 29th, in conjunction with Admiral Condouritis, announced a Provisional Government in Crete as an alternative to the Athens government, with the aim of bringing Greece into the war on the side of the Allies.

Ottoman Front
On 22 September, the Turkish garrison at Taif in the Hejaz surrendered to Arab forces under the Sharif of Mecca.

Africa
Allied successes continued in German East Africa as Dar-es-Salaam surrendered to British forces on 4 September. But on the 7th, General Smuts' British (South African) pursuit of retreating German forces was held at Kisaki when the German garrison used salvaged naval guns from the SMS Königsberg, (damaged by the Royal Navy in June 1915 in the Rufiji Delta and scuttled by her captain), and fired them on the South African units. Smuts called off the attack on 11 September.

Meanwhile Kilwa, on the coast, was occupied by the Royal Navy on the 11th and Lindi on the 17th.

Belgian forces from the Congo captured the German colony's strategically important town of Tabora on 19 September.

On a Lighter Note
On 6 September, the first true supermarket, the "Piggly Wiggly" was opened by Clarence Saunders in Memphis, Tennessee.

Part 40: October 1916

Purton men mobilised in October 1916

To France: William John Read, 1st Battalion Wiltshire Regiment at Thiepval, Somme.

To Salonika (Greece): Rupert Gilbert Woodward, Army Service Corps (MT).

Battle of the Somme
2 new phases of the battle were started: Transloy Ridges and Ancre Heights. Both were extensions of the successes at Thiepval in September.

Robert Stanley Grimes, *(right)* 29th Battalion Canadian Infantry (British Columbia Regiment) died at 1st Northern General Hospital, Newcastle on 13 October 1916, aged 30, of wounds sustained on 26 September at the battle of Thiepval Ridge. He is buried in St Mary's Church graveyard, Purton. His parents were Richard and Annie Grimes of Packhorse, Purton.

Stanley Frederick Haines, *(left)* 4th Battalion Seaforth Highlanders, Machine Gun Corps, son of Frederick & Winifred Haines, Railway Hotel, Purton, was wounded at Ancre Heights. He was transferred to hospital at Chatham where he died aged 26 on 19 October 1916. His body was returned to Purton by train and he was buried in St Mary's Church graveyard in a ceremony together with Robert Grimes.

Thomas Henry Embury, 2nd Battalion Wiltshire Regiment, was killed in action, aged 24, on 18 October 1916 at Flers 6 miles east of Thiepval. The son of Charles and Ellen Elizabeth Embury, of Church Path, Purton, he was buried at Warlencourt British Cemetery.

On 5 October, Adolf Hitler, serving with the 16th Bavarian Reserve Infantry Regiment, was wounded in the left thigh by an exploding shell during the Battle of the Somme in the Thiepval-Flers sector.

On 29 October, Lt.-Gen. Adolf Wild von Hohenborn was dismissed from his post as German Minister for War in the light of German failures at the Somme. He was succeeded by Lt.-Gen. von Stein, formerly Deputy Chief of the German General Staff.

Verdun
After the bloody but successful defence of Verdun at the end of August, the French armies started their "First Offensive Battle" of Verdun. Fort Douaumont was recaptured by the French Colonial Infantry Regiment of Morocco, supported by Senegalese and Somali troops after advancing 2 km through trenches under counter-attack. The entire regiment was awarded the Légion d'honneur for this action.

Austria
On 21 October, the Prime Minister of Austria, Count Karl von Stürgkh who had been in office since November 1911, was assassinated by Friedrich Adler, son of the Social Democratic party chairman. Emperor Franz Joseph appointed Dr Ernest von Körber as Stürgkh's successor.

The War at Sea
Submarine warfare had been a contentious issue for some years. On 7 October, a German submarine (U-53) arrived off Newport, Rhode Island (US).

While staying in international waters it sank 9 British merchant ships. America protested and on the 13th, in response to continued actions in the North Sea, the Norwegian government (neutral) ordered a prohibition of the use of submarines of belligerent nations in Norwegian waters. None of this lasted long as Germany resumed U-boat attacks on 15 October.

On 20 October the Russian battleship "Imperatritsa Mariya" (Empress Maria) suffered from a fire in the forward powder magazine while at anchor in Sevastopol. A team of sailors, led by Engineer-Mechanic Midshipman Ignatyev, managed to flood the forward shell magazine shortly before the powder magazine exploded but at the cost of their own lives. However, their action reduced the death toll to around 228 saving the rest of the ship's complement of 1,213.

Over the night of 26-27 October, 23 German torpedo boats raided the Straits of Dover to disrupt the Dover Barrage and destroy whatever Allied shipping could be found in the strait. The German torpedo boats were challenged by an ancient British destroyer HMS Flirt. The Germans sank Flirt and attacked the barrage's drifters (fishing boats similar to trawlers and cabled in a line). A flotilla of British destroyers was sent to repel the German flotilla. The Germans made a successful withdrawal. By the end of the night, the British had lost one destroyer, a transport, and several drifters while the Germans suffered minor damage to a single torpedo boat. This success encouraged Germany to plan more attacks and their raids continued until the British reinforced their fleet in November.

On 28 October, a British hospital ship "Galeka" hit a mine off Le Havre. Though not carrying any patients at the time, 19 Royal Army Medical Corps personnel died in the sinking.

The Air War

Now they knew how to do it, another German airship (L31) was shot down by aeroplane at Potters Bar, near London over the night of 1-2 October.

More in response to actions in France, the German Air Force was created on 8 October, combining various units of their mainly army-based air power. Flying Ace Hauptmann (Captain) Oswald Boelcke had introduced new tactics that were beginning to give the German Air Force greater aerial dominance especially using formation fighting rather than single combat. However, Boelcke was killed in action on 28 October.

Rumania

Although only recently joining the war on the allied side, and having some early victories, Rumania was now doing badly. The city of Brasov in Transylvania, was retaken by Austria on 7 October and German troops crossed into Rumania on the 14th. On 22 October, German and Bulgarian forces took Constanza, in the Rumanian heartland of Dobrudja province. 3 days later, Cernavoda in Dobrudja fell to the Germans.

Italian Front

We've ignored the Italian Front for too long so it's about time we looked at it. At the time Italy joined the allied cause, a treaty was signed (Treaty of London) in

April 1915. In return for her involvement, the Allies promised Italy territories of the Austro-Hungarian Empire which were mainly inhabited by ethnic Slovenes. Italy wanted land including the present-day Slovenia and the Italian army leader Field Marshal Luigi Cadorna had planned a frontal assault, breaking through into the Slovenian plateau. This would occupy Ljubljana and advance towards Vienna. The battle plan involved the area between the northernmost part of the Adriatic Sea and the inland sources of the river Soča (Isonzo). The plan was also to isolate Trieste, a major Austrian port on the Adriatic, and claim it as Italian territory. Twelve successive battles resulted.

Terrain was against the attackers but it did mean that Austria was forced to move forces from the Eastern Front (Russia and Rumania).

The 8th Battle of the Isonzo began on 8 October, lasting four days. 31 October saw the start of the 9th battle, lasting 5 days.

Greece

Greece was in a major crisis. On 3 October, Kalogeropoulos's new Greek Cabinet resigned. In the interim, Bulgarian and Austrian troops just to the north in Macedonia were being held by residual Serbian forces with French and Russian help at the Crna River and Monastir. The Allies needed full cooperation from Greece to keep this front going.

Eleftherios Venizelos had already set up a provisional Greek government in opposition in Crete and, on 9 October, he arrived back in Salonika - he was ardently in favour of the allied cause. The next day, the allied governments sent an ultimatum to the Athens Greek government to surrender the Greek navy. Under this pressure, the Greek government resigned and Professor Lambros formed a new government. He accepted the allied ultimatum on 11 October.

Things were moving fast and, on 19 October France formally recognised Venizelos's Provisional Government in Crete. The next day, an Anglo-French Conference was held at Calais to discuss Greek participation in the war.

Arabian Front

On 23 October 1916 at Hamra in Wadi Safra, Emir Faisal Hussein, son of Hussein bin Ali the Sharif of Mecca, met Captain T.E. Lawrence, a junior British intelligence officer from Cairo. Lawrence put forward the idea of an independent post-war Arabian state and was looking for the man to lead the Arabs. From 1916 until 1918, Faisal headed the army of rebellion that confronted the Turks.

The Sharif, Faisal's father, was proclaimed King of the Arabs on 29 October.

Part 41: November 1916

Francis John Burgess, 1st Battalion, Wiltshire Regiment and son of John and Mary Burgess, of High Street, Purton, died of wounds sustained on 7 July 1916 at the Leipzig Salient during the Battle of the Somme. He had a severe gunshot wound to the head and died, some 20 weeks later, aged 25 on 28 November 1916 in Bradford hospital. Francis was buried in St Mary's Church graveyard on 2 December. 4 Purton soldiers at home on leave carried the coffin at his funeral, Cpl E Ovens, L/Cpl B Woolford, Private F Lewis and Private F West. He was buried in a family plot so the grave is not marked by a Commonwealth War Graves Commission headstone, but his details are recorded on the plot surround.

Purton men mobilised in November 1916
To France:
  Valentine W Oakley Brown, 3rd Dragoon Guards (Prince of Wales' Own).

To Salonika (Greece):
  William Charles Griffen, 12th Battalion Hampshire Regiment, formerly with Berkshire Regiment.

The Somme & Verdun
The Battle of the Somme continued with fighting on the Ancre Heights, concluding when British forces took Beaumont Hamel on 13 November. 2 days later a British pilot, William George Barker, flying very low over the Ancre River, spotted German troops assembling for a counter-attack. He alerted artillery to fire on the target and the German infantry force of 4,000 men was broken up. Barker was awarded the Military Cross. On 18 November the British Expeditionary Force commander General Douglas Haig called off the battle, which had run for 4½ months, with over 1 million killed or wounded.

On 1 November, French forces recaptured Fort Vaux at Verdun.

Allied Strategy
On 15 November, the allies held a conference in Paris to discuss developments including the relations between Governments and Staffs, policy and strategy and war aims in Greece and Poland.

At Sea
2 British hospital ships were lost in November. On the 21st, HMHS Britannic, which had been designed as the third Olympic-class ocean liner for White Star Line, sister ship to the Titanic, sank in the Aegean Sea off the island of Kea after hitting a mine, with the loss of 30 lives. Britannic was the largest ship lost during the entire war (48,158 tons). 2 days later, the British hospital ship "Braemar Castle" also hit a mine in the Aegean Sea and was beached.

Two German commerce raiders "Seeadler" (Sea Eagle) and "Moewe" set out from Kiel in Germany during the month.

On 26 November, a second German naval raid was made on the port of Lowestoft in Norfolk. The same day, the French battleship "Suffren" was sunk by submarine in the Bay of Biscay. The torpedo exploded in an ammunition magazine and Suffren sank within seconds, taking her entire crew of 648 with her.

On 29 November, Admiral Sir David Beatty was appointed Commander-in-Chief of the Grand Fleet, replacing Admiral Sir John Jellicoe.

The Air War

On the night of 27/28 November during German Zeppelin raids, British aeroplanes destroyed airship L34 off Hartlepool and L21 off Yarmouth. But the Germans started new tactics with the first daylight aeroplane raid on London on 28 November.

Austria

On 21 November, Emperor Franz Joseph of Austria died after contracting pneumonia, aged 86. He was succeeded by his son Archduke Charles.

Eastern & Balkan Fronts

Rumania continued its losses in the face of Austro-German forces, culminating with the occupation parts of the Rumanian capital, Bucharest, on 23 November.

Greece was being pulled further into the war as the Entente governments demanded the expulsion of Central Powers embassy staffs from Athens (19 November) and the surrender of Greek military material to the Allies. Venizelos' Provisional Greek Government in Salonika declared war on Germany and Bulgaria on the 23rd. Allied forces landed at Piraeus, the port of Athens, on 30 November.

Russia

Between April and June 1916, Pavel Milyukov, a deputy in the Russian parliament (Duma) and leader of the moderate Kadet party, went to allied and neutral countries as part of a Russian parliamentary delegation. In July-September 1916, he went abroad privately, following up rumours about talks by the Russian government seeking a separate peace with Germany and Austria. Milyukov studied European newspapers and held meetings with Russian emigrés in Switzerland. The information he obtained was unreliable, but pointed towards his opinion.

On 1 November, Milyukov made a speech in the Duma known historically as "Stupidity or Treason?" He hinted at treasonable acts by Alexandra Fyedorovna, empress consort of Tsar Nicholas II, and Prime Minister Boris V. Shtyurmer. He told the government, "We will fight you ... by all legal means, until you leave."

On 7 November, Grand Duke Nikolai Nikolayevich warned the Tsar of a potential uprising. This led to pressure resulting in the resignation of Shtyurmer and his government on 24 November. It also led to the proposal by Mikhail Lvovich Mandelshtam in January 1917 to declare the State Duma as a Constituent Assembly.

The first steps towards the Russian Revolution had been taken.

Part 42: December 1916

The following men with Purton connections were mobilised in December 1916:

To France:
George Durnford, 11th Battalion Australian Infantry Force
Ernest Hesketh Harrison, 8th Battalion East Surrey Regiment

To Salonika:
George Hicks, Royal Garrison Artillery
William Slade, Royal Engineers

Lt. Leonard Dunsford, was born in Purton on 1 April 1889, the eldest son of Arthur and Blanche Maud Mary Dunsford, of Holly Lodge, Purton. He had emigrated to Canada where he enlisted. He was wounded in the thigh at Ypres Salient in April 1916 when he was a Sergeant with the 2nd Canadian Pioneer Battalion. He was fit for service again by November 1916 and transferred to the 4th Canadian Mounted Rifles, with a temporary commission as lieutenant. On 17 December 1916, aged 27, Leonard was inspecting sentry posts of his battalion near Écurie, north of Arras, with another officer. He was struck by an enemy trench mortar bomb and instantly killed. Leonard is buried in Louez Military Cemetery, Duisans.

The Battle of Verdun (the longest single battle of the war) ended on 18 December after 11 months, with the German troops defeated. No one really knows the overall cost in lives and suffering, but estimates vary from French deaths between 156,000 and 162,000, with around 143,000 Germans killed. Those wounded were about 3 times as many. Over a million men were fighting on each side during the conflict. No records seem to be available of the effects on the civilian population of the city, but at least they had some respite until the 2nd Battle of Verdun in August 1917, when France made a further push to regain its lost territory.

1916

Politics

On 4 December Herbert Asquith resigned as British Prime Minister to be replaced by David Lloyd George on the 7th. Lloyd George held his first meeting of the new War Cabinet on the 9th and on 11 December, in a coalition government, the full cabinet met for the first time. Lord Derby became Minister for War in place of Lloyd George and Balfour became Foreign Secretary succeeding Lord Grey. The Ministry of Labour was established the same day.

Then on 19 December, the new government instituted National Service, followed quickly by the establishment of new ministries of Food, Pensions and Shipping (22nd) with Lord Davenport being appointed as Food Controller on the 26th.

Changes were made in France too. On 12 December, General Joffre was replaced as Commander-in-Chief (Western Front) by General Nivells. Joffre became a technical military adviser to the government. Then on the 26th, Joffre was appointed a Marshal of France.

Surrender?

On 12 December, the German, Austro-Hungarian, Bulgarian and Turkish governments all simultaneously handed notes to the United States embassies in their countries. They stated they were ready to negotiate a peace. In response, US President Wilson send out a note to the allied governments, on 18 December, suggesting talks and asking what their war objectives were. The Central Powers agreed to Wilson's suggestion of negotiations on 26 December while an Anglo-French conference was discussing it in London. The Allied governments rejected the peace proposal on 30 December.

War in the Air

On 22 December, the Sopwith Camel air fighter made its maiden flight, having been designed to counter the German Fokker aircraft.

War at Sea

On 4 December, Admiral Sir John Jellicoe was appointed First Sea Lord, replacing Admiral Sir Henry Jackson.

Greece

While the Allies were trying to pull the official Greek government into the war, there was a Greek attack (1 December) on allied forces that had occupied Piraeus and parts of Athens. The Allied forces withdrew. On 6 December, there was a massacre in Athens of supporters of the Venizelos provisional government by troops of the official government. By the 8th, the Allies were in a position to enforce a naval blockade of Greece and on 11 December they sent a note to the Athens government demanding a complete Greek demobilisation. This was followed up by a demand that Greece remove all its forces from Thessaly, in eastern Greece (14th) which the official government accepted. But on 17 December, the official government issued a warrant for the arrest of Venizelos on charges of high treason. Britain countered by formally recognising Venizelos's provisional government in Salonika the next day.

Mesopotamia & Palestine

British forces in Mesopotamia commenced operations to recapture Kut-al-Amara on 13 December. On the Ottoman-Egypt border, the British Empire Desert Column occupied El Arish on 21 December during their advance across the Sinai Peninsula. 2 days later, the Desert Column captured the Ottoman garrison at Magdhaba.

Rumania

Rumania's foray into the war continued to do badly with the complete capture of their capital, Bucharest, on 6 December.

Russia

In one of the oddest incidents of the war, a pro-monarchist conspiracy was hatched to kill the mystic monk Grigori Rasputin who had been seen as a malign influence on the Russian Imperial Court since he had been allowed to treat the young Tsarevich (crown prince) for haemophilia. Rasputin was believed to have urged the Tsar, via the Tsarina, to make misguided orders for war plans.

On 30 December, one of the conspirators, Prince Felix Yusupov, nephew of Tsar Nicholas, invited Rasputin to the Moika Palace in Saint Petersburg where, supposedly, he would meet Yusupov's wife, Princess Irina Aleksandrovna Romanova. While there, Rasputin apparently survived being poisoned with cyanide-laced sweets, four bottles of poisoned wine, and a revolver wound through the chest, stomach and liver. Rasputin lurched from the palace and was then shot at again four times by another conspirator, Vladimir Purishkevich, though only one bullet hit. Rasputin never reached the gate. The body made a sudden movement, and a guard placed his revolver on Rasputin's forehead and pulled the trigger. The body was carried back inside, where Yusupov is said to have hit Rasputin in the right eye with his shoe ... just in case.

The body was thrown through a hole in the ice of the Malaya Nevka river but the conspirators didn't weight the body to make it sink and the corpse drifted into an ice mass. No one was ever charged with the murder. Of course, the two 1917 Russian revolutions in January and October probably added fancy to the story!

Other effects of war
Casualties in war are usually attributed to battles and sieges, but on 12 December in the Dolomites of southern Austria, now part of Italy, 100 avalanches in the Isonzo war zone buried 18,000 Austrian and Italian soldiers.

On the western front, manpower was in short supply with every able man used on the front line. On 30 December, the British and Chinese governments agreed a plan to allow employment of Chinese labour in the war areas of France.

- - - - - -

A CATCH-UP
While concentrating on Purton's involvement in the Great War, to date, I've not had much chance to write about the bigger picture of what was going on. We've looked at the War in Mesopotamia, Egypt and Africa. Also developments in the Balkans, Russia and the United States, which will become such key elements in the coming year, 1917.

But how did the War on the Western Front get to the situation that we would have found in December 1916 after 2 years and 5 months of conflict? I rather glossed over much of that because there was a lot of Purton and Wiltshire Regiment history to cover. Now, just over half way through the Great War, it is about time to give a bit of a summary.

During August 1914, the German forces advanced quickly through Belgium, capturing Brussels fairly early on. The Belgian army, despite its small size, managed to hold the massive German attack long enough to give France time to mobilise its forces and move them into place.

The British Expeditionary Force was very small - after all we were a naval power not keeping huge standing armies like the continental nations were used to. However, our input was very little, very late and served only to plug a few gaps in the French line. The British Commander-in-Chief, ironically General French, didn't seem to like the French ... nor command. The British defences at Mons were half-hearted at best and II Division on the BEF left flank was all but wiped out when I Division to their right were pulled back instead of supporting them. A few months later, the 2nd Battalion Wiltshire Regiment joined II Division. Had it been earlier, there would have been a lot more Purton deaths to report in August 1914.

In the face of German advances, the French retreated but couldn't keep up with the British retreating even faster. General French wanted to get west of Paris, away from the fighting, and even back to the Channel ports and England. The phase of the War called the Battle of the Frontiers was starting (i.e, the border between Belgium and France). Kitchener, on a visit to the front, laid down the law and General French eventually began to advance again with the subsequent push by France ... but painfully slowly.

The Germans continued to push forward towards Paris, Nancy and the heavily fortified city of Verdun. The Germans made what is seen as a terrible blunder by one of their armies, facing Paris, suddenly veering off to the east and leaving their right flank exposed. French forces took the opportunity to attack on 2 fronts splitting the German armies in two, and the BEF slowly wandered into the gap in the middle. The resulting Battle of the Marne saw a full retreat of German forces with massive loss of life. The new German line was formed at the River Aisne where another costly battle ensued.

Since the German forces couldn't now advance straight on to Paris, they fought their way west in what became known as the *Race to the Sea*, in order to secure North Sea and English Channel ports. The result of this was the stalemate that resulted in the trench war including the 1st battle of Ypres. No significant amount of territory was won or lost during the ensuing trench war. By late 1914, both sides had learnt that it was safer to defend that to attack.

Much reinforced and reorganised, the BEF became a more meaningful and respected fighting force during 1915 and 1916.

German forces continued to try to break through at Verdun but were eventually repulsed by French defending forces who eventually took the battle on to an offensive phase.

The Battle of the Somme, in 1916, was planned as a way of easing pressure on Verdun by diverting German forces away from the city, and of recovering lost French territory north of Verdun and east of Paris. This was successful ... but with terrible loss of life and maimed bodies.

As we see in the main article above, the Central Powers were looking for a way out of the War. The Allies had achieved a strategic push-back and didn't want a ceasefire that would consolidate German territorial gains as of December 1916.

Part 43: January 1917

The following men with Purton connections were mobilised in January 1917:
Francis P Bathe, 116th Battalion, Canadian Expeditionary Force
Frederick Thomas Bowden, Royal Field Artillery, Tank Corps
John Ranby Brown, 102nd Battalion, Canadian Infantry
Harry Lewis, 172nd Brigade Royal Field Artillery
Arthur Percy Richardson, 10th Battalion, Suffolk Regiment
Ralph Shailes, Royal Flying Corps

Ottoman Campaigns

In January 1917, the 5th (Service) Battalion Wiltshire Regiment was stationed in Mesopotamia (modern Iraq) involved in the Battle of Kut, which commenced on 9 January. On 11 January at 9 pm, they were at the River Hai taking over a line held by the South Lancashire Regiment on the east bank. While the Regiment dug an advanced trench "A" Company provided a covering fire. 5 men of the covering party were killed including **Thomas John Selwood** of Purton, aged 20 *(pictured)*. Thomas was the son of William and Sarah Jane Selwood of Pavenhill, Purton. 20 other officers and men were wounded.

1917

By the 25th the Battalion was advancing under cover of an intense bombardment as they attacked the Turkish front line. The objective was to capture and consolidate the Turkish first line. The engagement was considered a success with 234 Turkish dead. However, 35 officers and men of the 5th Wilts were killed including **Frederick Henry Litten**, aged 25, born in Purton the son of John and Ellen Litten. By the time of the war he was married to A E Litten and living at Inkpen Common near Hungerford. 114 other officers and men were wounded.

Both Thomas and Frederick are buried at the Amara War Cemetery. Thomas is remembered on the Purton War Memorial, and Frederick on the Kintbury (Berks) War Memorial.

Elsewhere, on 9 January, the last Ottoman Army garrison on the Sinai Peninsula was captured by the Egyptian Expeditionary Force's Desert Column at Rafah while the remaining Turkish troops withdrew into Palestine.

A Royal Navy flotilla captured Wejh in the Hejaz on the 24th and the position was consolidated by Arab forces under Faisal and T.E. Lawrence the next day.

Western Front

At the same time, the 6th (Service) Battalion Wiltshire Regiment was in the line at Hebuterne, near Thiepval. **Edward Harry Hedges**, born in 1898 and the son of John and Emma Hedges of Lower Pavenhill, Purton, contracted pneumonia and died, aged 19, on 29 January 1917. Edward was buried at Comie British Cemetery near Mondicourt. However, individual graves and small cemeteries were moved to larger communal cemeteries after the War by the Imperial War Graves Commission and battlefield clearance teams. He was moved to Couin

New British Cemetery. Edward is remembered on the Purton War Memorial.

On 3 January, the first contingents of the Portuguese Expeditionary Force landed at Brest in Brittany, France. Although not in any alliance with the joint Allied Powers, an alliance between England and Portugal had been in existence since 1386. It was and still is the oldest alliance in the world.

Also on the 3rd, General Sir Douglas Haig was promoted to the rank of Field Marshal.

Women's Land Army

With 3 million men away fighting in the war, there was an immense shortage of labour in agriculture, haymaking (horse fodder) and timber, all essential for the continued feeding of Britain and the needs of the war. The Board of Agriculture started activities in 1915, organising the Land Army in 1915.

In January 1917, the Women's Land Army was set up and by the end of 1917 there were over a quarter on a million women working as farm labourers, with 23,000 in the Land Army itself, doing chores such as milking cows and picking fruit.

Many farmers were against women workers so one of the early goals of the Board of Agriculture was to speak with farmers to encourage them to accept women's work on the farms. One sticking point was that the uniform of the Women's Land Army included trousers, which many at the time considered cross-dressing.

The first female Board of Agriculture inspectors were appointed and paid women officers were appointed in each county of England and Wales.

Munitions Accident

On 19 January, a blast at a munitions factory at Silvertown, West Ham in London, killed 73 workers and injured 400 more. The explosion and the resulting fire caused over £2 million worth of damage but was also a major set-back for armaments production.

Surrender?

In response to US President Woodrow Wilson's peace note in December 1916 and following an Inter-Allied conference in Rome on 5 January, the Allies sent formal note to Wilson outlining their war aims on the 10th. Belgium also placed itself in Allied hands.

On the 11th, Germany and Austria-Hungary issued a note saying they would not accept responsibility for the Allies' continuing the war. But they declared they would continue the war to a successful end if they had to.

In the face of the opposing views of the 2 power blocs, on 22 January Wilson made his "peace without victory" speech to the US Senate, effectively calling for an armistice.

However, in the background to this, saboteurs had set off the Kingsland Explosion at a munitions factory at Lyndhurst, New Jersey, on 11 January. On the 19th the German government sent a telegram instruction to its Ambassador in Mexico to negotiate an alliance with Mexico and Japan against the United States. Known as the Zimmerman telegram, it was intercepted by

British surveillance.

Far from ending the war, Germany appeared to be escalating it by dragging the USA in on the Allies' side.

At Sea

In separate actions, HMS Cornwallis was sunk by submarine in the Mediterranean (9 Jan); the Harwich flotilla was in action against the German 6th Flotilla in the North Sea when HMS Simoom was sunk (23 Jan); the British armed merchantman SS Laurentic was sunk by mines off Lough Swilly (Ireland) with the loss of 354 of the 475 aboard (25 Jan). German destroyers shelled Southwold and Wangford on the Suffolk coast on 25 January.

On 31 January, and against its stated position in surrender terms, the German government announced to the USA and other neutral powers that it would resume unrestricted submarine warfare and would not respect the status of hospital ships.

Rumania

In the first week of January, German forces captured Focsani and Braila in Rumania, and the last of the Russian and Rumanian forces evacuated the Rumanian heartland province of Dobrudja on 6 January.

Other News

J.R.R. Tolkien, had been on medical leave from the British Army suffering illness since the start of the Somme campaign in July 1916. In January 1917, he began writing "The Book of Lost Tales" which eventually became The Silmarillion, with the "Fall of Gondolin".

Part 44: February 1917

Only one man with a Purton connection was mobilised in February 1917 (to France):

William S Bathe, 116th Battalion, Canadian Expeditionary Force. Born Swindon and emigrated to Canada 1913. Next of kin listed as Eleanor née Linsell, of Purton.

Harry Lewis was born in Moredon in 1896. His parents were Francis and Harriett Lewis (of Common Platt by 1917). Harry served with the 172nd Brigade, Royal Field Artillery, was wounded in action on 31 January 1917 and died of those wounds, aged 20, on 1 February 1917. Harry is buried in Hazebrouck Communal Cemetery. He is remembered on the Purton War Memorial.

Western Front: Between 23 February and 5 April, German forces made strategic withdrawals from the front-line positions on the Ancre river to strong positions on the Hindenburg Line between Arras in the north and Laffaux, near Soissons on the Aisne.

Egypt and Mesopotamia

By the beginning of February, the Senussi troops of Libya, loyal to the Ottoman Empire, had withdrawn to their stronghold at the Siwa Oasis on the western frontier of Egypt. A British column including the Light Armoured Car Brigade (LACB) was dispatched to Siwa, where the armoured cars surprised and engaged the Senussi at Girba (3 February). The Senussi retreated overnight. The LACB entered Siwa unopposed on 4 February. The British force returned to Matruh on 8 February.

On 13 February, units of the Egyptian Expeditionary Force 13 began a raid on Nekhl in the Egyptian Sinai Peninsula to recapture that British regional administration centre that had been occupied by Ottoman forces at the beginning of the war.

In Mesopotamia, British and Indian forces reoccupied Kut-al-Amara on the 23rd and the Turkish garrison retreated towards Baghdad.

War at Sea

On 1 February, Admiral Tirpitz announced the resumption of unlimited German submarine warfare, rescinding the 'Sussex pledge', and 2 days later the United States severed diplomatic relations with Germany. That same day, 3 February, a US liner, the Housatonic, was sunk by a German submarine.

The neutral Scandinavian governments published a joint protest against German submarine warfare on 13 February.

On 21 February, a British troopship, the SS Mendi, was accidentally rammed and sank off the Isle of Wight, killing 646, mainly members of the South African Native Labour Corps.

On the 25th, German destroyers carried out a raid on the Kent coastal towns of Margate and Broadstairs.

Also on the 25th, German submarines sank the Cunard liner RMS Laconia, while returning from the USA to England. President Wilson called it the "overt act" for which he was waiting and next day asked Congress to authorise the arming of US merchant ships.

USA

In addition to the American reactions to the submarine war, a new constitution was adopted in Mexico on 5 February and, the same day, the last of the American troops commanded by General John Pershing left Mexico. The new Mexican President Carranza was installed.

In January, Britain had intercepted the Zimmermann Telegram, in which Germany offered to give the American south-west states back to Mexico if Mexico were to declare war on the United States. It wasn't until 24 February that the US ambassador to Britain was shown the intercept, but shortly after, on the 28th, the text was published in the American press.

War Aims

On 14 February, Britain informed the Japanese government that it would support Japanese claims to German territories north of the Equator if they would support British claims south of the equator.

Also on the 14th, the British government announced in Parliament that restoration of Alsace and Lorraine to France was a British war aim.

Espionage

Margaretha Geertruida "Margreet" MacLeod was born in Zelle in Holland on 7 August 1876. She is better known her stage name of Mata Hari, as an exotic dancer and courtesan. She was arrested in Paris on 13 February 1917 on charges of spying for Germany against the Allies. She was convicted and executed by firing squad in France on 15 October 1917.

My Family's War
A Deferment of Service

Rick Dixon writes:

This is a piece of local history with relevance to the history of my own house and the farm next door (up to 2017). It will be typical of similar small farms and businesses caught up by conscription in the Great War.

A Deferment of Service Tribunal was held in February 1917 on behalf of James Telling Selby an unmarried man, aged 37, and employed as a cowman by Mr Harry Dash of Quarry Road (now known as Quarry Farm, The Hyde). Mr Dash applied for deferment stating that Selby was his only remaining farmhand. The Tribunal's finding was a 'conditional exemption' and James was never enlisted.

As an additional flavour of Purton in the Great War is the following extract from "A history of Quarry House" by David Bisset & Rick Dixon. Harry Dash took over the lease at Quarry Farm in 1903. Dash continued for some years and was still listed in Kelly's Directory as the farmer in the 1915 edition. Edward and Elvira Matthews began farming at the beginning of the First World War while Dash continued to own Quarry House and the attached Honeymoon Cottage. Mervyn 'Blackie' Matthews was born at Honeymoon Cottage in January 1911. He told Rick that he remembered the line of pine trees being planted along Short Hedge footpath. The trees have grown a lot since but he said he was told off for playing leapfrog over those saplings with his mates!

The Great War saw the death of at least three of the Matthews men folk but someone may have brought back from France an 1897 five-centime coin to show family and friends. Unfortunately, this memento of strange faraway lands was lost in the front hedge of Quarry House, only to be found again in good condition when the driveway was widened in 1998. Up until 1922, Quarry Farm had always been farmed by tenant farmers under an absentee landlord. A momentous change came that year when Edward Matthews bought the farm outright from the landlord, by then one Henry Caleb Collingburn, for £2,000.

Harry Dash died at Quarry House in 1927 and was buried at St Mary's.

Part 45: March 1917

The only man with a Purton connection who was mobilised in March 1917 was Harry Tyler, Northamptonshire Regiment, Labour Corps, a groom, whose address was given as Stoke House, Purton Stoke, Wiltshire. His mother Sarah Tyler was listed as next-of-kin.

Edward James Williams *(pictured)* of Station Road, Purton, was serving with the 8th (Service) Battalion Gloucestershire Regiment. On 25 March 1917, the battalion was in trenches in the Dieppendaal Sector, some 5 miles southwest of Ypres. Edward was killed in action near Kemmel Hill in a dugout with 2 other men by a German shell; another 2 were wounded. He was aged 21. His Commanding Officer stated that he was a good man and a brave soldier. Edward was buried at Klein-Vierstraat British Cemetery. After the War, individual graves and small cemeteries were moved to larger communal cemeteries by the Imperial War Graves Commission and his burial is now at the British Cemetery, Bailleul. The son of Walter and Caroline, Station Road, Purton, Edward is remembered on the Purton War Memorial, and in the Memorials in St Mary's Church.

USA

On 1 March, the US government published the text of the Zimmermann Telegram via the newspapers; this telegram had contained a proposal for Mexico to join the war on the German side, with the offer of southwestern US states being ceded to Mexico. However, tensions between the US and Mexico had mostly passed and Mexico and the USA renewed diplomatic relations on 3 March. On the 11th, Venustiano Carranza was elected president of Mexico and the US recognised his government.

Woodrow Wilson was sworn in for a second term as President of the United States on 4 March. The Zimmermann scandal and the continued German naval hostilities against neutral ships were pushing the US towards war and on 12 March the United States announced the arming of all of its merchant vessels in the war zone by Presidential executive order after failing to win Congress approval.

The same day, a German submarine sank the Algonquin, an unarmed US merchant ship. By 20 March, after the sinking of 3 more American merchant ships, Wilson and his war cabinet, voted unanimously in favour of declaring war on Germany. This would still have to be accepted by Congress and Wilson planned to get that through in April.

In an unrelated deal, on 31 March the United States completed its $25 million purchase of the Danish West Indies, which were renamed the US Virgin Islands.

Russia

Events of major significance were also happening in Russia, with the outbreak of the February Revolution.

Confusingly this happened in March 1917 as the Russian Empire still used the old Julian calendar which was 13 days adrift from the modern Gregorian calendar. I have used the modern calendar here apart from noting the old calendar date of the start.

On 7 March, [old calendar 22 February], the Russian February Revolution broke out in Petrograd (now St Petersburg) with food riots in that starving city including a massed women's demand for increased bread supplies to be procured. Riots spread quickly through Petrograd, fuelled by unrest over the conduct of the war and poor to non-existent supplies of food, clothing and equipment to troops. A strike broke out at the Putilov factory, a major ironworks, producing steel, artillery shells, railway rolling stock. This could not be ignored and, by the 11th, Tsar Nicolas II ordered the army to put down the civil unrest by firing on them, but the army mutinied and joined the protesters.

In the face of mutiny, the Duma (parliament) set up a Provisional Government on 12 March. Revolutionary activists, Stalin, Kamenev and Muranov arrived in Petrograd and formed a rival soviet Executive Committee the same day. The Russian Provisional Government (RPG) removed the Premier and the Minister for War from office on the 13th.

On 15 March, the Tsar abdicated and dissolved his sons' claims of to the throne. His last act in power was to nominate his brother, Grand Duke Michael, to succeed him, but the Grand Duke declined and power passed to the RPG under the premiership of Prince Georgy Lvov. The Russian Empire had ended after 196 years.

The Provisional Government was recognised by Britain, France, Italy, USA, Rumania and Switzerland on 22 March.

While these negotiations were going on, mutiny broke out in the Russian Baltic Fleet on 16 March.

Other things started unravelling. Since the Tsar was no longer head of the Russian Orthodox Church, the Georgian Orthodox Church restored its independence (autocephaly) on 25 March, which had been denied to them by Imperial Decree in 1811. Then on the 30th, the Provisional Government acknowledged the independence of Poland.

Mesopotamia & Persia
While the Russian February Revolution was in progress, Russian activity in western Persia (Iran) against Ottoman forces continued, with the recapture of Hamadan, Kermanshah and Qasr-i-Shirin.

Meanwhile British and Indian forces crossed the Diyala river in Mesopotamia on 5 March, occupying Baghdad on the 11th.

Frank Sutton was born in 1891, the son of Frederick and Emily Sutton, Packhorse Farm, Purton. He had seen action at Loos in September 1915 and the North Wilts Herald at the time reported he was with the 1st Battalion Wiltshire Regiment. Bob Lloyd's investigations suggest that the 1st Battalion was not involved at Loos but the 2nd Battalion was. It is possible that Frank had been with the 1st Wilts when he was hospitalised following a gas attack at Hill 60 south of Ypres in April 1915. He was probably transferred to the 2nd Battalion after his recovery and in time to see action at Loos.

Frank was later sent to Mesopotamia to join the 5th Battalion Wiltshire Regiment. There, he suffered from dysentery and was hospitalised to India before returning to Mesopotamia and was present at the fall of Baghdad (11 March 1917).

On 29/30 March 1917, the Battalion diary records that they were at Deltawa having advanced from Jadida on the 25th. On 29 March, the Battalion was in action when it suffered 132 men wounded at Palm Tree Post. Frank Sutton is believed to have been wounded there and died the following day, 30 March 1917, aged 18.

Frank was perhaps buried south of Jadida village but is remembered on the Basra Memorial which commemorates more than 40,500 members of the Commonwealth forces who died in Mesopotamia between 1914 and August 1921 and whose graves are not known. His name is also inscribed on the Purton War Memorial and the Memorials in St Mary's Church.

Egyptian & Palestine Front

British forces began an offensive in Palestine on 24 March, which resulted in the 1st Battle of Gaza on 26 March. The British Egyptian Expeditionary Force troops virtually encircled the Gaza garrison but were ordered to withdraw, leaving the city to the Ottoman defenders on 27 March. On the 26th, the entire population of Tel Aviv and Jaffa, Jews and Arabs alike except for essential occupations, were expelled without notice by the Turkish authorities. They could go anywhere they liked except Jerusalem and Haifa. The Arab population were allowed to return soon after, but the Jewish population only after the British conquest in 1918.

The War at Sea

Three British hospital ships were mined or torpedoed in March: Glenart Castle (towed to Southampton), Asturias (beached) and Gloucester Castle (towed ashore). None was sunk but they were damaged and put out of action.

The German surface raider Leopard was sunk on 16 March in an action with British ships HMS Achilles and armed steamer Dundee. German destroyers raided Ramsgate and Broadstairs on the Kent coast on the 18th.

The French Dreadnought battleship Danton was sunk by submarine south of Sardinia in the Mediterranean on 19 March. 806 men were rescued by escort vessels, but 296 went down with the ship, including Captain Delage.

Austria-Hungary

The war had not been going well for Austria and on 31 March, the Austrian Emperor Charles sent a letter to President Poincaré of France containing a secret proposal to open peace discussions. This ran totally counter to the agreement between the Central Powers not to seek a separate peace.

Western Front

On 14 March, the German army began its planned withdrawal from the Somme front, strategically falling back on the Hindenburg Line defences to the east.

China

On 14 March, the Republic of China cut off diplomatic relations with Germany.

Part 45: April 1917

No men with Purton connections are known to have been mobilised in April 1917.

Western Front

By 5 April, the German withdrawal to the Hindenburg Line was complete but their positions were being attacked by Allied forces. **Albert Edward Hayward** of Cricklade had sailed from Southampton on 21 June 1916 to join the 2nd Battalion Wiltshire Regiment. On 9 April 1917, D Company of the Battalion was involved in attacking German positions on the Hindenburg line 2,000 and 2,400 yards away. At 11.38 am the 21st Brigade attacked with the 2nd Wilts on the right, the 18th King's (Liverpool) Regiment on the left, and the 19th Manchester Regiment in support. The Battalion advanced in artillery formation in 2 waves, each of 2 Companies.

With 2 sunken roads to cross and much barbed wire to negotiate, the advance was made under heavy shelling and machine gun fire. After relief from the 16th Manchesters, the remnants of the Battalion retired. The total casualties sustained by the 2nd Wilts in the attack was 2 Captains, 12 Subalterns and 328 other ranks. Albert was among those killed.

Albert has no known grave, and is remembered on the Arras Memorial.

On 9 April 1917, the Battle of Arras began - part of the Allied Spring Offensive. The battle lasted until May. During it, the Canadian Corps captured Vimy Ridge. British forces made long advances to Point du Jour and south of the Scarpe.

Arthur Henry Bridgman *(pictured)* of Kingston-on-Thames was the husband of Kate E Bridgman (née Selwood). Kate, known as Kit, was born in Purton in 1893, and she and Arthur married in 1914. Arthur was serving with the 9th Battalion Essex Regiment which was in action on 9 and 10 April at Feuchy Chapel near Arras. The casualty list as recorded in the Battalion diary included 33 men dead, 126 men wounded. 9th Essex records state these casualty figures as light! 80 German prisoners were  taken over the 2 days. Arthur was recorded missing during this action, later reported wounded and died of those wounds on 12 April 1917. He was buried in Duisans British Cemetery, Etrun. Arthur's name is remembered on the headstone of John and Elizabeth Kate Selwood in St Mary's Churchyard, Purton.

While the British and Empire forces were succeeding in the north, the French southern part of General Nivelle's Spring Offensive wasn't doing so well. Known as the 2nd Battle of the Aisne and the 3rd Battle of Champagne, it had a long front. The French offensive ground to a halt by 20 April due to serious casualties, gains well below Nivelle's expectations and a resultant mutiny in the French army. By 29 April, General Nivelle was dismissed and replaced by General Pétain as Chief of the French General Staff.

USA

On 2 April, US President Woodrow Wilson delivered his "War Address" to the

United States Congress for a declaration of war on Germany. 2 days later the Senate agreed by a majority of 82 to 6 and the United States of America declared war on Germany on 6 April 1917.

Over the next few days and weeks Cuba and Panama also declared war on Germany, while Brazil, Bolivia and Guatemala, siding with the US, cut off diplomatic relations. Not surprisingly, Austria-Hungary, Turkey and Bulgaria reciprocated by cutting off diplomatic relations with America.

Now at war, fury erupted over an ammunition factory explosion at the Eddystone Ammunition Corporation's artillery shell plant in Pennsylvania, on 10 April, which killed 133 workers and was suspected to be sabotage. Subsequent investigations suggested it was an accident and the plant reopened only two weeks after the explosion. As many as "900 girls" were reported to be ready to go to back to work and there were many new applicants. Applicants with German backgrounds were turned away.

The US Government was getting ready for the needs of war with Congress passing the Liberty Loan Act (24 April), so that the Treasury could issue a public subscription for $2 billion in bonds for the war. They followed that up on 28 April with an Act to raise an extra 500,000 men for the US Army.

Russia - *all dates are new calendar*

Following the "February" Revolution and the Russian Provisional Government's (RPG) declaration of an independent and united Poland, the British Government informed the RPG on 5 April of their support for that principle. On 8 April in Petrograd, the Russian capital, 40,000 ethnic Estonians demanded to have an autonomous province within Russia. On the 9th, the RPG confirmed to the Allied governments that they were in favour of self-determination of peoples and a durable peace. The Autonomous Governorate of Estonia was set up on 12 April formed from the Governorates of Estonia and northern Livonia.

The power bloc in Russia that formed the RPG was mainly composed of the Mensheviks ("smaller party") from the 1905 revolution. The oppositional Soviet Executive Committee had been set up in March by activists of the Bolsheviks ("larger party") from 1905, among whom was Stalin. On 16 April, another member of the Bolsheviks, one Vladimir Ilyich Ulyanov, better known as Lenin, arrived by train at the Finland Station in Petrograd, having travelled across Europe courtesy of the German railways. Lenin issued his radical paper known as the "April Theses" in which he demanded that the workers' committees (soviets) must take power from the RPG.

Middle East

A second attack by British and Egyptian forces in Gaza resulted in 10,000 casualties and led to a period of stalemate in Palestine.

There was better allied success further east into Mesopotamia with Russian forces taking Khanaquin, north east of Baghdad while Anglo-Indian forces took Samarra in Mesopotamia on 24 April.

War at Sea

Anglo-Japanese cooperation in the war led to a Japanese destroyer force being based in Malta in April 1917 to operate as anti-submarine convoy escorts. The force eventually totalled 14 destroyers with cruiser flagships.

British hospital ships and ambulance transports continued to suffer. HMHS Salta was sunk by mine off Le Havre on 10 April with the loss of 79 Medical Corps, nurses and crew. Two transports were torpedoed without warning in the English Channel on 17 April: Lanfanc sank with the loss of 22 British and 18 German wounded on board; Donegal sank with the loss of 41 British wounded and crew.

German destroyer raids were conducted against the Kent coast with Dover targeted on 20 April and Ramsgate on the 24th.

Propaganda

On 17 April, The Times and the Daily Mail, both owned by Lord Northcliffe, published a propaganda story about the supposed existence of a German Corpse Factory. The story, with no basis in fact, was based on the real shortage of fats in Germany due to the British naval blockade. Glycerine from rendered corpses of soldiers was said to be used to manufacture products such as nitro-glycerine (for armaments), candlewax, soap and lubricants.

Part 47: May 1917

The following men with Purton connections were mobilised in May 1917.

To France:

Walter Hunt, 2nd Battalion, Royal Marine Light Infantry.

John Jefferies, 1st Battalion Royal Welch Fusiliers

Western Front

On 2 May, the 3rd Battle of the Scarpe river and the Battle of Bullecourt began with British attacks. These were both parts of the Battle of Arras. Whereas the Scarpe was soon over, Bullecourt lasted until 17 May and, although it resulted in a victory for the Allies, it cost the Australian forces some 7,482 casualties. Together with the Canadians at Vimy to the northern end of the front, Empire forces made significant advances but couldn't achieve a breakthrough.

Further south, French forces recaptured Craonne on the strategic Chemin-des-Dames ridge on 4 May, but by the 9th the Nivelle Offensive was abandoned. General Nivelle was replaced as Commander-in-Chief of the French Army by General Philippe Pétain on 15 May. Pétain's role as Chief of the General Staff of the French Ministry of War passed to General Foch.

The mutinies in the French army continued and, on the 27th, more than 30,000 French troops refused to go to the trenches at Missy-aux-Bois, near Soissons.

USA

On 10 May, Major-General John J. Pershing was appointed to command the United States Expeditionary Force. He left New York for France on 28 May.

Conscription was introduced with the passing of the Selective Service Act in Congress on the 18th. On 19 May, the US Government announced it would send a Division of the United States Army to France at once.

Russia

On 16 May, Alexander Kerensky of the Socialist Revolutionary Party succeeded Alexander Guchkov as Russian Minister of War, with Mikhail Tereshchenko (no party alliance) taking over as Foreign Minister. A few days later, the Russian Provisional Government issued a declaration that they would not seek a separate peace with Germany and would continue to prosecute the war.

Italy

Italy was still struggling to make progress in its costly offensive in the Isonzo valley in modern-day Slovenia against Austrian defenders. On 12 May, the 10th Battle of the Isonzo began, with the 11th and 12th Battles in the next months, ending in Italian failure by 24 October.

Against this background, a month of civil violence in Milan ended on 23 May after the Italian army regained control of the city by force from anarchists and anti-war revolutionaries. During this 50 were killed and 800 arrested.

Greece & the Balkans

The Serbian government in exile was transferred from Corfu to Salonika on 20 May.

The Allies were still trying to get Greece to join the war on their side. On 28 May, an   Anglo-French conference was held in London to discuss the position of Greece's anti-war King Constantine. Actions considered were deposing Constantine and occupying Athens and the province of Thessaly.

Palestine

On 23 May, a raid on the Beersheba to Hafir-el-Auja railway, by the Desert Column of British Empire troops, destroyed large sections of the railway line linking Beersheba to the main Turkish desert base.

The War at Sea

On 4 May, a flotilla of US destroyers arrived in Queenstown in Ireland (now Cobh) to support convoys of ships between America and Britain. On the 17th, the British Admiralty in conjunction with the Ministry of Shipping set up a committee to draw up plans for merchant ship convoys.

The Allies had been maintaining a naval blockade at the 45-mile wide Strait of Otranto between the heel of Italy and Corfu in order to deny Austrian Empire ships access to the wider Mediterranean. The Otranto Barrage was a fixed barrier, composed of 47 lightly armed naval drifters with anti-submarine nets coupled with minefields and supported by Allied naval patrols. (Naval drifters are boats built like commercial fishing drifters but typically armed with an anti-submarine gun and depth charges.) On 14 May, fourteen British drifters were sunk in the Strait of Otranto when attacked by Austrian naval forces. Allied warships composed of British and Italian ships engaged the Austrian force. By the time they disengaged on 15 May, the Allies had lost 2 destroyers, 14 drifters and 2 supply ships sunk and with damage to a light cruiser and a destroyer. The Austrian navy had 2 light cruisers damaged. This battle was the largest surface action in the Adriatic Sea during the war. It was considered an Austrian victory but had little impact on Austrian access to the wider Mediterranean.

On 26 May, the British hospital ship HMHS Dover Castle was sunk by submarine in the Mediterranean. The initial explosion killed seven boiler stokers, but the crew was able to evacuate the wounded to their destroyer escort HMS Cameleon.

The War in the Air

The 7th saw the first night air raid on London, made by a single aircraft in moonlight.

The first great aeroplane raid over England on the 25th resulted in 290 casualties, more than half of whom were civilians, as German planes bombed Folkestone and other parts of Kent.

Other News

On 13 May, and then at monthly intervals until 13 October, a 10-year-old girl, Lúcia Santos, and her cousins Francisco and Jacinta Marto reported seeing apparitions of the Virgin Mary near Fátima in Portugal. These apparitions became known as Our Lady of Fátima.

Part 48: June 1917

The following men with Purton connections were mobilised in June 1917.

To France:
Ernest William Burgess, Royal Marines Light Infantry.

Western Front:

On 7 June, a major attack was launched on the Messines-Wytschaete Ridge. It started at 3.10 am with the detonation of 19 British mines that had been laid in advance under the ridge about 6 miles south of Ypres. The immensity of the explosion changed the landscape on the ridge and about 10,000 German soldiers died instantly in the blast. The sound of the explosion could be heard as far away as London (150 miles), some reports even saying as far away as Dublin (440 miles). It certainly ranks among the largest non-nuclear explosions of all time.

The initial advance in the sector was made by New Zealand forces under a creeping barrage of British shells landing up to 1,500 yards (1,400m) ahead of their advance, with support from tanks, cavalry patrols and aircraft. The

Australian 52nd Battalion moved beyond the New Zealanders' position into the German lines. Coming over the Messines ridge, the 52nd was struck by a German artillery barrage. The 49th Battalion was situated on their right flank, but the British 33rd Brigade, supposed to be on their left, had been delayed. The 52nd waited in shell holes for the order to advance. At 1.40 pm they crossed the Messines to Wytschaete road. Without the British 33rd, they needed to cover their section and also swing north to take the British unit's objectives and prevent German forces splitting the advance.

Richard Stanley Selwood was the son of John and Annie Selwood, of The Common in Purton. Richard was born in 1888 and attended school in Purton. After a period working in Swindon for the GWR, he emigrated to Australia in 1910 when 22 years old. He enlisted with the Australian Imperial Force in January 1916. Thus, he found himself in the Battalion's advance down the ridge where they immediately came under attack from a unit of machine guns located near the road. Casualty figures for the 52nd were heavy: 325 killed, wounded or missing in action. Richard was among those killed, aged 28. He has no known grave but is remembered on the Purton War Memorial, and on the Memorial Board and Memorial Book both located in St Mary's Church,

The 52nd Battalion eventually took up new positions as far forward as Wambeke, an advance of some 2 miles. The overall British offensive (7-14 June) secured the southern end of the Ypres salient in preparation for the 3rd Battle of Ypres and the advance to Passchendaele Ridge.

Also on the Western Front:

On 1 June in a further mutiny, a French infantry regiment seized the town of Missy-aux-Bois and declared an anti-war military government. They were soon captured by loyal French troops.

Portugal had been brought into the war in mid-1916 and had set up an Expeditionary Force (Corpo Expedicionário Português - CEP) in December 1916, with troops arriving in France during February 1917. On 30 May, the CEP 1st Infantry Brigade occupied the Neuve-Chapelle sector (between Béthune and Lille) at the front line which the Germans attacked on 4 June. On the 16th, the CEP 2nd Brigade occupied the Fauquissart sector of the front, 2 miles further north.

Having set off from New York in May, US Major-General John J. Pershing arrived in England on 8 June, transferring to France and setting up his HQ staff in Paris on the 14th. The 1st Division US Expeditionary Force arrived in France on 26 June.

USA

Back at home, conscription began in the United States on 5 June and 10 million Americans began registering for "The Draft". The US enacted the Espionage Act on 15 June "to prohibit interference with military operations or recruitment, to prevent insubordination in the military, and to prevent the support of United States enemies during wartime".

In support of the Espionage Act, Santo Domingo and Haiti cut off diplomatic relations with Germany.

The War in the Air
On 2 June, Canadian "air ace" Billy Bishop undertook a solo mission in France behind enemy lines. He shot down three aircraft while they were taking off and several more on the ground. Bishop was awarded the Victoria Cross.

On the 5th, Germany conducted a daylight aeroplane raid on the port of Sheerness and other naval establishments on the Medway. Then, during daylight on 13 June, they made the first major bombing raid on London by fixed-wing aircraft - Gotha G bombers. 162 were killed including 46 children, and 432 injured.

2 German airships were destroyed on 14 and 17 June - L43 over the North Sea and L48 over Suffolk.

The War at Sea
On 14 June, the British Admiralty approved the scheme for protecting merchant ships in convoy. On the 18th Admiral Sims, United States Navy, became acting Commander-in-Chief Irish Command at Queenstown (Cobh) in command of trans-Atlantic convoys.

About 240 miles south, the French cruiser Kléber was sunk by submarine off Brest, Brittany, on 27 June with the loss of 42 of her crew of 531.

Munitions Accident
An explosion on 13 June 1917 at the Hooley Hill Rubber and Chemical Works, Lancashire, manufacturing TNT killed 43 workers.

Greece & the Balkans
With Greece neither in nor out of the war, the Balkans was in a power vacuum with Austrian forces threatening territories further south of the conquered Serbia. On 3 June, Italy proclaimed a Protectorate over independent Albania. Then on the 8th they occupied Ioannina (Janina) 35 miles into Greece from the Albanian border.

To force Greece's hand, the Allied governments presented Greece with a demand for the abdication of King Constantine on 11 June. He did so the next day in favour of his second son who took the throne as King Alexander.

Corinth, 45 miles west of Athens, and Larissa, halfway between Athens and Salonika, were occupied by Entente forces on 12 June.

Following the abdication, the Greek Premier Alexandros Zaimis resigned on the 24th and was replaced by the pro-war Eleftherios Venizelos on the 26th. Venizelos immediately declared war on Germany, Austria-Hungary, Bulgaria and Turkey making his Provisional Government declaration (23 November 1916) apply to the whole of Greece. Greece was now in the war on the side of the Allies.

Russia
On 9 June, the Russian Provisional Government (RPG) refused a German proposal for an unlimited armistice. In opposition to the RPG, the 1st All Russian Congress of the Soviets was convened in Petrograd on 16 June.

Mutiny broke out in the Russian Black Sea fleet at Sevastopol on 21 June.

Other News
On 4 June, King George V inaugurated the Most Excellent Order of British Empire. This was set up to recognise the efforts of his subjects in the war. The Order continues and without it we wouldn't have the awards of BEM, MBE, OBE etc, that we have today.

To avert political problems in Ireland, the British government granted an amnesty (15 June 1917) to the prisoners taken during the Dublin Easter Rising of 1916.

On 28 June, General Edmund Allenby succeeded Murray as GOC commanding British forces in Egypt.

Part 49: July 1917

The following men with Purton connections were mobilised in July 1917.

To France:
Esaw Hawcutt, 69th Siege Battery. Royal Garrison Artillery.
William Jordan, 1st Royal Marine Battalion, Royal Marine Light Infantry.
Harry William Tuck, 1st Battalion Dorset Regiment.

Western Front
British and German representatives signed an agreement on 2 July at The Hague, in neutral Netherlands, for exchange of combatant and civilian prisoners of war.

From his Paris HQ, US General Pershing made his first request to the US Government on 2 July for provision of an army of 1 million men; he shortly revised it to 3 million.

Meanwhile British Command was preparing for the 3rd Battle of Ypres and on 22 July they bombed the German lines at Ypres with 4,250,000 grenades. By 27 July, British troops reached the Yser Canal near Boezinge north of Ypres. The 3rd Battle of Ypres commenced on 31 July. British and French armies attacked the German 4th Army and captured Pilckem Ridge and areas either side.

John Bertie Blackford was born in Purton in 1887 but by now was married and living in Swindon with his occupation given as butcher. He had joined the 8th Battalion Gloucestershire Regiment and on 28 July the battalion was in the line at Oosttaverne on the edge of the Messines ridge. At 1.25 am a strong German attack on the line was repulsed but with considerable loss. John was killed in action aged 41, by a German bomb during the raid. John has no known grave, but is remembered on the Menin Gate Memorial at Ypres. His name is included on Swindon's Roll of Honour. 22 men of the 8th Battalion died on this date. The 8th Glos was relieved by the 8th N. Staffs Regiment and was moved to defence of the ridge.

On 28 July, the Heavy Branch of the British Machine Gun Corps was reformed as the British Tank Corps.

Russia

On 1 July, the Russian General Brusilov attacked in Austro-Hungarian Galicia (the Kerensky Offensive), initially advancing towards Lemberg. German and Austro-Hungarian forces launched a counter-offensive on 18 July and captured Stanislau, Tarnopol and Zeleszczyki in Galicia between 24 and 30 July. These three cities are split today between Poland and Ukraine.

Russia continued to suffer civil and military unrest. Between the 16th and 17th of July, Russian troops mutinied, abandoning the Austrian front, and retreating to the Ukraine; hundreds of mutineers were shot by their officers during the retreat. There were serious clashes in Petrograd, known as "the July Days", between 16 and 18 July when the Bolsheviks intended to hold peaceful demonstrations at the Tauride Palace in Petrograd which housed the Petrograd Soviet. However, armed clashes broke out. Lenin escaped to Finland and Trotsky was arrested. Alexander Fyodorovich Kerensky of the Revolutionary Socialist Party succeeded Prince Lvov as premier of Russia on 21 July. General Kornilov succeeded General Brusilov as Russian Commander-in-Chief.

The Parliament of Finland, with a Social Democratic majority, passed a "Sovereignty Act" on 20 July, declaring the Grand Principality of Finland independent. The Russian Provisional Government (RPG) refused to recognise the act, as Russian sovereignty over Finland would be lost, with Russia left only with responsibility for the defence and foreign relations of an independent Finland. The RPG dissolved the Finnish Parliament on 30 July. New elections in the autumn resulted in a bourgeois majority.

On 20 July, the RPG enacted women's suffrage.

Greece & The Balkans

The June declaration of war by the Venizelos government came into effect on 2 July and Greece joined the war on the side of the Allies.

Viewing an end to the war that would see Austria collapse, the exiled Serbian government together with representatives of the Austrian provinces of Croatia-Slavonia and Carniola (Slovenia) signed the Corfu Declaration on 20 July, that would set up a post-war Kingdom of Yugoslavia.

The Allies worried that Russia wouldn't be able to continue the war. On 25 July, a full Inter-Allied Conference was assembled in Paris to discuss the Balkan situation to set plans in the event of a probable collapse of Russia.

Canada

The so-called Conscription Crisis of 1917 in Canada led to the Military Service Act being passed on 6 July in the Canadian House of Commons. Because of the financial costs of the war, the Canadian Finance Minister, Sir William Thomas White introduced Canada's first income tax as a "temporary" measure on 25 July. The lowest tax bracket was set at 4% and the highest at 25%.

The War at Sea

Atlantic convoy methods had been agreed in June and the first regular merchant convoy sailed for Britain from Hampton Roads, Virginia, on 2 July. Convoys from Great Britain back to the USA did not start till August.

A concerted attack by German submarines on United States transports on 4 July was defeated.

The British battleship HMS Vanguard was destroyed and sank while at anchor at Scapa Flow on 9 July as a result of an internal explosion of faulty cordite. 840 men were killed. As Vanguard sank in relatively shallow water, the wreck was heavily salvaged in search of non-ferrous metals before it was declared a war grave in 1984.

On 19 July, Sir Edward Carson, First Lord of the Admiralty, resigned to be appointed Minister without Portfolio and member of the War Cabinet. Carson was leader of the Irish (later Ulster) Unionist Party from 1910 to 1921.

The War in the Air
A major aeroplane raid on 7 July on Margate and London resulted in 250 casualties, most of them civilian. It was the last daylight raid on London of the war.

Germany
A parliamentary revolt in the German Reichstag, by an alliance of the Social Democratic, Progressive, and Zentrum Parties, looked certain to pass a Peace Resolution for "a peace without annexations or indemnities". On 14 July, the Imperial Chancellor Theobald von Bethmann-Hollweg resigned and was replaced by the relatively unknown Dr Georg Michaelis. The Foreign Minister Dr Arthur von Zimmerman resigned the following day. The Peace Resolution was passed by the Reichstag on 19 July.

Egypt, Turkey & Mesopotamia
The forces of the Arab Revolt, led by Auda Abu Tayi and advised by T.E. Lawrence ("of Arabia") captured the Ottoman Empire's Red Sea port of Aqaba on 6 July.

With little support from the RPG, Russian forces in Western Persia were in a state of collapse. They began to withdraw from western Persia on 8 July and Qasr-i-Shirin was evacuated.

Between 8 and 13 July, British troops make unsuccessful attacks on Ramadi in Mesopotamia. The majority of British casualties were due to the extreme heat. In an unusually hot summer, temperatures reached 50°C in the shade and several degrees higher in tents and dug-outs. There were a total of 566 British casualties out of the Brigade strength of 1,000 men.

On 27 July, the French and Italian Governments signed an agreement defining their respective post-war zones of influence in Asia Minor.

Other News
Following the Gotha bomber raid on London in June, King George V bowed to public pressure and announced on 17 July that the British Royal Family of the House of Saxe-Coburg Gotha would renounce its German names and titles. From then on it would be known as the House of Windsor. Other names that were changed included Battenberg which became Mountbatten. Various other changes around this time might seem amusing to us now, but the German

Shepherd dog was renamed as the Alsatian, and in the US the Frankfurter was renamed the Hot Dog. The German Ocean had been renamed the North Sea well before the mid-1800s.

During July, the first "Cottingley Fairies" photographs were taken in Yorkshire, apparently depicting fairies. The children who created the hoax only admitted it in 1981!

Three girls had seen apparitions of the Virgin Mary near Fátima in Portugal. On 13 May 2017, Pope Francis declared 2 of the girls to be saints - Francisco and Jacinta Marto. The third girl is also on the way to sainthood.

Part 50: August 1917

The following men with Purton connections were mobilised in August 1917.

To France: Victor Rowland Lovelock, 2nd Battalion Wiltshire Regiment.

Royal Navy: Ernest R. Holder, R.N. (transferred from Devonport RN Barracks to HMS Cornwall)

Edward Selby received a letter of exemption for conscription as he was already working at the Purton Remount Depot at Manor Hill.

Western Front

The British offensive of the 3rd Battle of Ypres continued with successful actions at Pilckem Ridge and the Ypres Canal at Boesinghe, but indecisive results at Langemarck. The Canadian Corps fought the Battle of Hill 70 (15-18 August) capturing the hill and establishing a defensive position which prevented the Germans from sending further forces towards Ypres. Hill 70 saw the first use of Mustard Gas by the German Army. However one might view a "successful action", the total casualties in this first month of the 3rd Battle of Ypres were perhaps 78,500 killed or wounded on the Allied side and 79,000 on the German side.

French forces began the 2nd offensive battle at Verdun, capturing Mort-Homme and Cote 304.

Richard Thomas Bartlett, husband of Mabel with 3 children, and son of John and Phoebe Bartlett, of Pavenhill, Purton was born in 1879 in Ashton Keynes. He had enlisted with the Wiltshire Regiment, but transferred to the 11th Battalion Somerset Light Infantry. The 11th Battalion moved to France in May 1916 having carried out Garrison Service since its formation in January 1917. They were placed into the 59th (2nd North Midland) Division which had been reduced by heavy losses during the German spring offensive. The Division was used in rear defence construction until sufficiently trained to be used in the front lines in late July. Thomas was wounded in action and subsequently died of tetanus on 15 August 1917, aged 39, at the No.2 General Hospital in Le Havre.

Thomas is buried in Ste. Marie Cemetery, Le Havre and is remembered on the Purton War Memorial, and on Memorials in St Mary's Church.

Herbert Gladstone Brown was born in Purton in 1881 though living at Biddlestone near Chippenham. He was serving with the 20th Hussars in the 2nd Cavalry Division. Herbert died aged 38 on 17 August 1917 and is buried at St Hilaire Cemetery, Frevent, Pas-de Calais. The 1891 census records him living at Lydiard Tregoze.

USA: The Green Corn Rebellion, an uprising by several hundred farmers against conscription, took place in central Oklahoma during August. On the 5th, the entire US National Guard was taken into national service, and became subject to presidential rather than state control.

Canada: The Military Service Act was passed the Canadian House of Commons on 29 August, giving the Government of Canada the right to conscript men into the army.

Russia

On 3 August, Czernowitz (Bukovina) was retaken by Austrian and German forces.

In an inflammatory article, on 4 August, the Bolshevik revolutionary newspaper, Pravda, called for the killing of all capitalists, priests and officers.

Germany

Mutiny broke out in the German fleet at Wilhelmshaven on 2 August. 400 sailors marched into town demanding an end to the war and refusing to continue fighting. The demonstration was quickly brought under control by the army. Some sailors returned to their ships without violence but 75 of were arrested and imprisoned. The ringleaders were subsequently executed after trial.

Rumania

On 22 July, Rumanian forces with Russian assistance commenced an offensive against the Austro-Hungarian 1st Army at Mărășești and the Siret river. After initial success, a German and Austrian counter-offensive in August initially halted the Rumanians. Then between 6 August and 3 September, the Rumanian army fought their most significant battle of the 1917 campaign. The Rumanian 1st Army, together with Russian forces, managed to halt the German advance and forced the German attack towards the north west. From 16 August, the Rumanian army took over command of the battle from the Russians and completely held the German advance. This was the last major battle between Germany and Rumania during the Great War. Although most of Rumania was still occupied by the Central Powers, the Battle of Mărășești kept the north-eastern region of the country free from occupation. Over the campaign, Rumania lost over 27,000 men, including 610 officers, while Germany and Austria-Hungary lost over 47,000.

War in the Air

HMS Furious, a cruiser, had been modified with a single "fly-off" flight deck. During trials at Scapa Flow, Squadron Commander Edwin Dunning landed his aircraft successfully on 2 August although the ship's superstructure mad the manoeuvre difficult. However, he was killed 5 days later during a third landing attempt. The ship was modified in November 1917 by removing the rear gun turret to add an extra "land-on" deck,. In 1921 she was converted with a full length flight deck.

The German airship L23 was shot down by British aircraft over North Sea on 21 August and, on the 22nd, Germany launched a daylight aeroplane raid on England which would prove to be the last such raid of the war.

Other News

On 1 August, Pope Benedict XV sent a Note to belligerent Governments appealing for peace. This may have fallen on deaf ears since the Republic of China and Liberia declared war on Germany and Austria-Hungary during August, and Italy declared war on the Ottoman Empire.

On 10 August, the Labour Party decided to send a representative to a consultative conference in Stockholm. The British Government refused to issue passports for the Conference.

On the 18th, the British, French, and Italian Governments concluded provisional arrangements regarding future policy in former territories of the Ottoman Empire. A Ministry of Reconstruction was formed in Great Britain on the 21st.

On 18 August, the Great Thessaloniki Fire (Greece) destroyed 32% of the city, leaving 70,000 people homeless.

Part 51: September 1917

The following men with Purton connections were mobilised in September 1917.

To France:

Herbert Willie Ponting, Royal Field Artillery.

To Egypt:

Herbert Henry Stone, 1/4th Battalion Wiltshire Regiment. He had been serving with the Battalion in India since 1916 and was transferred with the Battalion to the Egypt Expeditionary Force. (Herbert had been in the army since 1898 in the Boer Wars though on the reserve list between 1905 and 1916.)

Western Front

The French Premier Alexandre Ribot resigned on 9 September and was replaced by Paul Painlevé on the 12th.

In the 3rd Battle of Ypres, British Empire forces attacked the strategically important Menin Road Ridge on 20 September, succeeding in holding he ridge on the 25th with losses of about 20,255 killed or wounded. German casualties were similar. From 26 September until 3 October, British and Australian forces attacked at Polygon Wood capturing positions from the Germans, with 21,000 lost to the British and Australians and 13,500 German troops.

Russia

German forces attacked in the Battle of Riga on 1 September capturing the city on the 3rd. They continued on to attack Jacobstadt in Courland (Latvia) on the 22nd.

On 8 September, General Kornilov headed a revolt against the Russian Provisional Government (RPG) under Prime Minister Kerensky and organised a march on Petrograd. Two days later Kerensky assumed dictatorship of Russia under the RPG and proclaimed Kornilov a traitor. Kerensky declared Russia to be a republic on 14 September. Leon Trotsky was elected Chairman of the oppositional Bolshevik Petrograd Soviet on the 23rd. On the 25th, the Mossovet (Moscow Soviet of People's Deputies) voted to side with the Bolsheviks.

As the fringes of Russia continued to disintegrate, the Central Powers proclaimed a temporary constitution for Poland on the 12th. Trans-Caucasia was proclaimed a federal republic on 20 September by a committee known as the Council of Trans-Caucasian Peoples (representatives from Armenia, Georgia, Azerbaijan and Daghestan).

Mesopotamia

In the 2nd Battle of Ramadi (28-29) September, British troops took Ramadi from Ottoman Empire control.

War in the Air

Although daylight air raids on England ended in August, several moonlight raids were conducted by German aeroplanes, notably on the 2nd with the first raid by more than a single aeroplane, and attacks on Kent and London between 3 and 4 September.

On 6 September, the French pilot Georges Guynemer shot down his 54th German aircraft.

War at Sea

On 4 September, Scarborough on the Yorkshire coast was shelled by a German submarine. On the 6th, Sir Eric Geddes was appointed as First Lord of the Admiralty.

Italy

An Anglo-French conference was held in London on 4 September to discuss military assistance for Italy, which was still struggling with the Isonzo river valley battles against Austro-Hungary. The 11th Battle of the Isonzo ended on 12 September.

A further Anglo-French Conference assembled in Boulogne on 25 September to discuss an Italian offensive and the extension of the British front in France.

Other News

A first party of British POWs was repatriated through Switzerland and reached England on 11 September,

On 21 September, Costa Rica severed diplomatic relations with Germany.

Part 52: October 1917

The following men with Purton connections were mobilised in October 1917.

To France:
Walter John Selwood, 3rd Battalion East Lancashire Regiment.

Western Front

The Battle of Polygon Wood ended on 3 October and on the 4th the II ANZAC (Australian and New Zealand Army Corps) attacked in the Battle of Broodseinde. The ANZACs reached the high ground just below the summit of the Broodseinde Ridge overpowering the German 4th Army's defences.

Percy Thomas Hedges, the son of Nelson Thomas and Sarah A Hedges of Locks Lane in Purton, was serving with the 6th (Service) Battalion Wiltshire Regiment near Zillebeke, 2 miles south east of Ypres. The Battalion War Diary records that the enemy shelled their positions on 4 October 1917. During work to strengthen and repair the front line and defensive wire at Fusiliers Wood, two men were killed and three wounded. Percy was one of those killed, aged 25.

Percy was buried at Fusiliers Wood, near Klein Zillebeke. After the war, individual graves and small cemeteries were moved to larger communal cemeteries by the Imperial War Graves Commission and battlefield clearance teams. Oxford Road cemetery *(pictured)* holds the combined burials from several cemeteries to the east and south-east of the Ypres salient. Percy is also remembered on the Purton War Memorial and on the Memorial Board and Book held in St Mary's Church.

I have resisted referring to the entire 3rd Battle of Ypres as Passchendaele, which is properly attributed to two battles within the 3rd Ypres campaign. Passchendaele* is village on a ridge east of Ypres, close to a railway junction which was important to the German 4th Army supply system. A dry September became a wet October and much of the campaign was bedevilled with mud. In a preliminary engagement at Poelcappelle, on 9 October, ground opposite Passchendaele was won and then lost again in a battle costly to both sides. The 1st Battle of Passchendaele itself commenced on 12 October 1917 when the allied forces attacked a German defensive position and failed, with the biggest loss of life in a single day for New Zealand forces. Over 845 New Zealanders were killed that day. Considering the small size of that nation at the

---

* During the 1920s, Holland (neutral in the war) instigated a spelling reform for the Dutch language which was taken up by the closely related Flemish speakers in Belgium. Passchendaele is spelled Passendale today, and is the way it had always been pronounced (Pass-un-dah-ler). Throughout this series, I have kept to the spellings of the time with notes as appropriate especially for locating war

time, that was about 1 in 1000 of their entire population.

On 13 October, the British called off the offensive in the hope of better weather. The aim became to reach and hold a line for the winter and to keep German forces tied up and away from planned French offensives on the Chemin des Dames, south of Arras - the Battle of Malmaison.

The captured ground made a starting off point for the 2nd Battle of Passchendaele on 26 October, fought between 26 October and 10 November 1917. The Canadian Corps relieved the exhausted II Anzac Corps and captured Passchendaele village. The overall battle captured the high ground along the Passchendaele to Westrozebeke ridge but stopped just short of Westrozebeke. The Austro-German victory against the Italian Army at Caporetto *(see below)* and the planned Battle of Cambrai forced the British to divert forces from the Ypres Salient.

USA

Major-General Pershing, commanding the United States Army in France, was promoted to General on 6 October. American forces of the 1st Infantry Division, known as the "Big Red One" after the design of their shoulder patch, entered the front lines for the first time (under French command) on 21 October and their first shell of the war was fired towards German lines on 23 October. On the 25th, the 2nd Battalion of the 16th Infantry suffered the first American casualties of the war.

Russia

Leon Trotsky was named chairman of the Petrograd Soviet on 8 October as the Bolshevik party gained control.

German operations in the Baltic provinces commenced. The island of Ösel, in the West Estonian archipelago, was captured by German forces on the 12th and Moon and Dagö Islands on the 18th. The Russian battleship *Slava* was sunk in the Gulf of Riga on the 16th and the German conquest of the archipelago was completed on 20 October.

During these operations, the Petrograd Soviet accepted the establishment of a Petrograd Military force. Lenin made a speech on 23 October against the political actions of Kamenev, Kollontai, Stalin and Trotsky, and a pan-Russian Congress was opened in Petrograd on the 25th.

On 15 October, the Polish Regency Council was appointed as part of the intended autonomy of that country.

If you're expecting the October Revolution in Russia, you'll have to wait until Part 53. The name of the revolution was based on the old Julian calendar still operating in Russia and it actually happened in November by the modern calendar.

Italy

The Italian campaign against Austria-Hungary along the Isonzo River valley continued and on 24 October the Austrians with German assistance launched the 12th Battle of the Isonzo. This is variously known as the Battle of Caporetto, Karfreit or Kobarid, depending on whether you are Italian, Austrian or Slovene.

Although the battle continued until 19 November, it was obvious early on that it was going to be a major defeat for the Italians. Paolo Boselli's government collapsed as a result of the impending disaster on 25 October. A new administration was formed by Vittorio Emanuele Orlando on the 29th.

However on the 28th, Austrian forces had already pushed through and retaken Gorizia and Udine, in Venice province.

War at Sea
The cruiser HMS Drake was torpedoed by a German submarine at Rathlin Island off Northern Ireland on 2 October following completion of convoy duties. The ship was beached and the crew taken off before it capsized. In further convoy raids, on 17 October, two destroyers, HMS Strongbow and HMS Mary Rose, were sunk in the North Sea.

War in the Air
On 17 October, the Royal Flying Corps carried out the first British bombing raid on Germany. Meanwhile a squadron of 11 German airships carried out a bombing raid on England on the 19th, which proved to be the last such raid.

Munitions Accident
On 1 October at White Lund Shell Filling Station, Morecambe an explosion occurred involving more than 20,000 shells, wholly or partly filled and 3000 tons of TNT. 10 workers were killed in the explosion.

Mesopotamia & Palestine
Ottoman forces attacked an Arab stronghold at Petra, but the Arab forces repulsed the attack on 21 October. On the 27th, the Turks attacked the Desert Mounted Corps which was holding the el-Buqqar ridge. British and Commonwealth forces launched the 3rd Battle of Gaza aimed at breaking the Turkish defensive line that stretched from Gaza to Beersheba. The battle is best known for the charge of the 4th Australian Light Horse Brigade, which was the last successful cavalry charge in the history of modern warfare.

Other Events
In line with the USA's entry to the war, Peru and Uruguay cut off diplomatic relations with Germany. A Brazilian ship was sunk by a German U-Boat on 23 October and as a result Brazil declared war on Germany on the 26th.

On 13 October, a large crowd gathered near Fátima, Portugal. The three shepherd children who said they had witnessed the Virgin Mary earlier in the year, prophesied that "Our Lady of Fátima" would perform miracles on that day. People claimed that the sun had danced and was seen in radiant colours. The event known as the Miracle of the Sun was dismissed by unbelievers as the result of staring at the sun too long, but declared a miracle by believers.

On 15 October, the Dutch dancer Mata Hari was executed by firing squad at Vincennes, near Paris, for spying for Germany. The story was introduced in Part 44 (February 1917).

On 30 October, Count Hertling succeeded Dr Michaelis as German Imperial Chancellor.

Part 53: November 1917

The following men with Purton connections were mobilised in November 1917.

To France:

William James Haines, Tank Corps, to action at Cambrai.

To Italy:

Edward John Woolford, 1/4th Battalion Royal Berkshire Regiment. Transferred with the battalion from training in France to Italy.

Royal Navy:

Harold Raleigh Molden, to HMS Dido, 10th Destroyer flotilla at Harwich.

Western Front - Passchendaele & Cambrai

On 6 November, Canadian forces took Passchendaele village. It was strategically important with a ridge at a height of 60 m (200 ft) and a railway supplies junction, so taking Passchendaele effectively completed the objectives of the 3rd Battle of Ypres which was officially concluded on 10 November.

3rd Ypres was fought between 31 July and 10 November 1917 with involvement of British and Empire forces including English, Welsh, Scottish, Irish, Canadian, Belgian, New Zealand, Australian and Indian troops under the command of Field Marshal Douglas Haig. During October and November, incredibly heavy rainfall meant a significant number of those killed or wounded were the result of the weather as much as of enemy action.

Shell craters and continuous rain created a battlefield with the consistency of porridge. Shell holes filled with water, bodies and other debris, and everything became coated with slime. Contaminated water supplies led to dehydration and sickness amongst troops on both sides. Guns sank into the earth and troops drowned in the soft mud as they tried to charge the line.

After 16 weeks of fighting in conditions which varied from rain, mud, and slime, to hot and dry weather with clouds of dust, the initial objective of Passchendaele Ridge had been gained at a cost of 270,000 Allied lives, including 17,000 officers. German casualties were just as appalling, with 217,000 German soldiers lost. The village of Passchendale itself was totally destroyed.

Cambrai, 50 miles south of Ypres, was an important supply point for the German Hindenburg Line. The British attacked German lines between 20 November and 7 December in order to capture the town and the nearby Bourlon Ridge. The 1st Battle of Cambrai saw the first use of large numbers of tanks in battle. However, after British successes on the first day, mechanical failures, German artillery and infantry defences showed the Mark IV tank had weaknesses. On the second day, only about half of the tanks were still operational and British advances ground to a halt. The Germans quickly reinforced their defences on Bourlon Ridge and made a counter strike on the 30th recapturing much of the ground lost on the 20th.

About 44,000 men were lost on each side. Disproportionately many of the British Empire losses were in the Newfoundland battalions.

Frederick Nelson Daniels was born in 1898, son of Joseph and Hannah Daniels of West Lodge, Braydon, Purton. Frederick had enlisted with the 2nd Battalion Coldstream Guards (2nd CG) and was in action with them at Cambrai, while the Battalion was assigned to the 1st Guards Brigade. On 30 November, 2nd CG moved forward as the German counter-attack at

Cambrai started. 2nd and 3rd CG attacked Gouzeaucourt from the south, and 1st CG from the north. They met heavy machine gun fire from the village, but the objective was secured within an hour. However, Frederick was killed in action, aged 19, along with 82 Coldstream Guardsmen and officers. Frederick has no known grave, but is remembered on the Cambrai Memorial at Louverval *(above)* and in the Memorial book in St Mary's Church. A memorial plaque for Frederick was mounted in Braydon Church but later moved to St Mary's.

Outstanding Service

Geoffrey Charlton Paine Rumming *(pictured)* was born in Purton on 2 December 1888, the son of William and Mary Nellie Rumming. By 1915 he was an assistant and runner for a miller in Calne, when he enlisted with the Royal

Naval Air Service (RNAS), initially as an engineer. He was later transferred to armoured cars as Petty Officer Mechanic and served at Gallipoli. He was severely wounded in the head and discharged from the RNAS in October 1915.

Geoffrey felt fit for duty again and re-enlisted in March 1916, just short of 29 years old, with the Machine Gun Corps (MGC) as the Armoured Car sections had been disbanded in the meantime. After training in Ayrshire and Grantham, Geoffrey was discharged on medical grounds suffering from epilepsy, and no longer physically fit for War Service. On discharge his address was given as Quemerford, Wiltshire, where he had returned to his father's mill.

Geoffrey died on 4 November 1917 having never really recovered from the effects of his wounds and was buried in Curzon Street Cemetery, Calne. He is also remembered on the War Memorial in Calne.

Geoffrey was posthumously awarded the French Medaille Militaire, by a warrant dated in Paris in April 1918.

Italy

Following the disastrous defeat of the Italian army at Caporetto in October, reinforcements of French troops arrived in Italy on 3 November and British troops the next day. General Cadorna was replaced as Italian Commander by General Diaz.

While the French and British troops were still being mobilised, Austro-German forces reached the River Piave just north of Venice, on 11 November, after advancing from Caporetto.

Egypt, Palestine & Mesopotamia
On 1 November, the British XXI Corps of the Egyptian Expeditionary Force (EEF) began the 3rd Battle of Gaza with the Desert Mounted Corps moving towards Hebron and Jerusalem. The British XX Corps and Desert Mounted Corps attacked Ottoman defences on the Gaza to Beersheba road allowing XXI Corps to occupy Gaza after the Ottoman garrison withdrew.

On 7 November, the Battle of Jerusalem began with the EEF attacking Ottoman forces in the Judaean Hills. **George Hicks** was born in Purton in 1887 and enlisted with the 303rd Brigade Royal Field Artillery. He was married to Lilian Hicks and living at Westmill, Cricklade. George was killed in action on 7 November 1917 during the assault on Jerusalem. He has no known grave, but

is remembered on the Jerusalem Memorial *(right)* along with 3,300 Commonwealth servicemen from operations in Egypt or Palestine. George is also remembered on the War Memorial in Cricklade.

The EEF attacked retreating Turkish forces on 16 November during the Battle of Mughar Ridge, taking 50 miles (80 km) of Palestine territory. Tel-Aviv and Jaffa were occupied by British forces on the 16th. Following these actions, the ANZAC Desert Mounted Corps won the Battle of Ayun Kara against Ottoman forces bolstered by German rear-guards.

Russia - The "October Revolution"
On 5 November, Estonian Bolsheviks seized power in Tallinn, taking over the Autonomous Governorate of Estonia. This prompted the Russian Provisional Government (RPG) to attempt to close 3 Bolshevik printing presses. In response, troops of the Petrograd Soviet seized RPG buildings (6 November) and arrested members of the RPG. On 7 November (25 October under the Julian calendar) they bombarded and stormed the RPG headquarters at the Winter Palace in Petrograd. In this coup, Lenin made himself Premier, deposing Kerensky, and Trotsky became Foreign Minister. Kerensky's forces attempted a counter-coup on 13 November but were defeated by the Bolsheviks. Kerensky fled from Petrograd on the 15th. Lenin issued decrees abolishing private property ownership and all ranks, titles and privileges from tsarist days.

The new Soviet government immediately set about holding talks with Germany and Austria-Hungary (at Brest-Litovsk) to end the war.

Finland declared itself independent of Russia on 15 November, the Ukraine on the 20th and Estonia on the 28th.

In response to the October Revolution, Persia (modern Iran) which had been providing armaments to Russia, refused to support the Allied Forces from that point.

War at Sea
On 7 November, two United States Navy destroyers captured a German submarine U-58 off the south-west coast of Ireland. This was the first combat action in which U.S. ships took a submarine. U-58 was then scuttled.

Israel
On 2 November, the British Foreign Secretary Arthur Balfour published a Declaration proclaiming British support a Zionist national home for the Jewish people in Palestine, which was to be removed from Ottoman control at the end of the war. The letter read, "His Majesty's *[George V]* government view with favour the establishment in Palestine of a national home for the Jewish people, and will use their best endeavours to facilitate the achievement of this object, it being clearly understood that nothing shall be done which may prejudice the civil and religious rights of existing non-Jewish communities in Palestine, or the rights and political status enjoyed by Jews in any other country."

Suffragism in the USA
On 6 November, New York State adopted a constitutional amendment giving women the right to vote in state elections. Then on the 10th, 41 suffragettes of the Silent Sentinels were arrested in front of White House, Washington DC, where they had ben holding a long-term protest in favour of votes for women. On the night of 14-15 November, the "Night of Terror", 33 of the Silent Sentinels imprisoned at Occoquan Workhouse, Virginia, were assaulted and tortured by their guards.

Other News
Georges Clemenceau became prime minister of France on 16 November.

The People's Dispensary for Sick Animals was founded in the United Kingdom on 17 November.

Part 54: December 1917

Rationing
Germany increased its use of submarines, in January 1917, to sink all ships headed to Britain in an attempt to starve the country into submission. Voluntary rationing of food was introduced in February 1917 and bread was subsidised from September 1917. Some local authorities took rationing into their own hands, but the government introduced a compulsory rationing scheme in stages between December 1917 and February 1918. By December 1917, Britain's supply of wheat had fallen to just six weeks' worth. To make rationing work, ration books were later introduced in July 1918 for butter, margarine, lard, meat, and sugar. For the most part, rationing benefited the health of the country and during the war, average energy intake decreased by only 3%, but protein intake by 6%.

Western Front

The 1st Battle of Cambrai ended on 3 December. **William James Haines** was born in Purton in 1886, the son of Henry and Mary Jane Haines. By the time he enlisted, before 1915, he was married to Renee Haines, giving his address as Jasmines Cottage, The Packhorse, Purton. Originally with the Royal Wiltshire Yeomanry, he was serving with "B" Section, Tank Corps at Cambrai in November 1917 and was killed in action on 10 December 1917*, aged 31.

William is buried in Rocquigny-Equancourt Road Cemetery, Manancourt. This Cemetery was used for the period of the Battle of Cambrai that took place 10 miles away to the north-east. William is remembered on the Memorial Board in St Mary's Church, (recorded as Haynes) and in the in the Memorial book in the church.

*This is the date given on the CWGC memorial at Manancourt and the Tanks Museum confirms he was killed in action. We can only assume he died in a follow-up action a full week after the battle. RD.

On 7 December, the American 42nd 'Rainbow' Division arrived in France. Among its ranks was one Colonel Douglas MacArthur later to become famous in the Japan campaigns of the Second World War. The Division's distinctive shoulder patch is pictured.

On 22 December, the Flanders Council (Raad van Vlaanderen - RVV) led by Pieter Tack declared independence from the rest of Belgium for the Flemish region - nominally the northern half of the country with the division being a line east to west from a position on the French border some miles south of Ypres to the Dutch Limburg border near Maastricht. Brussels was and is a French speaking "island" within the Flemish-speaking area. The Council hoped for (victorious) German support after the war to implement their independence. The armistice in November 1918 led to the end of the Council and many of its members were arrested and imprisoned as collaborators.

Russia

Following the "October" Revolution in Russia and the agreement to hold talks, hostilities between Russia and the Central Powers nominally ceased on 2 December. In actual fact, fighting ended on dates agreed between local commanders in anticipation of a truce. The first session of peace talks started on 3 December at Brest-Litovsk, in German-held former Russian territory in modern day Poland. Rumania, in alliance with Russia, was isolated and agreed a ceasefire on 6 December in line with the overall Brest-Litovsk truce.

The talks were briefly adjourned with the truce in place (confirmed to last until 14 January 1918), and resumed on 13 December in advance of an Armistice being signed between Russia and the Central Powers. A Secret Convention was signed on the 22nd concerning the future of an independent Poland.

As a result of the loss of authority in Russia, Finland, German-occupied Lithuania and Bessarabia (modern Moldavia) declared their independence. A local plebiscite voted to transfer some western areas of the Petrograd region into Estonia.

The new Russian Constituent Assembly (parliament) met in Petrograd on 11 December. Unfortunately, the elections that created it had not given the Bolsheviks the majority they had expected and so the Assembly was broken up by Bolshevik forces two days later. On 20 December, a decree by Lenin set up the Cheka, a Soviet state security force and forerunner to the KGB, under Felix Dzerzhinsky.

Palestine & Mesopotamia
On 9 December, the British Egyptian Expeditionary Force (EEF) accepted the surrender of Jerusalem by the mayor, Hussein al-Husayni and General Edmund Allenby formally entered the city on the 11th leading units of the EEF on foot through the Jaffa Gate. On the 26th, Turkish forces made a counter-attack but by the 30th the British defence was successful.

The British government gave a written assurance on 11 December to the King of the Hejaz of independence after the war.

Munitions Explosions
An explosion occurred at the National Shell Filling Factory in Barnbow, Leeds on 5 December 1916. 35 women were killed and many more seriously injured by a blast in one of the shell fusing rooms. It was the first major loss of female civilian workers during the war and the worst disaster resulting in loss of life in Leeds' history. A further two were killed in an explosion on 21 March 1917 and three men lost their lives in a blast on 31 March 1918.

On 6 December, at Halifax, Nova Scotia in Canada, two freighters including a French munitions ship Mont Blanc collided in the harbour. The resulting explosion killed at least 1,963 people, injured 9,000 and destroyed part of the city. It was the biggest non-natural explosion in recorded history until the Trinity nuclear test in 1945.

War at Sea
The United States Battleship Division, under Rear-Admiral Rodman, joined the British Grand Fleet at Scapa Flow on 6 December. On the 12th, German destroyers raided a British convoy in the North Sea and sank one of its destroyer escorts, HMS Partridge. 97 of the crew were killed and 24 rescued. A French troop ship (cruiser) Château-Renault was sunk by submarine on 14 December. Most of the troops and ship's complement were rescued by accompanying ships and local trawlers.

Admiral Sir John Jellicoe resigned as First Sea Lord on 26 December to be replaced by Admiral Sir Rosslyn Wemyss.

Portugal & Portuguese Territories
While the war in Europe had continued to flare, so had the war in Africa, the home to many Portuguese overseas territories. In the war against German East

Africa (Tanganyika, later Tanzania), the last German forces were driven out of that territory into Portuguese Mozambique on 1 December.

At home, there was a military coup: Afonso Augusto da Costa resigned as Prime Minister on 10 December to be replaced by Sidónio da Silva Pais . Pais' coup of 11 December deposed the President, Machado Guimaraes, and da Silva Pais was appointed acting President on the 28th.

Meanwhile, Funchal, the capital of Portuguese Madeira, was shelled by a German submarine on 12 December. Madeira held a strategic position in the North Atlantic.

Italy

Austro-German forces launched an offensive against the Italians on the western end of their line, around Asiago on 5 December. On the 9th, an Italian naval raid on Trieste harbour resulted in the sinking of the Austrian battleship Wien.

A French troop train derailed in the French Alps on 12 December killing 543.

USA

The United States declared war on Austria-Hungary on 7 December. Panama and Cuba also declared war on Austria-Hungary while Ecuador severed diplomatic relations with Germany.

The 18th Amendment of the Constitution, prohibiting alcohol, was approved by the US Congress on 18 December. It was ratified by the required number of states by 16 January 1919, and came into effect another year later in 1920.

US President Woodrow Wilson used the Federal Possession and Control Act on 26 December to place most US railroads under federal administration, with the aim of transporting troops and war materials more efficiently.

My Family's War

Three Cookery Books

from Purton Magazine in April 2012 (Rick Dixon)

In the Exhibit of the Month series, I described a set of three books of household hints and recipes. These were the Best Way Book compiled from pages of the Woman's World and Home Companion. The first 2 volumes are signed on the flyleaf by the owner "M Miles 1912" so are over 100 years old. Book 3 doesn't have a date but refers to Wartime Economies so may be from late 1914 or so.

The original volume (let's call it Book 1) has a red cover which proclaims it contains 850 "practical and tried recipes and household hints" and has the strap line "The cheapest Cookery Book in the World". It was priced at 6d (2½p).

Book 2 with a yellow cover has a further 1000 entries. The blue-covered Book 3, although still 6d and containing 1200 entries, has perhaps been undercut in price since the strap line has changed to "Every Home should have this Book." By this time, the source material had been extended to the Family Journal and the Weekly Friend.

Adverts inside are for some products still familiar to us today (Brown & Polson's cornflour, Atora shredded suet, Bird's custard) and others that have fallen by the wayside (Symington's pea flour and Icilma Fluor Cream guaranteed to clear the skin without hair growth while preventing sunburn, chapping and washday redness).

Recipes include a breakfast dish of Brain Rissoles (Book 2, page 51): take the skin off some calves' brains and simmer for ½ an hour, then cut into slices and dip in egg and breadcrumbs. Mix a saltspoonful of mixed herbs with the breadcrumbs. Fry to golden brown in boiling fat.

"An Inexpensive Dish" from Book 3, page 13 suggests you boil some sausages in their skins for about 20 minutes, just covered with water, then remove the skins. Line the bottom of a pie dish with mashed potatoes, put in a layer of sausage meat, then a layer of sliced tomatoes seasoned with salt and pepper. Repeat until the dish is full but the top layer should consist of potato.

Mark with a fork and bake in a hot oven until golden brown.

Household Hints from Book 1 include how to clean a tiger's skin rug with water, a clothes brush and some benzoline and Book 3 has a lemon juice, glycerine and borax anti-freckle lotion.

Book 3 also suggests rubbing the lead of a pencil (graphite) against the joint of a squeaking door hinge ... this one at least should work! Also a topical tip on how to renovate a feather boa: if a feather boa gets limp while out in the damp, curl it as soon as you get home by shaking it over a bowl of boiling water in which a handful of salt has been dissolved.

I hope that these tips will be of assistance ... but please don't use benzoline on your tiger's skin rug!

Part 55: January 1918

Yet another new year in the "War that would be over by Christmas" ... of 1914.

War at Sea

On 4 January, a British hospital ship HMHS Rewa, with wounded from Salonika, was sunk by submarine in the Bristol Channel. 4 engine room ratings were killed in the explosion, but all others were evacuated to lifeboats. German destroyers bombarded Yarmouth on the Norfolk coast on the 14th.

The keel of HMS Hermes, the first ever purpose-designed aircraft carrier, was laid down on the Tyne on the 15th.

In a naval action (Battle of Imbros) outside the Dardanelles, the German cruiser Breslau and two British monitors, HMS Raglan and M28, were sunk. A Turkish cruiser struck a mine and was beached, but refloated on 27 January.

Herbert Ernest Martin, son of George and Bessie Martin, The Square, Purton, was serving with the Royal Navy on board HM Submarine K4 as a Stoker. K class submarines had been specially designed to operate with a battle fleet. They were large boats for their time, at 339 feet (103 m) long, powered by steam turbines, and could make 24 knots on the surface, to keep up with the fleet.

On 31 January, a night-time naval exercise was held by the Grand Fleet (Operation EC1) near the Isle of May in the Firth of Forth. It was misty with only stern lights on each ship, which maintained radio silence. Two K class submarine flotillas were involved: the 12th led by a cruiser HMS Fearless (K3, K4, K6 & K7) and the 13th led by a destroyer HMS Ithuriel (K11, K12, K14, K17 & K22).

Off the Isle of May, the 13th Flotilla encountered the outbound 12th. Fearless collided with K17 which sank in 8 minutes, though most of her crew escaped by jumping into the sea.

The submarines following Fearless turned to avoid their stationary leader, but the battlecruiser HMAS Australia narrowly missed K12 which turned to get out of the way, and headed towards K6. K6 turned but hit K4, which was nearly cut in half and sank with all hands. Herbert had been on board K4 on 31 January 1918 and was among those that died.

Other warships, unconnected with the exercise, passed through the area unaware of the accident and cut through the survivors of K17 struggling in the water. Only nine of the 56 of K17's crew survived and one of these later died of injuries.

This self-inflicted naval disaster became known, with black humour, as the Battle of May Island. Within 75 minutes, two submarines had been sunk and 4 damaged as well as the damage to HMS Fearless. 104 men were killed on K4, K17 and K14.

Herbert is commemorated in St Margaret Pattens Church, Eastcheap, London, together with rest of the K4 crew. The memorial was erected by K4's Commanding Officer's widow. Herbert is also remembered on the Purton War Memorial and in the Memorials in St Mary's Church.

The accident was kept secret during the war, and a memorial cairn was finally erected 84 years later, on 31 January 2002, opposite the Isle of May.

Western Front

William Jordan, husband of Elizabeth (Netta), 9 Clarence Cottages, The Square, Purton, was serving with the 1st Battalion Royal Marine Light Infantry. In October the Battalion had been in action at Passchendaele before being withdrawn to Ypres.

On 1 January 1918, the Battalion was in support near Villers Plouich, supplying working parties for consolidation of the defensive line. Under incoming fire, William was killed in action and is buried in Metz-en-Couture Communal Cemetery, British extension, France.

The Chief of the General Staff, British Expeditionary Force, Lieut-Gen. Kiggell resigned on the 24th and replaced by Lieut-Gen. Sir Herbert Lawrence.

Prisoners of War

Herbert Fisher, son of Albert and Mary Fisher, Church Path, Purton, had been serving with the 2nd Battalion Wiltshire Regiment when he was taken prisoner by the Germans on 24 October 1914 at the 1st Battle of Ypres. He had been successively held at POW Camps at Gottingen, Celle and Hameln. It was at Hameln that Herbert died of consumption (tuberculosis) on 10 January 1918, aged 24.

Herbert is buried in Niederzwehren Cemetery, Hessen, Germany and is remembered on the Purton War Memorial and in the Memorials in St Mary's Church.

War Aims

On 5 January, the Prime Minster David Lloyd George published a demand for a unified peace in a speech to Trade Union delegates. However, the Russian Soviet Government was already in talks with the Central Powers for a separate peace.

On the 8th, US President Woodrow Wilson outlined to Congress his Fourteen Points for peace, broadly in line with Lloyd George's. Many of these points concerned freedom of the seas and trade, arms reductions and independence after breaking up of empires. Other specific statements covered national boundaries after the war and the 14th Point called for the creation of a League of Nations. The speech was translated into many languages and copies were dropped behind German lines. Ten days later, on 24 January, the German Chancellor Count Herling and Austrian Foreign Minister Count Czernin made public replies to both Wilson's and Lloyd George's speeches calling them mere propaganda.

However, Austria and Germany were disrupted by strikes on 16 January amid national impatience with the continuing war. Between 25 and 28 January there were strikes in metals and ammunition factories in Berlin, inspired by revolution in Russia. 400,000 workers went on strike and the action spread to other industrial centres across the country. The army arrested the strike's leaders and dispatched many of them to the front.

Air War
On 2 January, the Air Ministry was formed in Britain and, the following day, the Air Council took over the functions of the former Air Board.

Russia
On 4 January, the Bolshevik Government recognised the independence of Finland and France, Sweden and other countries followed soon after. On the 12th, Finland granted Finnish Jews full civil rights.

The left-right split in Finland resulted in Civil War at the Battle of Kämärä Railway Station on the 27th. Leftist (red) rebels seized control of the capital, Helsinki, and members (white) of the Finnish Senate fled to safety.

The Russian Constituent Assembly met on 18 January in Petrograd and proclaimed a Democratic Republic. But the Bolsheviks yet again forcibly dissolved the Assembly and declared Russia to be a Republic of Soviets on 25 January.

The peace negotiations at Brest-Litovsk were delayed first when the Bolsheviks demanded the talks be moved to neutral Stockholm, but later withdrew the demand. Another delay was caused by the Russians accusing the Central Powers of falsifying reports of the negotiations, but again resumed.

As the month progressed, the British government sent a note to the new Russian Government supporting the creation of an independent Poland. Latvia and Estonia declared independence and, on the 22nd, Ukraine proclaimed itself a free republic though it was really a German puppet state. The Bolsheviks declared war on Ukraine (Ukrainian-Soviet War) with the Battle of Kruty on 29 January.

Palestine & Mesopotamia
On 4 January, the British government wrote to the King of the Hejaz (Hussein bin Ali) confirming Palestine would be removed from Ottoman control following the war.

Arab regular forces under the command of Jafar Pasha al-Askar began actions against Tafileh (southeast of the Dead Sea) on 1 January 1918. The battle of Tafileh itself (23-28 January), was a defensive engagement that turned into an offensive rout, and was described as a brilliant feat of arms. T.E. Lawrence, who was British liaison officer with the Pasha's forces, was awarded the Distinguished Service Order for his leadership at Tafileh and was promoted to lieutenant colonel. 400 Turks died in the battle and 200 were taken prisoner.

Arab camel forces seized the Turkish Dead Sea Flotilla at El Mezran on the 27th.

Horrors yet to come ...
In January, a disease later to be known as "Spanish 'flu" was first observed and diagnosed in Haskell County, Kansas. This was to become pandemic around the world and as big a killer as the Great War itself.

Other News
In the US, in the face of worldwide food shortages, Herbert Hoover, then the US Food Administrator, on 26 January called for "wheatless and meatless" days for the US war effort.

The first Tarzan film, "Tarzan of the Apes", premiered on Broadway in New York on the 27th.

Woodrow Wilson's 14 Points

I. Open covenants of peace, openly arrived at, after which there shall be no private international understandings of any kind but diplomacy shall proceed always frankly and in the public view.

II. Absolute freedom of navigation upon the seas, outside territorial waters, alike in peace and in war, except as the seas may be closed in whole or in part by international action for the enforcement of international covenants.

III. The removal, so far as possible, of all economic barriers and the establishment of an equality of trade conditions among all the nations consenting to the peace and associating themselves for its maintenance.

IV. Adequate guarantees given and taken that national armaments will be reduced to the lowest point consistent with domestic safety.

V. A free, open-minded, and absolutely impartial adjustment of all colonial claims, based upon a strict observance of the principle that in determining all such questions of sovereignty the interests of the populations concerned must have equal weight with the equitable government whose title is to be determined.

VI. The evacuation of all Russian territory and such a settlement of all questions affecting Russia as will secure the best and freest cooperation of the other nations of the world in obtaining for her an unhampered and unembarrassed opportunity for the independent determination of her own political development and national policy and assure her of a sincere welcome into the society of free nations under institutions of her own choosing; and, more than a welcome, assistance also of every kind that she may need and may herself desire. The treatment accorded Russia by her sister nations in the months to come will be the acid test of their good will, of their comprehension of her needs as distinguished from their own interests, and of their intelligent and unselfish sympathy.

VII. Belgium, the whole world will agree, must be evacuated and restored, without any attempt to limit the sovereignty which she enjoys in common with all other free nations. No other single act will serve, as this will serve, to restore confidence among the nations in the laws which they have themselves set and determined for the government of their relations with one another. Without this healing act the whole structure and validity of international law is forever impaired.

VIII. All French territory should be freed and the invaded portions restored, and the wrong done to France by Prussia in 1871 in the matter of Alsace-Lorraine, which has unsettled the peace of the world for nearly fifty years, should be righted, in order that peace may once more be made secure in the interest of all.

IX. A readjustment of the frontiers of Italy should be effected along clearly recognizable lines of nationality.

X. The people of Austria-Hungary, whose place among the nations we wish to see safeguarded and assured, should be accorded the freest opportunity to autonomous development.

XI. Rumania, Serbia, and Montenegro should be evacuated; occupied territories restored; Serbia accorded free and secure access to the sea; and the relations of the several Balkan states to one another determined by friendly counsel along historically established lines of allegiance and nationality; and international guarantees of the political and economic independence and territorial integrity of the several Balkan states should be entered into.

XII. The Turkish portion of the present Ottoman Empire should be assured a secure sovereignty, but the other nationalities which are now under Turkish rule should be assured an undoubted security of life and an absolutely unmolested opportunity of autonomous development, and the Dardanelles should be permanently opened as a free passage to the ships and commerce of all nations under international guarantees.

XIII. An independent Polish state should be erected which should include the territories inhabited by indisputably Polish populations, which should be assured a free and secure access to the sea, and whose political and economic independence and territorial integrity should be guaranteed by international covenant.

League of Nations

XIV. A general association of nations must be formed under specific covenants for the purpose of affording mutual guarantees of political independence and territorial integrity to great and small states alike.

Part 56: February 1918

Western Front

The British Government announced the enlargement of powers of the Supreme War Council at Versailles on 3 February and on the 18th, General Sir W. Robertson, Chief of the British Imperial General Staff, resigned to be replaced next day by General Sir H.H. Wilson.

In early 1916, the 12th Battalion, Sherwood Foresters, was stationed in the front line at Ypres, Belgium, and came across a printing press abandoned by a Belgian who had, in the words of the editor, "stood not on the order of his going, but gone." A sergeant who had been a printer in peacetime salvaged the press and printed a sample page. Eventually they produced the *Wipers Times*, named after Tommy slang for Ypres itself (Wipers). This trench magazine was published in the Ypres Salient until the end of 1918. Publication was held up from February 1918 by the build-up of German attacks, but they later restarted with two issues of "The Better Times". The second of these was billed as the "Xmas, Peace and Final Number."

The front page of most issues had an advert for a spurious concert or event; even an advert for the sale of property such as this one for the whole of the Front Line:

For Sale
The Salient Estate
Complete in every detail
Intending purchasers will be shown round anytime day or night.
Underground residences ready for habitation.

Splendid Motoring Estate! Shooting Perfect!
Fishing Good!!!
Now's the time. Have a stake in the country.
No reasonable offer refused.

Do for Home for Inebriates or other Charitable Institution.

Delay is Dangerous! You might miss it!!
Apply for particulars etc., to
Thomas, Atkins, Sapper & Co., Zillebeke and Hooge.
Housebreakers: Wooley, Bear, Crump & Co.
Telegrams: "Adsum, Wipers"

Politics & Women's Suffrage

On 6 February, the Representation of the People Act was passed which gave most women over 30 the vote.

On the 21st the Ministry of Information was formed in Britain.

War Aims

On 11 February, US President Woodrow Wilson addressed Congress and added Four Principles to his Fourteen Points of January. These included the freedom of navigation and an end to secret diplomacy.

Russia

On 1 February, Russia abandoned the old Julian Calendar and adopted the western Gregorian Calendar. Thus, 1 February 1918 was followed by 14 February. Finland, since incorporation into the Russian Empire, had used both systems in parallel and merely dropped the Julian dates from documents on independence. Estonia, Latvia and Lithuania also changed to the new calendar. All dates below are in the new calendar, including those leading up to 14 February.

On 4 February (22 Jan - Julian) General Alexeyev led a move with forces from the Don Cossacks towards Moscow against the Government (Bolshevik) forces. Alexeyev's force was defeated by 13 February and Alexeyev committed suicide.

The Soviet government declared the separation of church and state on 5 February.

The Finnish Civil War continued as General Carl von Mannerheim gathered an army known as the White Guard to mount a counter revolution against the Bolshevik Red Guard (10 February).

Armenia, Azerbaijan, and Georgia declared independence calling themselves the Transcaucasian Democratic Federative Republic.

A Military Convention was signed between Germany and Poland on 25 February at Bobruisk.

Brest-Litovsk and continuance of war:

Talks at Brest-Litovsk continued and, on 9 February, a peace treaty was signed between the Ukraine and the Central Powers including Bulgaria and Turkey. A supplementary treaty defined the borders of the new Ukrainian State. Britain announced it would not recognise this treaty.

On 10 February, Leon Trotsky, the Russian Foreign Minister, announced that the state of war between Russia and Central Powers, Bulgaria and Turkey had ended, but that Russia would not sign a formal peace treaty. However, in the absence of a peace treaty the Armistice on the Russian front expired on the 18th. The German armies resumed hostilities and advanced rapidly against disorganised and dispirited Russian troops, capturing Dvinsk. On the 19th, the Russians indicated they would sign the peace treaty with Germany. But early in February, Lithuania declared independence from the new Russian Soviet Republic. Then, on 22 February during the talks, Germany claimed all the Baltic states, plus Finland and Ukraine from Russia. Anticipating the loss of Estonia in the imminent treaty, the Russian Navy evacuated Tallinn in Estonia through thick ice over the Gulf of Finland.

The treaty negotiations did not stop hostilities and on 23 February the new Red Army achieved its first victory over German troops near Narva and Pskov. This date became commemorated as Red Army Day from 1923. But German forces occupied Dorpat and Tallinn in Estonia on the 24th-25th, and went on to capture Pernau, Reval and Pskov.

The Russians resumed negotiations on the 28th and military operations halted.

Rumania
The German government sent an ultimatum to Rumania on 6 February demanding peace negotiations within four days. The Rumanian Prime Minister Bratianu resigned and a new Cabinet was formed the next day. Peace negotiations started in Bucharest on the 25th.

War at Sea
The SS Tuscania was the first ship carrying American troops to Europe to be torpedoed and sunk (5 February) off the Irish coast. The former luxury liner had a capacity of over 2,500 passengers. About 210 of the troops and crew were killed, but many were rescued by Royal Navy destroyers Mosquito and Pigeon.

A third German destroyer raid in the Straits of Dover occurred overnight on 15th/16th February, and Dover was shelled by submarine on the 16th.

Hospital ship HMHS Glenart Castle was sunk by submarine the Bristol Channel on 26 February. Of 200 men and women aboard, only 38 survived.

Palestine, Mesopotamia & Persia
The British government made another declaration to the King of the Hejaz, on 4 February, reaffirming pledges regarding freedom of the Arab peoples after the end of the war.

On the 19th, the British occupation of the Jordan Valley began with the capture of Jericho by the Egyptian Expeditionary Force.

On 1 February, British forces extended their East Persia Cordon into Khorasan in relief of Russian forces withdrawn by the Bolshevik Government. However, Trebizond (Trabizon) in northern Turkey, on the former Russian front, was retaken by Turkish forces on the 24th. British forces occupied Kermanshah in western Persia on 25 February.

Revolts
On 1 February, Austrian sailors, led by two Czech Socialists, mutinied in the Gulf of Cattaro (Kotor), on the Adriatic coast of Montenegro. Sailors on about 40 ships joined the mutiny demanding political change and an end to the war. The mutiny failed to spread and was put down by the loyal 3rd Fleet on 3 February. About 800 sailors were imprisoned and four were executed. The Commander-in-Chief of the Austrian fleet was replaced.

Part 57: March 1918

The following men with Purton connections were mobilised to France in March 1918.

Arthur John Selby, 127th American Expeditionary Force. Born in Purton in 1887, he was the son of Robert and Lydia Selby, Fox Road, Purton, but had emigrated to the USA. The 127th were part of the American 32nd Division, and arrived in Brest, France on 4 March 1918. They saw action in Alsace, Aisne-Marne, Oise-Marne and Meuse-Argonne before they marched to the Rhine and became part of the Army of occupation.

Edward Boyekin Bletso, Worcestershire Regiment.

Stanley Lewis Kibblewhite, Royal Naval Air Service (amalgamated as RAF from 1 April 1918).

Western Front

The German military command had seen a disastrous end to 1917, a cold beginning to 1918 and the arrival of fresh American troops. With the end of major hostilities against Russia, 50 Divisions were freed up from action on the Eastern front and moved to the west. The German Spring Offensive, starting with Operation Michael (or *Kaiserschlacht*) was intended as an all-or-nothing gamble to break the British 3rd and 5th armies, capture Paris and win the war before the Americans could be fully mobilised.

On the first day (21 March), a giant German cannon (the Paris Gun or *Kaiser Wilhelm Geschütz*) began to shell Paris from a distance of 71 miles (114 km). The German offensive attacked British positions on a long front, from Picardy to the Somme. It failed to break through as planned, but the British Army lost nearly 20,000 dead on the first day.

The Germans advanced to the River Somme, taking Peronne, Bapaume, Noyon, Albert, Chaulnes and Roye by the 26th. **John Reginald Lane** of Bagbury Farm, Purton, and son of Frederick and Sarah Lane, was serving with the 6th Wilts and was reported missing in action at Bapaume on the 23rd. In the face of the German advances, a crisis meeting between the Allies appointed General Ferdinand Foch as co-ordinating authority over the entire Western Front. The German advance continued, taking Rosières and Montdidier by the 27th. (See map on inside front cover.)

Albert Job Lewis *(pictured)* was the son of Francis and Caroline Lewis of High Street, Purton. He was serving with the 2nd Battalion Wiltshire Regiment in the St Quentin sector of the Somme. The German Spring offensive "fell upon the Wiltshire's line" causing massive casualties. The Battalion War Diary entry for 21 March 1918 records "an intense enemy bombardment of our trenches and back areas with high explosive and gas shells at 4.30am [which] continued throughout the day. The enemy attacked at 10am with two Divisions on our Battalion front [which] broke through on our flanks and surrounded the Battalion. ... A message was received by pigeon [that they were] still holding out ... with 50 men. The Battalion Transport moved back from Fluquières to Dury at 4.40am ..."

Albert was one of those killed in action that day (21 March), aged 29. He has no known grave, but is remembered on the Pozières Memorial, Somme, and in the Memorial Book at St Mary's Church.

Walter Hunt of Locks Lane, Purton, was serving with the 2nd Battalion, Royal Marine Light Infantry. During the Spring Offensive, the Battalion carried out numerous rear-guard actions attempting to stall the German advance. On 27 March, the Battalion was in positions counter-attacking along the Martinsart-Mesnil Road and through Aveluy Wood, where they repulsed the enemy. Walter *(pictured)* was killed in action during these attacks. He has no known grave but his name is recorded on the Arras Memorial, Pas de Calais, France.

A subsidiary German offensive, Operation Mars, on 28 March against the British Third Army at Arras was repulsed with "few British casualties".

Palestine, Mesopotamia & Persia

On 3 March, troops of the British East Persia Cordon occupied Meshed in Persia. In the former Russian sector, Hamadan in western Persia was evacuated by the Russians on the 16th.

Arthur Anthony Brown *(pictured)* was serving with the 271st Brigade, Royal Field Artillery as Lieutenant (Acting Captain). He was the son of John and Amelia Elizabeth Brown, The Close, Purton and had married Edith Gore (née Holdship, from Sydney) in Purton on 24 October 1916. He had been awarded the Military Cross in 1916 with the citation including "For conspicuous devotion to duty throughout the operations before Gaza and subsequently during the advance culminating with the action securing the Jaffa-Jerusalem Line".

Arthur died suddenly of a heart attack on 4 March 1918 at a village just north of Jerusalem. He was buried in Ramleh War Cemetery, Palestine, and is commemorated on a grave surround in St Mary's churchyard and in the Remembrance Book in St Mary's Church.

On 8 March, units of the British Army's Egyptian Expeditionary Force (EEF) launched an attack against Ottoman defences from the Mediterranean Sea, across the Judaean Mountains to the edge of the Jordan Valley. Known as the Battle of Tel Asur, it ended on 12 March having pushed much of the Ottoman front-line northwards.

The EEF crossed the River Jordan on 21 March, moving through Es Salt in Palestine and attacking Amman on the 27th. However, the EEF was forced to withdraw to the Jordan Valley on 31 March.

Further east, on 9 March, British forces occupied Hit on the Euphrates, and attacked Khan Baghdadi (26th) before taking Ana in Mesopotamia on 28 March.

War at Sea

On 7 March, the Allies sent a final Note to the (neutral) Netherlands Government regarding surrender of all Dutch ships in Allied ports. The Dutch Government accepted the demands 'with reservations' on the 18th. The Allied Blockade Committee was formed on 20 March. As a result, Dutch ships in British and US ports were requisitioned on 21 March by the British and US governments.

Allied shipping losses continued: HMS Calgarian, an armed merchant cruiser, was torpedoed and sank on 1 March off Rathlin Island, Northern Ireland. Calgarian had been at Halifax, Nova Scotia, when the Halifax Explosion took place on 6 December 1917 and had assisted with rescue and medical relief.

On 6 March, USS Cyclops disappeared in the Bermuda Triangle while carrying a cargo of 11,000 tonnes of manganese ore for munitions. The German navy denied responsibility and storms may have been the cause.

HMHS Guildford Castle, a British hospital ship, survived a German U-boat attack in the Bristol Channel and reached port.

As a new development, SS Faith, the 1st ever concrete ship and an 8000-ton freighter, was launched in California on 14 March. It was later the first concrete ship to cross the Atlantic. *[You may be interested to know that your present author, served as mate on a concrete schooner, Pen y Ddraig, during 1996. Concrete, just like steel, is heavier than water - but both float like a bowl will in a sink..]*

War in the Air

On 6 March, the first pilotless drone aircraft, the Hewitt-Sperry Automatic Airplane had its test flight at Long Island, New York. The drone never came into active use and development was scrapped in 1925 as the guidance system was unreliable.

On the 7th, German aircraft made their first "moonless night" air raid over England.

Brest-Litovsk

The Treaty of Brest-Litovsk was signed on 3 March 1918. Under the terms of the treaty, Russia renounced all territorial claims in Finland, Estonia, Latvia, Lithuania, White Russia (now Belarus), and Ukraine. The Kingdom of Poland was not mentioned in the treaty.

Germany and Austria-Hungary said that the future of all those territories would be settled in agreement with their populations. However, the treaty ceded most of them to Germany - they would become little more than puppet states. Their previous local declarations of independence had little effect in reality as ambitions were swallowed by the treaty. In each territory, the ethnic German residents (*Volksdeutsch*) were to become the ruling elite. A Germanic monarchy was created in Lithuania, and Latvia and Estonia were amalgamated as the United Baltic Duchy under a German duke.

Before the treaty was signed, German forces captured Kiev in the Ukraine on the 2nd and went on to occupy the rest of the Ukraine and the other treaty territories shortly after. In the power vacuum between the Russians and the Germans, Ukrainian mobs massacred Jews at Seredyna-Buda on the 9th.

The Allied Governments issued a Note refusing to recognise the Brest-Litovsk Treaty on the 18th.

Turkey didn't get much out of the Treaty, other than return of the districts of Erdehan, Kars, and Batum which it had lost in the Crimean War. Russian troops evacuated the area and Turkey took over Erezum on the 12th.

Russia

As a result of the Brest-Litovsk Treaty, Leon Trotsky was appointed Minister for

War on 8 March, his former post of Foreign Minister going to Georgy Vasilyevich Chicherin. Next day, the Russian Bolshevik Party renamed itself the Communist Party. Then, because Petrograd was only 100 miles from the German treaty territories of Estonia and Finland, the Russian Government moved from Petrograd to Moscow, which was also 300 miles from German-held White Russia (Belarus).

In his new post as Minister for War, Trotsky took back overall control of the Red Army on 12 March. The Treaty of Brest-Litovsk was ratified by the Congress of Soviets at Moscow on 14 March.

Russian (RSFSR) and Armenian Revolutionary Federation forces suppressed a Muslim revolt in Baku, Azerbaijan on 30 March (the "March Days") with the result of some 30,000 deaths.

Finland
Unlike most of the Russian Brest-Litovsk nations, Finland fared comparatively well. While the now Finnish Social Republic of Workmen signed a Treaty of Peace and Amity with the Russian Federal Soviet Republic on 1 March, it also requested that a German force take over the Aaland Islands off the south-western coast of Finland. These had once been Swedish and a local ethnic Swedish minority population had wanted the islands transferred back to Sweden. On the 3rd, the German Government notified Sweden of the occupation.

The Finnish Army Corps of Aviation was founded on 6 March, adopting a blue swastika as its symbol. This was a tribute to Eric von Rosen, a Swedish explorer and aviator who donated the first plane and who saw the Viking symbol as his personal lucky insignia. The Finnish Air Force was later established in 1928.

Peace was signed at Berlin between Germany and Finland on 7 March, including terms of alliance.

Rumania
Rumania signed a peace treaty at Buftea with the Central Powers, Bulgaria and Turkey on 9 March. In a change of government, Premier and Foreign Minister General Averescu was replaced on 21 March by Alexandru Marghiloman as Premier, and Constantine Arian as Foreign Minister.

Bessarabia (Moldova) was confirmed as a new Rumanian territory on the 27th.

USA
The US Army's Distinguished Service Medal was authorised by Congress on 7 March, perhaps in anticipation of someone needing to be awarded it as US forces were soon to be in action in France and Belgium.

The US had managed to muddle along without official Time Zones up until now, but on 19 March Congress established time zones across the country. Daylight Saving Time was approved and went into effect on 31 March.

Spanish 'Flu
First recorded in January, Spanish 'Flu was spotted at Funston Army Camp, Kansas and then the first confirmed cases were reported on 11 March at Fort Riley, Kansas.

My Family's War
Herbert Dubrey

Mrs Jean Robson was researching her uncle Herbert Dubrey, killed on 21 March 1918 at "The Somme" and enquired to the Museum of the Royal West Kent Regiment, Maidstone. Herbert had been serving with the West Kents.

The Curator of the Museum wrote back to Jean:
Herbert was in the 7th Battalion of the Royal West Kents. The battalion saw a lot of action and bitter fighting along the Somme.

On the date of his death, 21/3/18, his battalion suffered terrible losses as the cutting below describes. I [the curator] know the Pozières region quite well as my partner's boat was moored nearby on the Somme for 2 years. The mist hangs about near the river (in fact we had to delay trying to take photos of the Memorial because of the visibility) so I can well imagine that awful morning of the 21st March [1918].

[Press Cutting]
THE GERMAN ATTACK
When, on March 21st, 1918, the long-expected German attack at last developed The Queen's Own had two battalions in the front line, exposed to the full weight of the terrific bombardment which ushered it in. For both the 7th and 8th Battalions March 21st began a time of severe trial; both were to suffer terribly, the 7th indeed was almost wiped out, both were to do splendidly and add greatly to their laurels. Before the fighting on the front of the Third and Fifth Armies died down in the middle of April two more battalions had become involved, the 6th coming down from the Lys Valley to stem the hostile advance across the Ancre, the 10th, newly returned from Italy, being thrown in at an earlier stage.

The 7th, as already mentioned, had returned to the "Forward Zone" in its Divisional sector South of St. Quentin two days before the attack. It had barely settled down before, on the afternoon of the 10th, the warning "Prepare for attack" came round. A raid on the front of the neighbouring Corps had revealed the fact that the enemy were massing near St. Quentin and must be on the point of attacking.

A night of anticipation was followed at 4.30 next morning by the outburst of the heaviest bombardment the 7th had ever experienced. At that hour it was still dark, but as dawn came nearer it became evident that the morning was going to be shrouded in the thickest of mists, under cover of which the enemy would be able to approach undetected to within 30 or so yards. The mist was the greater disadvantage because it presented the conditions which the new system of defence was least well adapted to meet. [Continuing page not available.]

Herbert was killed in action on 21 March 1918 and is remembered on the Pozières Memorial, Somme.

Jean writes in her note to me:
The museum of the Royal West Kent Regiment at Maidstone has helped me a lot in my research. I enclose here some of my correspondence with them and the full description of the fighting on 21ˢᵗ March - it makes very sombre reading.

The one tiny piece of good news is that the Germans were amazed by the wonderful British food supplies they captured. At least young Herbert was not hungry when he was killed - little consolation though.

Part 56: April 1918

Only one man with a Purton connection was mobilised in April 1918.

To France: George Arthur Smith, Royal Engineers, transferred to BEF.

Western Front
It was a heavy month for Purton losses - 7 deaths, of which 2 were in one family.

French and British forces repelled the German attack on Amiens (Battle of the Avre, 4 April). But this was followed by the Battle of the Ancre on the 5ᵗʰ. **Frederick Charles Lane**, son of Frederick and Sarah Lane, of Bagbury Farm, Purton, was serving with the 5ᵗʰ Battalion Royal Berkshire Regiment at Albert - the River Ancre runs through the town. The 5ᵗʰ Royal Berks was in trenches with the 36ᵗʰ Brigade in front of Albert and was heavily shelled for 2½ hours. The Germans attacked the entire front but were repulsed with help from the 9ᵗʰ Royal Fusiliers. A second attack got into the trenches and reinforcements were sent in over open ground - half the reinforcements were killed by machine gun fire. Frederick was reported missing in action, aged 28, on 5 April 1918. His body was found and he is buried in Bouzincourt Ridge Cemetery, Albert. The first phase of the German Spring Offensive (Kaiserschlacht) was halted at Bouzincourt Ridge. Frederick is remembered on the Purton War Memorial and in the Memorial book in St Mary's Church.

John Reginald Lane, younger brother of Frederick Lane *(entry above)* had been reported missing in action at Béthune on 23 March 1918 serving with the 6ᵗʰ Wilts. He was taken Prisoner of War and died of wounds in a German field hospital, aged 23, on 13 April. Perhaps his wounds were from the 23 March conflict or maybe in forced POW labour behind German lines and ironically wounded by British fire. (This is discussed in greater depth in Bob Lloyd's book.) John was buried at Marquion Grove German Cemetery, France and later moved to the Honourable Artillery Company (HAC) Cemetery, Ecoust-St-Mein. He is also remembered on the Purton War Memorial and in the Memorial book in St Mary's Church. The Lane family had lost two sons within 8 days.

The German "Operation Georgette", phase 2 of the Spring Offensive, was launched on the 9ᵗʰ, against British and Portuguese forces of the 2ⁿᵈ Army between Armentières and Givenchy - the Battle of the Lys (4th Battle of Ypres). German forces took Neuve-Chapelle, then widened the offensive almost to Ypres and took Messines on the 10th, Armentières and Merville next day. **William Charles Eveleigh**, serving with the 6th Battalion Wiltshire Regiment, was taken Prisoner of War on the 10th at Wytschaete, while the Battalion was holding trenches east of the Messines-Wytschaete ridge. (See Part 64.)

The same day, **Frederick Walter Sutton**, son of Frederick and Emily Sutton, of Packhorse Farm, Purton, was also with the 6th Wilts at Wytschaete. During the 10 April attack, he was reported missing in action, aged 26. Frederick has no known grave but is remembered on the Tyne Cot Memorial and on the Purton War Memorial as well as the memorials in St Mary's Church. There is also a memorial stone placed on top of his parents' grave in St Mary's Churchyard.

Mervyn Howard Tom Green, son of George and Hannah Green, New Road, Purton, was also with the 6th Wilts. He was severely wounded and had a leg amputated. His condition worsened and he died on 16 April 1918 of heart failure, aged 22, at Pendleton Hospital, Manchester, to which he had been transferred. Mervyn is buried in St Mary's churchyard, Purton, in a family plot so not marked by a CWGC headstone. He is also remembered on the Purton War Memorial and in the memorials in St Mary's Church.

On 12 April, Field Marshal Sir Douglas Haig commanding the British forces issued a Special Order of the Day known as "Backs to the Wall" announcing the seriousness of the situation and ordering his forces to stand fast and fight it out. Meanwhile German actions started against Hazebrouck and Bailleul (taken by the Germans on the 15th). **William James Sainsbury**, born in Wootton Bassett but resident in Purton, was serving with the 15th (Service) Battalion (1st Birmingham), Royal Warwickshire Regiment at Morbecque, just south of Hazebrouk. William died of wounds received on 14 April 1918, aged 34. He is buried in Morbecque British Cemetery and remembered at the Memorial Hall in Wootton Bassett.

William John Edmonds was the son of Alfred and Alice Edmonds of Lydiard Green, Purton. He was serving with the 1st Battalion Wiltshire Regiment, having previously served with the 5th Battalion at Gallipoli in 1915. On 12 April, the Battalion was in trenches around Neuve Eglise and after dusk marched to Bailleul and was then dispatched to hold a position at Crucifix Corner between Neuve Eglise and the Ravelsberg. In the ensuing action, 2 officers and 4 other ranks were killed, 16 wounded and 282 reported missing. William was among those missing but was later confirmed killed in action, aged 23. William has no known grave, but his name is remembered on the Ploegsteert Memorial, Comines-Warneton, Belgium and on the War Memorial in Lydiard Millicent.

General Foch was appointed Commander-in-Chief of Allied Armies on the Western Front on the 14th, though Belgian forces were not placed under his command. The British Secretary of State for War, Lord Derby, was against inter-Allied command and Lloyd George replaced him with Viscount Milner on 20 April.

Under pressure of the Georgette Offensive, the British 2nd Army withdrew in the Ypres salient on 16 April to release reserves for use at the Lys, and so German forces were able to retake Passchendaele. The German offensive against Kemmel Ridge, 17 to 19 April, was followed by actions against Béthune. German forces attacked Villers-Bretonneux on the 24th but were forced back by a British and Anzac forces counter attack.

Charles Christopher Lander was serving with the 1/6th North Staffordshire Regiment. He was the husband of Susan Lander, 61 Regent Place, New Swindon, though when called up they had lived in High Street, Purton. He had 5 living children. Charles had been wounded in France in 1914 but was re-enlisted in 1917 when he re-joined the Battalion. On 21 April 1918 he received a gunshot wound to the upper right arm and was transferred back to hospital in Newhaven, Sussex, where his arm was amputated. He was transferred to the City of London Hospital but septicaemia set in and he died on 18 May 1918, aged 33. Charles is buried in Swindon (Radnor Street) Cemetery and is listed on Swindon's Roll of honour.

German troops again stormed Kemmel Ridge on the 24th (2nd Battle of Kemmel) capturing the high ground. **George Edward Butcher** *(pictured),* son of Sarah Butcher, Battlewell, Purton, was serving with the 2nd Wilts on an outpost line near Kemmel Ridge east of Wytschate. After heavy bombardment, German forces attacked at dawn driving the outpost line back. The Germans took Kemmel Hill and 2nd Wilts withdrew to a defensive flank by the Ypres-Comines Canal then to rear positions. George was reported "died", aged 28, on 26 April. He has no known grave, but is remembered on the Tyne Cot Memorial and on Swindon's Roll of Honour.

An attempt by the Germans to advance from Kemmel was held back and marked the end of the Battle of the Lys.

April's actions in the German Spring Offensive had been disastrous for the 2nd Wilts who had lost so many dead and wounded that they were down to 2 Companies in strength. The 2nd Berkshires were in a similar position and the two battalions were merged into a single command under 2nd Berks direction. However, the Germans had also suffered 330,000 casualties in the Michael and Georgette offensives and had almost no reserve troops left.

The first contingent of Italian troops arrived on the French front on 27 April.

During the Battle of the Lys, the Portuguese Expeditionary Corps was slaughtered and the Portuguese government couldn't arrange reinforcements. Even at the end of the war, Portugal couldn't transport its troops back to the country and social conflict at home increased.

Britain & Ireland

The 3rd Military Service Act was passed by Parliament on 10 April, raising the upper age limit for conscription to 51 and extending conscription provisions to Ireland. The Act came into effect on 18 April. The result of this in Ireland was a one-day general strike on 23 April in protest and affecting railways, ports, industry, transport, public services and even shipyards and Government munitions factories. It also further fuelled the calls for Irish Home Rule.

The Air War

On 1 April, the Royal Flying Corps and the Royal Naval Air Service were amalgamated into a new and separate service - the Royal Air Force. The aviation industry supporting the air force was itself the world leader, by that time.

The 12th saw the last German airship raid on England to cause casualties (27).

The German air ace, Manfred von Richthofen, known as The Red Baron, shot down his 79th and 80th victims on 20 April. The most successful fighter pilot of the war, he was himself shot down and killed over Morlancourt Ridge near the River Somme on the 21st. A Canadian pilot, Arthur Roy Brown, was credited with shooting him down.

The War at Sea

In response to Liberia's declaration of war in January 1918, a German submarine bombarded the capital, Monrovia, on 10 April. This didn't deter Guatemala, with a coast on the other side of the Atlantic, from declaring war on Germany on the 23rd.

Royal Navy activity included a raid by naval light forces on the Kattegat which was followed by blockading raids on Zeebrugge and Ostend in unsuccessful attempts to seal off German U-boat bases at both locations.

Russia

On 10 April, a Settlement Treaty between Germany and Turkey was ratified in Berlin, agreeing their spheres of influence over the defeated Russian state. During the month, German forces captured Ekaterinoslav and Kharkov in Southern Russia, and the Crimea.

To protect Allied interests in the east from potential German actions, British and Japanese marines landed at Vladivostock in the Russian far east on 5 April.

Rumania

Bessarabia (modern Moldova) passed an Act of Union with Rumania on 9 April. The territory had been part of Russian Ukraine, so the new Ukraine Government protested against the union on the 16th, as did Russia on the 23rd.

The New Republics

In Finland, the government had been taken over by the Bolshevik party backed by the Red Guards. A German Expeditionary Force left Danzig on the 1st arriving in Finland on 3 April and capturing Helsinki on the 13th. The Finnish government now announced that all German troops in Finland had landed at their request. Vyborg in Finland, but close to the Russian border by Petrograd, was captured by German forces with Finnish White Guards on the 30th. Several British submarines had been at Helsinki and were destroyed by their crews to avoid capture by Germany.

Latvia proclaimed independence from Russia on 9 April and joined the other Baltic Provinces in agreeing to form themselves into a confederated state within the German Empire.

The Trans-Caucasian Council (Azerbaijan, Armenia and Georgia) declared independence from Russia on the 22nd and hoped Turkey would stay away. Turkish forces had taken over Van in Armenia, and Sarikamish, Batum and Kars in Georgia, under the Settlement Treaty with Germany.

Meanwhile Germany established a military dictatorship in Ukraine on the 29th.

Palestine
On the 30th, the British Egyptian Expeditionary Force (EEF) made a 2nd attack across the Jordan towards Ottoman-held Shunet Nimrin and Es Salt. Again, the action was unsuccessful and the EEF withdrew to the Jordan Valley on 4 May.

Other News
Gavrilo Princip who assassinated Archduke Franz Ferdinand of Austria in June 1914, and sparked the Great War, died of tuberculosis on 28 April after 3 years in prison in Theresienstadt in the Austro-Hungarian province of Bohemia (now Terezín in the Czech Republic).

Part 59: May 1918

Western Front
Victor Rowland Lovelock was serving with the 2nd Battalion Wiltshire Regiment, under the command of the 2nd Bedfordshires - the two had been merged after enormous losses during the German Spring Offensive. By that time the 2nd Wilts could only muster 2 companies - full strength would be 4 companies. Victor was the son of George and Mary Jane Lovelock, Pavenhill, Purton. After the Battle of the Lys, 2nd Wilts had moved to trenches on the Front Line near Vierstraat where they relieved the South African Composite Brigade while under active artillery fire. Early on 8 May, after gas shells and a mortar shell barrage, the Germans attacked the French to 2nd Wilts' right with rifle fire. The French had to retire leaving the battalion's right exposed and the Front Line fell back. A counter-attack by the French and 2nd Wilts/Berks failed and the Germans kept up an intense bombardment causing very heavy Battalion casualties. Victor was killed in action, aged 20, and has no known grave. He is remembered on the Tyne Cot Memorial, on the Purton War Memorial and in the Memorial book in St Mary's Church.

William George Vizer was serving with the 157th Siege Battery, Royal Garrison Artillery attached to the 1st Army in the area south of Armentières. His next of kin was given as his grandfather, John Godwin of the Royal George, Pavenhill, Purton. He was the son of the late William and Annie Mary Vizer of Minety. William died of wounds, aged 26, on 12 May 1918 and is buried at Sandpits British Cemetery, Fouquereuil, Pas de Calais.

The German attacks against the French 6th Army at the 3rd Battle of the Aisne commenced on 27 May 1918, with the aim of capturing the Chemin-des-Dames Ridge before the American Expeditionary Force were action-ready in France. The attack began with a bombardment from over 4,000 German artillery guns, followed by a poison gas drop and an infantry attack. The French wouldn't retreat in the face of the German attacks as they had captured the ridge with heavy losses in 1917. Instead they massed together in the front-line trenches, an easy target for artillery and causing heavy losses to British units trying to support them.

The attack took the Allies by surprise. With Allied defences spread thin, the German army advanced through a 25-mile gap in the Allied lines and reached the River Aisne in under six hours. They broke through eight Allied divisions between Reims and Soissons, gaining an extra 9 miles of territory by the end of the day.

This amazing success made General Ludendorff see the chance to change direction towards Paris hoping to draw the Allies into a final battle and win the war. He captured over 50,000 Allied soldiers and 800 guns, advancing to within 35 miles of Paris by 3 June. But their advance was stalled by shortages of supplies, fatigue, lack of reserves and casualties. In May, the Germans captured Craonne, Soissons, Fère-en-Tardenois, Château-Thierry and Dormans and approached the River Marne.

28 May was an important date in the War marking the first major action by US forces, the 28th Regiment (1st Division), which gained a victory at the Battle of Cantigny.

Britain & Ireland
On 5 May, Field Marshal Sir John French was appointed Lord Lieutenant of Ireland.

A German Plot was "uncovered" in May when the British arrested Joseph Dowling, put ashore (April) on the Irish west coast by a German U-boat. Dowling, of the Irish Brigade, involved in the 1916 Easter Rising, said under questioning that Germany was planning a military invasion via Ireland to open a new front against Britain. 150 leaders and members of Sinn Féin were arrested and interned on the night of 16-17 May. Internment backfired on Britain - those gaoled were of the political movement rather than the Irish Republican Brotherhood (IRB) who saw physical force as the route to republicanism. Michael Collins was able to take control of the IRB and focus on armed actions. The "German Plot" was seen, even at the time, as black propaganda against Sinn Féin rather than revealing a real plot.

The War in the Air
In retaliation against air raids over British towns, the new RAF conducted its first air raid on Germany on 18 May, bombing Cologne during daylight. The following day, a German night aeroplane raid was made on London. It turned out to be the last one in which casualties were inflicted - 49 killed and 177 wounded. Over the war years, nineteen aeroplane bombing raids had been

made on London alone.

A German air raid on British camps and hospitals at Étaples near Boulogne caused heavy casualties on 19 May.

The War at Sea
On 9 May, a second Royal Navy raid was made to seal off the German U-boat base at Ostend. The cruiser HMS Vindictive, already severely damaged at Zeebrugge, in April, was positioned, scuttled and sunk to block Ostend harbour. Even though the sinking of the ship was intentional, lives were lost from enemy fire. Vindictive had a skeleton crew of 55 and 38 survivors were picked up by HM Motor Launch 254. The Zeebrugge and Ostend raids resulted in a large number of VC awards: the Navy perpetuated Vindictive's name in a new aircraft carrier under construction as the new HMS Vindictive. (It was to have been HMS Cavendish.)

On the 15th, a German submarine bombarded St Kilda in the Hebrides. And German U-boats were seen in US waters for the first time on 25 May.

USA
Rather surprisingly, the US Congress passed the Sedition Act on 16 May. It made it a criminal and imprisonable offence to criticise the US government.

Even on the home front, war wasn't easy - a TNT explosion on 18 May killed 200 at a chemical factory in Oakdale, Pennsylvania. But technology was advancing as the world's first electrically propelled warship was announced in New Mexico on 20 May. The US Military went on to announce that the Army Aviation Section would be separated from the Signal Corps and form two new sections: the Division of Military Aeronautics and the Bureau of Aircraft Production.

Russia
At the beginning of May, German forces occupied Sevastopol in the Crimea and, with it, captured the Russian Black Sea fleet. A few days later they took Rostov.

Recent events in Russia convinced the British and French governments that military intervention via North Russia was essential. There were several objectives and one was to prevent Allied war stockpiles in Arkhangelsk falling into German or Bolshevik hands. The pro-Allies Czechoslovak Legion was stranded along the Trans-Siberian Railway - if they could be rescued and the Bolshevik army defeated, perhaps the Eastern Front could be re-formed with the Czechs and local anti-communist militias. On 24 May, General Poole landed at Murmansk with the aim of organising a North Russian Expeditionary Force.

The New Republics
Frederickshamn in southern Finland was captured on 7 May by the White Guards (anti-Bolshevik). This is officially the date of the end of the Finnish Civil War which had started on 1 March. Outposts of resistance made the effective date 15 May.

Finland signed peace agreements with Turkey on 11 May in Berlin, and with Austria-Hungary in Vienna on the 29th.

Ukraine signed an armistice with Russia at Koronevo on 4 May. Ustemovich became President on the 9th. But Ukraine was still under a German dictatorship.

In the Caucasus, German and Turkish (Ottoman) delegates arrived at Batum on 6 May to negotiate peace with the new Trans-Caucasian Federal Government (Georgia, Azerbaijan and Armenia). However, Ottoman forces in the meantime occupied Alexandropol in Georgia on the 18th. Trans-Caucasia was dissolved on the 26th as Georgia, Azerbaijan and Armenia all declared full independence. That same day Armenia defeated the Ottoman Army in the Battle of Sardarapat.

On 11 May, the "Mountainous Republic of the Northern Caucasus" declared independence from Russia - this was a confederation of Chechnya, Ingushetia, North Ossetia-Alania, Kabardino-Balkaria, Dagestan and part of Stavropol Krai, many of which were much in the news in the 1990s and 2000s.

Portugal
Sidónio da Silva Pais, acting President of Portugal since December 1917 after a military coup, was elected President on 9 May. But army losses at the Battle of the Lys (April 1918) had caused massive social conflict at home and Pais resigned on 15 May. J.T. de Souza Barboza was appointed President and Secretary of the Interior.

Other Theatres
A final peace treaty was signed between Rumania and Bulgaria, the Central Powers and Turkey on 7 May.

On 8 May, Nicaragua declared war on both Germany and Austria-Hungary. Costa Rica declared war on Germany on the 23rd.

On 12 May, a military treaty, *der Waffenbund*, was signed between Germany and Austria-Hungary combining their armies under a single command.

British forces captured Kirkuk in Mesopotamia from Ottoman forces on 7 May but were forced to retreat on the 24th.

Between 29 and 30 May, the Battle of Skra-di-Legen was fought north-west of Thessaloniki, on the Macedonian front. The battle was the first large-scale employment of Greek troops of the newly established Army of National Defence and resulted in the capture of the heavily fortified Bulgarian position.

Other News
The Three-Minute Pause, was initiated in Cape Town, South Africa, by the Mayor Sir Harry Hinds and the Noon Gun was fired daily on Signal Hill. It inspired the two-minute silence for Remembrance introduced in November 1919.

The Allies signed military and naval agreements with Japan and China on 15 May to counter German penetration in the Far East and Bolshevik hostilities, following the fall of Russia.

Part 60:   June 1918

Western Front

The German offensive on the River Aisne continued and they pushed towards the River Marne. They reached the north bank of the river at Château-Thierry, 95 kilometres (59 miles) from Paris, on 27 May. On 31 May, the US 3rd Division held the Germans at Château-Thierry. But on 1 June, Château-Thierry and Vaux fell, and the German troops moved into Belleau Wood. The U.S. 2nd Division, with a brigade of US Marines, faced them. The Marines attacked the woods six times before the Germans finally withdrew on 26 June. The battle marked the first US victory of the war, but also one of their bloodiest and most ferocious battles with 9,777 casualties, including 1,811 killed. Many are buried in the nearby Aisne-Marne American Cemetery. The battle also became a key story in the history of the United States Marine Corps recounting how they fought off parts of five divisions of Germans, often reduced to using only their bayonets or fists in hand-to-hand combat.

By that time, 650,000 US troops had arrived in France, with 10,000 more arriving each day.

Richard Beassant, the son of Richard and Louisa Beassant of Lydiard Millicent was serving with the 88th Brigade, Royal Field Artillery. He had been badly gassed earlier in 1918 but had returned to his unit which was at the Battle of the Aisne, at Bligny and Bois-des-Buttes. Richard was killed in action by an enemy shell, aged 21, on 6 June 1918 and is buried in Marfaux British Cemetery, Marne, France. He is remembered on the Purton War Memorial, the Memorials in St Mary's Church in Purton and also on the Lydiard Millicent War Memorial. The Battle of the Aisne ended that same day.

Albert Painter *(pictured)* was born in Purton in 1892 and had emigrated to Australia.   He enlisted with the 25th Battalion Australian Imperial Force in 1915 and saw action at Gallipoli, then in France at Pozières during the Battle of the Somme of July 1916.   There he took a gunshot wound to the buttock and convalesced in Leicester.   By December 1916, he had re-joined his battalion in France and was soon promoted to corporal, then to sergeant. By 10 June 1918, he was in action in the 3rd Battle of Morlancourt attacking German positions between Sailly-Laurette and Morlancourt.   His platoon was  caught by machine gun fire in no-man's-land. 42 were killed, 156 injured and 8 missing.   Albert was killed in action, aged 26.   He is remembered on the Villers-Bretonneux Memorial, France. He was initially buried near Morlancourt. During the post-war battlefield clearances, it is possible that Albert's body was reburied at CWGC Beacon cemetery, which holds many who died around that same date, including many unidentified Australians whose original identifying marks had been lost. Albert is also remembered on Swindon's Roll of Honour.

On 9 June, the Germans launched the fourth operation of the Spring Offensive known variously as the Noyon-Montdidier Offensive, Operation Gneisenau and the Battle of Matz. They planned to push their Front Line west between Amiens and the Aisne. Although they made progress on the first day, a counter-attack on 11 June by 3 French and 2 American divisions plus tanks halted the offensive after 3 days.

Frank George Merchant, was the son of Albert and Isabella Merchant, of Pavenhill, Purton. He was serving with the 1/7th Battalion, Lancashire Fusiliers (Territorial Force) who were in the Hebuterne and later the Beaumont-Hamel sectors. Frank died, aged 18, on 24 June 1918 of wounds received during a German air raid and is buried in Gezaincourt Communal Cemetery, Somme, France. He is remembered on the Purton War Memorial and Memorials in St Mary's Church.

The War in the Air
Between 30 May and 1 June, Canadian ace William (Billy) Bishop downed 6 German aircraft, including that of German ace Paul Bilik. Bishop was credited with 72 victories, making him the top Canadian ace of the war. He had been awarded the Victoria Cross in 1917, survived the war and died in 1956 (aged 62) in Florida.

The Royal Air Force had been created in April 1918. The Independent Air Force (IAF), was set up on 6 June as a strategic bombing group within the RAF to strike against German railways, aerodromes, and industrial centres without co-ordination from the Army or Navy.

The first aeroplane bombing raid by an American unit in France was made on 12 June.

The War at Sea
An example of the perils of operating at sea in war-time is the story of RMS Kenilworth Castle. Kenilworth was homeward bound to England in company with the Durham Castle and convoyed up the English Channel with an escort of the cruiser HMS Kent and five destroyers. In morning darkness on 4 June, and with all ships without lights, Kent left the convoy, 35 miles out from Plymouth, and changed course as planned. However, that put her on a collision course with the Kenilworth Castle. Kenilworth swung over to avoid Kent but hit the convoy destroyer HMS Rival cutting off Rival's stern which held depth charges for submarine attack. The depth charges exploded underneath Kenilworth Castle causing a large hole in the hull. Kenilworth limped towards Plymouth with her passengers. 15 were drowned including some of the 36 nurses on board.

Seven were killed when a Dutch hospital ship Koningin Regentes was sunk on 6 June by a German submarine en route from Boston (Lincolnshire) to Rotterdam.

On 10 June, the Austrian battleship SMS Szent Istvan was sunk by two Italian motor torpedo boats off Premuda Island on the Dalmatian Adriatic coast.

An Australian steamer Wimmera was sunk, on 26 June, off Cape Maria van Diemen near the northern tip of New Zealand by a mine laid a year earlier by the German raider Wolf. 26 of its 151 passengers and crew were killed.

On 27 June, a British hospital ship HMHS Llandovery Castle, one of five Canadian hospital ships that served in the First World War, was torpedoed and sunk off the coast of Ireland. The sinking was the deadliest Canadian naval disaster of the war. 234 doctors, nurses, members of the Canadian Army Medical Corps, soldiers and seamen died in the sinking and subsequent machine-gunning of lifeboats. Only 24 people survived, all occupants of a single life-raft. The incident became infamous internationally as one of the war's worst atrocities. After the war, Llandovery Castle was one of six British cases presented at the Leipzig war crimes trials in 1919. (2 officers of U-86 were each sentenced to four years in prison. Their captain had fled to the Free City of Danzig and was never prosecuted.)

Italy
The Battle of the Piave began on 15 June as Austrian forces attacked at the request of Germany. Austrian forces crossed the river and opened a 12-mile front, but they couldn't hold it: they were suffering from a lack of food, horses and supplies, and were facing a refreshed Italian Army with support from British forces at Asiago, sent to Italy after Caporetto late in 1917. The Austro-Hungarian attack was halted at the Asiago Plateau and the Austrians withdraw after suffering 150,000 casualties. Austrian soldiers in Italy begin deserting. The Battle of the Piave ended on 24 June.

The first contingent of United States troops arrived in Italy on 30 June.

Russia
The Allies continued to see Russia as a corridor for German ambitions into the far north and east. The North Russian Expeditionary Force (NREF) created in May was bolstered by a section of British marines landed at Pechenga on the north Russian coast on 4 June. Another British force landed at Kem on the 7th.

On the same day, the Czech troops in Siberia captured Omsk, an important city on the Trans-Siberian railway. The local Bolshevik secret police had been guarding the imprisoned Grand Duke Michael Alexandrovich of Russia, together with his secretary, Nicholas Johnson, in Perm, since the revolution. The police decided that the Czech advances were a threat to the Grand Duke's imprisonment and that he might become a focus for counter-revolution if freed. On 13 June 1918, they drove him and Johnson by horse-drawn trap to Motovilikha near the railway, where they were murdered by hand gun fire. The Ural Regional Soviet approved the executions after the event as did Lenin. The Grand Duke was the first of the Romanovs to be executed by the Bolsheviks and a forerunner of later events. Neither his nor Johnson's remains were ever found.

Allied actions continued despite the 8th June order by the Russian Bolshevik Government that Allied forces must leave North Russia. Instead 2 new British forces joined the NREF on 23 June. On 30 June, Allied forces took control of the railway from Murmansk to Soroki and the local Murman People's Soviet decided to support the Allied forces against the Bolshevik Government. At the far eastern end of the Trans-Siberian Railway, a provisional government, opposed to the Bolsheviks, was set up on the 29th at Vladivostok, the Russian port on the Sea of Japan.

The Cossacks in the River Don region (Don Cossacks) declared their own independence on 4 June.

As the bulk of the Russian Black Sea Fleet had been captured by the Germans in May, the crew of the Russian battleship Svobodnaya Rossiya (*Free Russia*) scuttled the ship in the Black Sea to avoid it falling into German hands.

The New Republics

On 3 June, the British, French and Italian governments declared support for the national freedom aspirations of the Poles, Czecho-Slovaks and Yugo-Slavs within the German and Austro-Hungarian Empires. The US Government echoed this on 29 June, announcing that all branches of the Slav races should be completely freed from German and Austrian rule. And a treaty was signed on 30 June between Italy and Czecho-Slovak Council delegates recognising the Council's jurisdiction over the Czech and Slovak peoples.

On 8 June, a German force landed at Poti in Georgia. That day the Georgian government and the Armenian Council both signed peace agreements with Turkey and Georgia with Germany. German troops occupied Tiflis in Georgia on the 12th and Turkish forces occupied Kurdamir in Azerbaijan.

An armistice was agreed at Kiev on 12 June between the Ukraine and the Russian Bolshevik Republic.

Spanish 'Flu

Between June and August, Spanish 'flu spread and became pandemic. Over 30 million died in the following 6 months.

Prisoners of War

The first sitting of an Anglo-German Conference at The Hague concerning prisoners of war was held on 9 June.

Part 61: July 1918

Albert Page, serving with the Army Service Corps, was mobilised to France in July 1918 with No.6 Section, 937 Motor Transport Company and was then promoted to Sergeant with the 76th Auxiliary Motor Transport Steam Company.

Mervyn Harry Price *(pictured)*, the son of Henry and Ann Price of Restrop, Purton, had been serving with the Royal Garrison Artillery in the 153rd Siege Battery in France. He was awarded the Médaille Militaire by the French government for saving a French officer whilst under enemy fire. Mervyn's certificate is dated 21 July 1918, when he would have been 23, and is held at Purton Museum.

Western Front

Australian Army and US Army infantry, supported by British tanks made a successful attack at Le Hamel on the Somme (4 July 1918) against German positions. It was planned and commanded by the Australian Imperial Force, and lasted 93 minutes. The 5 Australian infantry brigades were augmented by 10 US Army companies to give the newly-arrived American Expeditionary Force (AEF) combat experience. Le Hamel was the first operation in which AEF troops were under a non-US command.

The final campaign of the German Spring Offensive commenced on 15 July at the River Marne (2nd Battle of the Marne) with a front stretching down to Reims (4th Battle of Champagne). 52 German divisions were assigned to the attack. However, the German attack was held. By 18 July, the German Army began to collapse on the Western Front as the battle turned into a joint French, US and Italian counter-attack (Aisne-Marne). Together with British forces in Marfaux and Buzancy (south west of Reims), they pushed the German forces back north of the Marne, retaking Château-Thierry, Soissons and Fère-en-Tardenois. (On 4 August, Corporal Adolf Hitler was presented with the Iron Cross (first class) for bravery at Soissons on the recommendation of his Jewish superior, Lieutenant Hugo Gutmann.)

Edward Pritchard McNellee was serving with the Australian Imperial Force. He was first mobilised to France in 1916 and married Ada Alice (née Bartlett) of Hillside, Purton on 18 March 1918 in Purton while on leave. He returned to France and re-joined his unit at La Kreul in May. He was wounded in the right side, chest and thigh by a shell on 20 July while taking ammunition to the front line. He died the following day, 21 July 1918. Edward is buried in Louenesse Souvenir Cemetery, St-Omer, Pas-de-Calais.

Britain

Ration books were introduced in the UK for butter, margarine, lard, meat, and sugar during July 1918. Although the war ended some 4 months later it took a while for supplies to return to normal so rationing didn't end immediately. Butter, for example, remained on ration until 1920.

As Britain was also trying to cut German access to imported food and goods, Sir Laming Worthington-Evans succeeded Lord Robert Cecil as British Minister for Blockade on 18 July. The British government had already protested to the Netherlands government (14th) against the Dutch agreement, made in May, to supply Germany with sand and gravel.

Eight tons of TNT exploded on 1 July 1918 at a National Shell Filling factory at Chilwell, Nottinghamshire. 134 people were killed, of whom only 32 could be positively identified, and a further 250 were injured. The blast was reportedly heard twenty miles away.

Russia

The Siberian Intervention was launched by the Allies on 3 July to save the Czech Legion in the Russian Civil War. The Siberian Soviet (Council) declared independence from Russia on the 4th but withdrew the declaration two days later. France, Britain and the USA signed an agreement with the Murman (Murmansk) Soviet to conduct their anti-Bolshevik expedition on the Russian north coast. Meanwhile the Czech Legion occupied Irkutsk (Siberia) on the 13th and Kazan on the 14th. A provisional government was set up at Vladivostok on the east coast on 10 July.

On 26 July, most of the French Expeditionary Force troops had arrived at Murmansk to join the North Russia Expeditionary Force. British troops took control of Archangel on the 31st.

The German Ambassador to Moscow, Count Mirbach, was murdered on 6 July at the request of the Central Committee of the Left Socialist-Revolutionaries, who wanted to reignite the war between Russia and Germany. Mirbach's assassination started the revolt of the Socialist-Revolutionaries in Moscow.

More startling on the world stage were the events over the night of 16 to 17 July, when a Bolshevik firing squad, under the command to the Cheka (secret police), executed Tsar Nicholas II, his family and several staff at the Ipatiev House (Дом Ипатьева) in Ekaterinburg in Siberia.

The War in the Air

On 9 July, the English flying ace James McCudden was killed, aged 23, in a flying accident when his plane crashed into a wood in France. In his flying career, he had downed 57 enemy planes and had been awarded the Victoria Cross, Distinguished Service Order and Bar, Military Cross and Bar, the Military Medal and the French Croix de Guerre.

Another English ace, Edward 'Mick' Mannock was killed in action on 26 July, aged 31, when his plane was hit by massive volley of ground-fire from German trenches he was flying across. He had previously been awarded the Victoria Cross, Distinguished Service Order and two Bars, and the Military Cross and Bar

A German air raid on England on 20 July caused no damage but turned out to be the last attempt to attack the British Isles with aeroplanes. During the course of the war there had been a total of 59 aeroplane raids against the British Isles during which bombs were dropped. There had also been 11 reconnaissance flights over parts of Great Britain or in the vicinity of the coast when no bombs were dropped.

The War at Sea

On 12 July, the Japanese battleship Kawachi suffered an explosion in her ammunition magazine while in Tokuyama Bay, Yamaguchi, western Honshu and sank with the loss of over 600 officers and crewmen.

RMS Carpathia, famous for having rescued survivors of the RMS Titanic in April 1912, was torpedoed and sunk off the east coast of Ireland, on 17 July, by German submarine U-55. Carpathia had departed Liverpool 2 days earlier in a convoy bound for Boston. 5 crewmen were killed but 218 of the 223 on board were rescued.

On the 19th, United States cruiser San Diego was sunk by a mine off Fire Island, Long Island USA. She sank in 28 minutes with the loss of six lives but was the only major warship lost by the United States during its involvement in the war.

On 21 July, a German submarine U-156 shelled Nauset Beach (Orleans, Massachusetts). A tug and 2 barges were destroyed but no one killed or injured.

Turkey
The Ottoman Emperor, Sultan Mehmed V Reşâd died on 3 July having reigned since 1909. His half-brother Mehmed VI Vahidettin became emperor.

Other News
Haiti and Honduras both declared war on Germany during July, on the 12th and 19th respectively.

Part 62: August 1918

The War at Sea
On 3 August, Australian troop ship HMT Warilda was carrying wounded from Le Havre to Southampton and was clearly marked by red crosses. It was sunk by a German submarine and 149 aboard lost their lives. One of these was **Reginald Arthur Jones**, aged 30, a former gamekeeper of Braydon, Purton. He had been serving in Egypt with the Army Service Corps, 2nd Battalion the Loyal North Lancashire Regiment and was being returned to England via France with malaria. Reginald's grave is the English Channel but he is remembered on the Hollybrook Memorial, Southampton.

Western Front
The 2nd Battle of the Marne had turned from defence into an Allied offensive in July. Three French armies and 5 American divisions forced the Germans to withdraw their armies from the Marne by 3 August. French forces had already retaken Soissons on 1 August. General Ferdinand Foch was declared a Marshal of France on the 6th as a result of these victories under his command.

On the 8th, Canadian, Australian, British and French forces broke through German lines with 600 tanks at the Battle of Amiens (Montdidier in the French sector). The RAF dropped 1,563 bombs and fired 122,150 rounds of ammunition in support of ground troops who forced the German troops back to the Hindenburg Line. German General Ludendorff referred to this as the "Black Day of the German Army". The German command threw in their final reserves, but the Allies continued to push forward in a string of victories which became known as the "Hundred Days Offensive".

On 11 August, the 15th Battalion Tank Corps was at Dog Wood, near Villers-Bretonneux, where they were resting and maintaining tanks for the next operation. **Albert Leach**, son of Thomas and Sarah Leach, of Wootton Bassett Road, Purton, died of wounds, aged 31, on 11 August. A family story tells that Albert was run over by his tank while he was sleeping underneath it together with another tank man. Albert was buried in Adelaide Cemetery, Villers-Bretonneux. Albert is remembered on the Purton War Memorial and on the memorials in St Mary's Church.

The Battle of Amiens ended on 12 August and is regarded as the last great battle on the Western Front. The last bombardment of Paris by the Kaiser Gun occurred on 15 August.

The French began a new offensive on 17 August (2nd Battle of Noyon) and the British advanced in Flanders on the 18th (Outtersteene Ridge). Over the next few weeks, Allied forces retook Merville, Noyon, the Aisne Heights, Albert and Roye with particular successes for the Canadians who broke through the Hindenburg Line on 28 August.

The 2nd Batle of the Somme started on 21 August with the 2nd Battle of Bapaume. **Frederick Thomas Bailey** *(pictured)* was born in Purton, though his parents had moved to Brinkworth and his family home by 1918 was at Cambria Place in Swindon. Frederick was serving with the 10th Battalion, Tank Corps attached to the New Zealand Division which had 8 tanks in action on 25 August. Their objective was to secure the Bapaume road and move east if possible. Five tanks reached their objectives and the New Zealanders occupied Bapaume the next day. The highly strategic position of Mount Kemmel was evacuated by the Germans on 31 August.

Frederick was killed in action on 25 August, aged 30, and is buried in Grevillers British Cemetery, Pas de Calais. His name is included on Swindon's Roll of Honour.

The War in the Air
A raid on England on 5 August was the last one and the airship involved (L70) was destroyed. Over the war there had been 51 airship raids (plus 8 attempted raids) against the UK in which bombs had been dropped. On 11 August, L53 became the last German airship to be destroyed in the war when it was shot down off the Dutch Frisian coast.

USA
The only battle of the Great War to be fought on United States soil occurred on 27 August, when US Army forces skirmished against the Mexican Army and militias and their German advisors at Nogales, Arizona. The American victory resulted in the establishment of a permanent and agreed border between Mexico and the USA.

Britain
20,000 London policemen went on strike on 30 August for increased pay and union recognition. Inconceivable in previous years, it showed the growing strength of the union movement as well as a realisation at home that the end of the war was close.

Russia
The allied intervention in Russia continued with the Expeditionary Force capturing Archangel on 1 August and sparking a pro-Entente (anti-Bolshevik) revolution there on the next day.

On the Pacific coast, British troops landed at Vladivostok on 3 August and were reinforced by the arrival of Japanese troops on the 11th. Meanwhile the British government had issued a statement (6 August) to the Russian people that it had no intention of interfering with Russian politics, despite its already having troops in north and south Russia and at Vladivostok. In fact, on 10 August, the British commander in Archangel received instructions to help the White Russians (anti-Bolsheviks). Not everything was going the allies' way and on 16 August a force of US troops were overrun at Archangel by Bolshevik troops.

The same day, however, the Czechoslovak legion fought a successful battle at Lake Baikal (Siberia) against the Red Army.

On 24 August, the White Russian leader at Vladivostok, General Dmitry Horvath, organised a coup d'état and on the same day, at Dukhovskaya (130 miles north of Vladivostok), Bolshevik forces were defeated by a combined allied force of French, Czech, Cossack and Japanese troops together with one British battalion.

The Russian capitals were not safe either. On 17 August, Moisei Uritsky, the Petrograd head of the secret police (Cheka) was assassinated. Lenin himself was shot and wounded, in Moscow on 30 October, by Fanny Kaplan a member of the Socialist Revolutionary Party, but he survived. These events spurred the Soviet government to reinstate the death penalty after it had been abolished in October 1917 - Fanny was executed by firing squad on 3 November.

On the 31st, Captain Cromie, the British Naval Attaché, was murdered by Bolsheviks at the British Embassy in Petrograd.

The New Republics
On 13 August, the Czecho-Slovak people declared war on Germany and the British government formally recognised them as an Allied nation. Czechoslovakia didn't become an independent country until October 1918 after declaration of independence from Austria-Hungary at Prague.

Part 63: September 1918
The following men with Purton connections were mobilised in September 1918.

To France: Walter Evelyn Ovens, Tank Corps.

Royal Navy: Laurence Leonard Mills, Royal Marine Artillery.

Western Front
By 3 September, British, Canadian and Australian forces had recaptured Péronne, Drocourt, Quéant, Lens, Arras and Bapaume. Canadian troops continued to advance in their sector past the Hindenburg Line and the Allied objectives of the 2nd Battle of the Somme were completed.

The first large-scale Allied offensive carried out separately by the American Expeditionary Force (AEF) on the Western Front commenced on 12 September at St Mihiel. The US forces cleared the St Mihiel salient, during which the greatest air assault of the war was launched by the US with 1,476 Allied aircraft. US forces occupied St Mihiel on the 16th.

A series of Allied offensives to overcome the Hindenburg Line also began on 12 September with the Battle of Havrincourt, and on the 18th with the Battle of Epéhy. **Ernest Hesketh Harrison** *(pictured)* was serving with the 8th (Service) Battalion East Surrey Regiment. He was the husband of Alice (née Partiger) of Hill House, Purton and the son of the Vicar at St Mary's the Reverend Robert and Mrs Marguerite Harrison, of the Vicarage, Purton. Ernest was promoted to full Captain having been temporary captain. He was Brigade Bombing Officer,  responsible for maintaining stocks of grenades in the front-line trenches, and training hand-grenade specialist Bombers within the Brigade.

Ernest was killed in action, aged 26 on 18 September 1918, during the Battle of Épehy, involving the British Fourth Army against German outpost positions in front of the Hindenburg Line. He is buried in Peronne Communal Cemetery Extension, Somme, France, having originally been buried at Lieramont near Épehy. He is also listed on the War Memorial in Aston Abbotts near Aylesbury and on the Purton War Memorial and the Memorials in St Mary's Church.

On the 15th, the German Government made a peace offer to Belgium, which was rejected.

The Allied advances on the Hindenburg Line continued through late September with the Battle of the Canal du Nord, the Battle of the Flanders Peaks and the 5th Battle of Ypres, breaking out of the Ypres salient and recapturing Messines, Passchendaele and Diksmuide by the 28th.

John Ranby Brown was serving with the 102nd Battalion, 4th Canadian Division with the rank of temporary Lieutenant. John was born in Harleston, Suffolk, and was married to Azeela Ellen Brown of Rose Cottage, Purton. His parents were Edward Cyril and Isabel Brown of The Cottage, Church End, Purton.

On 26 September 1918, the Battalion moved to its assembly point prior to "the most glorious operation" in its history, the capture of Bourlon Wood. The Battalion was in the Hindenburg support line from which they advanced to Inchey-en-Artois and into action at 06:00 hrs on the 27th. The Battalion suffered 8 officers and 44 other ranks killed, with 8 officers and 151 other ranks wounded. The Battalion Diary recorded the day a "great success" with 157 Germans captured along with 15 field guns and 18 machine guns. John was among those killed in this action, aged 38, when he was struck by fragments from an enemy shell while advancing his platoon along the south edge of the wood. He is buried in Bourlon Wood Cemetery, Pas-de-Calais, France and is remembered on the Purton War Memorial and the Memorials in St Mary's Church.

On the 29th, the Battle of the St Quentin Canal was one of the "finest feats of arms" as British forces crossed the canal at Riqueval, and General Haig's forces achieved a decisive breakthrough of the Hindenburg Line. On 30 September, the German Imperial Chancellor Count Hertling resigned.

Further south, on 26 September, French, Siamese and US forces began the Meuse-Argonne offensive in Champagne and Argonne. This was the final Franco-American offensive of the war but, with more than 1.2 million American soldiers, it was their largest and most costly: 26,277 Americans were killed, 95,786 wounded, 70,000 French casualties and 19 killed from the Siamese Expeditionary Force. (Siam entered the war in July 1917 and Siamese contingent began operations on the Western Front in September 1918. Siamese troops also contributed to the initial occupation of the Rhineland, occupying Neustadt an der Haardt.)

The War in the Air
A German aeroplane raid on Paris on 16 September was the last one of the war.

The War at Sea
HMS Glatton was a coastal defence ship originally ordered by the Norwegian navy but never delivered because of the outbreak of war in 1914. Recently completed and never having seen service, the ship suffered a fire in one of her gun magazines in Dover harbour on 16 September resulting in a massive explosion. The ship was scuttled to prevent an even larger explosion which would have destroyed the harbour. Between 57 and 80 men died on board. The wreck was moved after the war to the north-eastern end of the harbour where it would not obstruct shipping. It was buried under landfill during the construction of the current car ferry terminal.

Austro-Hungarian Fronts
French and Italian forces began an offensive in Austrian-occupied Albania on 6 July, capturing Berat soon after. However, the offensive came to a halt on 22 August and the Austrians counter-attacked on the 26th, retaking Berat.

The Serbian army started a new front against Austria on 14 September in coordination with Allied operations in Macedonia (15-16 September). The Battle of Dobropolje was followed by expansion into Macedonia at Monastir and Doiran, occupied by British forces on 22 September. French forces captured Prilep in south Serbia on the 23rd and the Serbs took back Ishtip and Veles on the 25th. The Italian government recognised an independent Yugo-Slav State on the 25th.

The Battle of the Vardar saw Serb, Czech, Italian, French and British forces fighting Bulgarian forces, Austria's ally, on 26 September. This offensive was so successful that the Bulgarian government asked the Allies for an Armistice on 27 September. Negotiations were swiftly concluded and the armistice was agreed. Hostilities between Bulgaria and the Entente Powers ended at noon on 30 September. King Ferdinand I of Bulgaria abdicated on 3 October and was succeeded by his son Boris II.

The loss of its ally put Austria-Hungary under added pressure. They had already send a note to US President Wilson on 15 September requesting peace discussions. Wilson rejected the request on 16 September.

Palestine & Mesopotamia

The Ottoman Empire also came under renewed pressure from British and Arab forces. The Battle of Megiddo (18-19 September) broke the Ottoman front from the Mediterranean coast to the Judaean Mountains. The Allied forces moved into the Jordan Valley and towards Nazareth and Beisan which were occupied by the British Indian Army's 4th and 5th Cavalry Divisions on the 20th. By the 23rd, British and Australian forces had captured Jenin, Haifa, Acre and Es Salt in Palestine and the Turkish garrison abandoned Ma'an near Amman on the Hejaz railway to Arabia. British forces cut the Hejaz railway line at Amman on 25 September.

The 3rd Transjordan attack ended on 25 September: the ANZAC Mounted Division was victorious at the 2nd Battle of Amman and captured more than 10,000 Ottoman and German prisoners.

Russia

Further landings were made early in the month by US and Italian troops in the north (Murmansk and Archangel) and in the far east at Vladivostok. The Allied Expeditionary Force made territorial gains in these areas. A Canadian contingent landed at Archangel on 30 September.

The Russian Red Army defeated the White Army at Kazan on the River Volga between 5-10 September consolidating the city under Soviet control and solidifying the Red Army's power in Russia over the White Army and enabling strategic Red Army offensives westwards.

The New Republics

The United States government recognised the Czech-Slovak people as having a *de facto* government on 3 September.

Part 64: October 1918

Western Front

It was a dark month for Purton with the deaths of 10 men.

Allied offensives continued on the Western Front. In the north, French forces recaptured Saint-Quentin, and the British took the Canal du Nord and the St Quentin Canal by 2 October. The 5th Battle of Ypres ended on 2 October and British forces recaptured Armentières on the 3rd. **William New** was born in Purton in 1894, the son of Richard and Annie New who lived at Westcott Place, Swindon by the time of William's enlistment. He was serving with 'D' Battery, 84th Brigade, Royal Field Artillery and died of wounds on 3 October 1918 aged 24. He is buried at Tincourt New British Cemetery, Somme, France and is named on Swindon`s Roll of Honour.

A new British offensive started on 3 October, the Battle of the Beaurevoir Line which lasted until 5 October. **Herbert Stanley Woolford** was the son of Alfred and Catherine Woolford of Widham. He had served with the 6th (Service)

Battalion, Royal Munster Fusiliers at Gallipoli in 1915 and later in Palestine. The 6th was absorbed into the 2nd Battalion and by 2 October was near Épehy. On 4 October, at 02:00 hrs, the Battalion was ordered to attack and capture the village of La Pannerie. The Munsters moved forward to Le Catelet at 05:10 hrs and were involved in street fighting that led to heavy casualties. Herbert, aged 23, was among those killed in action. He is buried in Templeux-le-Guerard British Cemetery, Somme and is remembered on the Purton War Memorial and in the Memorials in St Mary's Church.

Mervyn Thomas Webb was born in 1896, the son of James and Sarah Webb of Upper Square, Purton. He was serving with 'A' Battery, 186th Brigade Royal Field Artillery. Mervyn died of wounds caused in action on 5 October 1918, aged 23, and is buried at Terlincthun Cemetery, Wimille, Pas-de-Calais, France. He is remembered on the Purton War Memorial and the Memorials in St Mary's Church, and is listed on Swindon's Roll of Honour.

British and Canadian troops pushed forward in the 2nd Battle of Cambrai (8-10 October). Cambrai itself was captured on the 9th and British troops advanced to the last line of trenches in the Hindenburg Line. **Herbert Martin** was born in Hilmarton in 1891, the son of Edward and Annie Martin of Widham Cottage, Purton. He was serving with the 13th (Service) Battalion (2nd Rhondda), Welsh Regiment and was killed in action, aged 23, on 8 October 1918. Herbert was buried at Villers Cotterets, Cambrai. After the war, his grave was moved to a larger cemetery, Prospect Hill Cemetery, Gouy, Aisne, France. Herbert is remembered on the Purton War Memorial and in the Memorials in S Mary's Church.

Albert Victor Fishlock was born in Purton in 1898, the son of Henry and Dorcis Fishlock. His Service record shows his father living "somewhere in Swindon" whilst his mother (recorded as Jane Spanerwicke), brothers and sister all lived in Pontnewydd, Monmouthshire. Albert had served with the 1st Battalion (Territorial force) Monmouthshire Regiment at the 2nd Battle of Ypres (1915) where he was wounded in action, with a gunshot wound (shrapnel) to his hand, thigh and chest. By June 1918 he was serving again in France with the Machine Gun Corps. Albert was killed in action, aged 20, on 8 October 1918 and is buried at Sequehart British Cemetery No.1, Aisne and is named on Swindon's Roll of Honour.

Valentine W Oakley Brown was born in Cheltenham in 1896, the son of Mr A C Oakley Brown and Alice Oakley Brown, Norbury, Purton. He was serving with the 6th Cavalry Brigade of the 3rd Dragoon Guards (Prince of Wales' Own). On 9 October, his brigade was ordered to attack and take the villages of Honnechy and Reumont and push onto the ridge west of Le Cateau. Valentine was killed in action during the cavalry charge at Honnechy, aged 22. During the action which lasted only a few hours, 2 officers and 2 other ranks were killed with the loss of 90 horses. Valentine is buried in Busigny Communal Cemetery, Nord, France and is remembered on the War Memorial in Cheltenham as well as the Purton War Memorial and the Memorials in St Mary's Church.

Edward George Mills was the son of George E and Mary Mills of Lower Pavenhill, Purton. He was serving with 'K' Battery Royal Horse Artillery and was killed in action on 10 October 1918, aged 25. Edward is buried in Highland Cemetery, Le Cateau, Nord and is remembered on the Purton War Memorial and the Memorials in St Mary's Church.

On 8 October, in the Argonne offensive (started 26 September) U.S. Corporal Alvin C. York was one of a group of 17 US soldiers assigned to infiltrate German lines and silence a machine gun position in the Argonne Forest. After capturing a large group of German soldiers, the US patrol came under small arms fire killing 6 Americans and wounding 3. York took charge of the patrol. He left his men guarding the prisoners, and single-handedly attacked the machine gun position, killing many German soldiers with his rifle. He was out of rifle ammunition by then and, when attacked by 6 more Germans, he shot them with his pistol. The German officer in charge of the machine gun position surrendered. York and his men marched back to their unit's command post with more than 130 prisoners. York was immediately promoted to sergeant and was awarded the Distinguished Service Cross, later upgraded to the Medal of Honor. York became a national hero. The Argonne offensive ended on 15 October.

Further advances were made in Belgium with French and British forces recapturing Craonne on the Chemin des Dames ridge on 12 October followed by Laon, La Fère, Courtrai (Kortrijk), Roulers (Roeselare), Menin, Lille, Douai, and Ostende by the 17th. On 14 October, German troops had started to abandon the Belgian coastline. Belgian forces recaptured Zeebrugge and Bruges and secured the entire Belgian coast by the 20th.

Charles Henry Skuse was serving with the 10th (Service) Battalion, Sherwood Foresters. He was born in Purton in 1879, the son of Henry and Elizabeth Skuse who are recorded as living in Birmingham. Charles was killed in action, aged 39, on 20 October 1918, and is buried in Neuvilly Communal Cemetery Extension, Nord. 16 men of the 10th Battalion died on that date.

Alfred W Matthews was born in Purton in 1894, the son of Mr Alfred W and Mrs Emily J Matthews of Marston Meysey, Cricklade. He had served with the 5th Wilts at Gallipoli in 1915 and later transferred to the 2nd Battalion, Leinster Regiment. On 19 October 1918, the 2nd Leinsters crossed the Lys between Courtrai and Harelbeke, and the following day captured the villages of Staceghem and Steenbrugge. They faced heavy fire east of Staceghem but by 9.20a.m. the Leinsters had gained 5000 yards and captured 40 prisoners, 6 machine guns and 1 field gun. 3 officers and 70 other ranks were wounded and 6 other ranks killed. Alfred was one of the casualties in this action and died of wounds received, aged 22, on 21 October 1918. He is buried in Dadizeele New British Cemetery, Moorslede, Belgium.

Prisoner of War

William Charles Eveleigh, was born in Somerset, the son of Thomas and Mercy Eveleigh. His father was a railway signalman which possibly brought the family to Wiltshire. William's wife, Eva, lived at 5 Station Road, Purton. Serving with the 6th Battalion Wiltshire Regiment, he had been taken Prisoner of War on 10 April at Wytschaete, while the Battalion was holding trenches east of the Messines-Wytschaete ridge. He was held in Freidrichsfeld POW camp in Germany run by the German 7th Army Corps. William *(pictured)* died, whilst a Prisoner of War, aged 30, on 24 October 1918. There is no recorded grave but he is remembered on the Tyne Cot Memorial, Flanders, Belgium. The POW records held by the Red Cross in Geneva do not record any details of William's death but

1918

family record had it that he was moved by train as the Germans fell back and he was put into a cattle truck for the move. At Potsdam he was found to have died and removed from the train. He may indeed have died of starvation, as many POWs did, due to a general lack of food as Germany was squeezed under the Allied naval blockade. The story is covered in more detail in Bob Lloyd's book.

William is remembered on the Purton War Memorial and in the Memorials in St Mary's Church.

Austro-Hungarian Fronts
Italian forces recaptured Berat in Albania on 1 October and the Strait of Otranto between the heel of Italy. The Albanian coast was closed by an Allied sea mine and net barrage, isolating Austrian Adriatic ports from outside assistance. Durazzo on the Albanian coast was bombarded by British and Italian warships on the 2nd.

Major advances were made by Serbian, Italian, French and British forces recapturing Vranje, Pristina, Prizren, Nish and Novi Bazar in Serbia, Elbasan, Durazzo, San Giovanni di Medua and Scutari in Albania and Ipek in Kosovo.

The Battle of Vittorio Veneto started on 24 October on the Italian front, capturing the city on 30 October, and ending on 3 November. (See Part 65.)

On 16 October, the Austrian Emperor issued a manifesto proclaiming a Federal State for the Austrian half of the empire on the principle of Nationality, - this did not cover Hungary which was autonomous.

The last few days of October saw the Empire fall apart. On 30 October the Hungarian government surrendered Fiume (Rijeka) to the local Croatians: but the self-styled National Council of Fiume proclaimed the independence of the city and announced their wish for union with Italy while the Croatian Congress (Sabor) held firm to the Yugo-Slav declaration of independence.

There were Revolutions in Vienna and Budapest on the 31st and Count Tisza, a Hungarian pro-Empire politician, was assassinated in Vienna. The Hungarian government terminated the union with Austria, officially dissolving the Austro-Hungarian Empire the same day. Also on the 31st, the Austrian Emperor handed over control of the Adriatic fleet to the Yugo-Slav National Council.

Requests for Armistice
Germany and Austria-Hungary both sent notes (3-4 October) to US President Woodrow Wilson requesting an armistice based on Wilson's 'Fourteen Points'.

The German note was received by Wilson on 6 October and the Austrian one on the 7th.

Kaiser Wilhelm II of Germany formed a new and more liberal government to pursue a peace policy. Key to this was the appointment of Prince Maximillian of Baden as Imperial Chancellor of Germany on 4 October with the combined role of Foreign Minister.

President Wilson replied to the German and Austro-Hungarian notes on 8 October demanding evacuation of occupied territories as a first condition of any armistice. The German government replied on the 12th that it would accept those conditions. Wilson added military conditions for talks (14 October) and stated he would deal only with a democratic government. This was accepted by Germany on the 20th and Germany ceased unrestricted submarine warfare on the 21st. On this basis, Wilson replied on 23 October that he would submit the matter to the Allied governments.

Germany's supreme commander General Eric Ludendorff resigned on 26 October in protest against the terms to which the German Government had agreed prior to negotiating an armistice.

On the 27th, the Austrian government asked Italy for an armistice and also asked President Wilson for an immediate general armistice "without awaiting the result of other negotiations."

Ottoman Empire

Allied forces advanced through Palestine, Transjordan and Syria. Damascus was captured on 1 October by Australian forces of the Desert Mounted Corps and the Arab forces of the Sharif of Mecca's third son Prince Feisal, with Lt-Col T.E. Lawrence as his advisor and British liaison officer.

In the following days, the Allied forces advanced through Sidon, Beirut (taken by French forces), and Tripoli in Syria. On 14 October, the Turkish Government sent a Note to President Wilson requesting an armistice.

Homs in Syria fell to British cavalry on 15 October. British forces advanced on Mosul in northern Mesopotamia and took Kirkuk on the 25th. Meanwhile Prince Feisal's forces captured Aleppo.

Turkey and the Allied powers met at the end of October at Mudros on the island of Lemnos and signed an armistice on 30 October ending the war with the Ottoman Empire. The Turkish army surrendered on the River Tigris and the Mutawakkilite Kingdom of Yemen was granted independence from the Ottoman Empire by the Mudros treaty. Hostilities officially ceased at noon on the 31st.

The War at Sea

Armed merchant cruiser HMS Otranto sank on 6 October following a collision with HMS Kashmir off the Isle of Islay, Scotland, with the deaths of 425 crew. The Mail Ship Leinster was sunk in the Irish Sea on the 10th by German submarine with the loss of 501 lives.

On 15 October the British Q-ship Cymric sank a British submarine (J6) in error. Q-ships were merchant vessels with heavy armaments, intended to lure German submarines to the surface and then sink them. In this incident, Cymric mistook the conning tower identity lettering 'J6' for a German 'U6'. 5 crew on J6 were killed.

Russia

In the east of Russia, British forces advancing from Vladivostok occupied Irkutsk on 14 October and Omsk on the 18th. The Red Army was more successful in the west when the Russian 10th Army drove the White armies out of Tsaritsyn (later named Stalingrad, now Volgograd).

The New Republics

The Polish Regency Council declared Polish independence from the German Empire on 7 October and demanded that Germany cede the provinces of Poznań, Upper Silesia and Polish Pommerania. On the 12th, the British government recognised the Polish national army as autonomous and a member of the allied nations. On 28 October, the Poles declared a new government in Western Galicia.

Yugoslavia proclaimed itself a republic on 17 October and the King of Montenegro declared his support on the 26th for a confederated Yugoslavia. On 29 October the Yugo-Slav National Council declared the independence of the Yugo-Slavs from Austria-Hungary.

The Czechs declared independence from Austria-Hungary on the 18th and Slovakia was included in the formation of the Czechoslovakian state on the 30th. A short-lived Banat Republic was founded on 31 October in territory on the borders between Rumania, Hungary and Serbia.

Other News

On 4 October, an explosion at Morgan Munitions Factory in New Jersey killed 100 workers and destroyed enough ammunition to have supplied the Western Front for 6 months.

Sir Cecil Chubb, the last private owner of Stonehenge, donated the monument to the British nation on 26 October.

The Spanish 'flu virus killed 21,000 people in the USA in the last week of October 1918 alone.

Part 65: November 1918

Western Front

Following Cambrai, the British First Army advanced on Valenciennes on the way to Mons. The battle lasted two days and Valenciennes was captured on 3 November.

On 4 November, British forces attacked at the River Sambre, in Picardy. **Joseph John Woolford** was the son of Arthur John and Clara Frances A Woolford of 1 Stanley Cottages, Pavenhill, and serving with "A" Battery, 312th Brigade Royal Field Artillery. Joseph died, aged 19, on 8 November 1918 of wounds received at the Sambre. The North Wilts Herald reported he had been in

EVENING SWINDON ADVERTISER

MONDAY, NOVEMBER 11, 1918.

THIRD EDITION.

4.30 p.m.

LATEST TELEGRAMS.

(Per Exchange Telegraph Company and from Our Own Correspondents.)

THE ARMISTICE TERMS.

BELGIUM TO BE EVACUATED

RHINELAND TO BE EVACUATED

ALSACE AND LORRAINE AND LUXEMBOURG TO BE FREED

ALLIES TO OCCUPY HELIGOLAND.

The Prime Minister on entering the House of Commons, this afternoon, was greeted with tremendous cheering by a full House.

Mr. Lloyd George rose, when the cheering had subsided, to announce the terms of the Armistice as follows :—

The immediate evacuation of Belgium, Alsace and Lorraine and Luxembourg.

Evacuation by the enemy of Rhineland to be completed within 16 days.

The release of Alsace and Lorraine to be immediate.

Repatriation by the Germans of Allied and United States prisoners.

All German troops in Russia, Rumania and elsewhere to be withdrawn. Complete abandonment of the Treaties of Bukharest and Brest-Litovsk.

Immediate cessation of all hostilities at sea. Handing over to Allies and United States of all submarines.

The surrender by the German government of the following equipment : - 5000 guns, of which 2500 will be heavy and 2500 field guns. 30,000 machine guns, and a large number of trench mortars.

Six battle cruisers. ten battleships. eight light cruisers. and "other services" are to be disarmed. and the Allies reserve the right to occupy Heligoland to enable them to enforce the terms of the armistice.

OTHER CROWNS GONE.

(Per Exchange Co.)
Paris. Monday.

A message from Geneva says that Hesse has declared for a republic.

Berne reports that the King of Wurtembug, fearing a hostile attitude of the people, left for an unknown destination.

THE KAISER'S ABDICATION

FLIGHT TO HOLLAND.

(Admiralty, per Wireless Press)

The following historic announcement was made on Saturday through the German wireless service :—

The German Imperial Chancellor, Prince Max of Baden, has issued the following decree :—

"The Kaiser and King has decided to renounce the Throne.

"The Imperial Chancellor will remain in office until the questions connected with the abdication of the Kaiser. the renouncing by the Crown Prince of the Throne of the German Empire and of Prussia, and the setting up of a Regency have been settled.

"For the Regency, he intends to appoint Deputy Ebert as Imperial Chancellor, and he proposes that a Bill be brought in for the establishment of a lawproviding for the immediate promulgation of general suffrage, and for a Constitutional German National Assembly which will settle finally the future form of government of the German nation and of those peoples which might be desirous of coming within the Empire.

– The Imperial Chancellor, Prince Max of Baden.

Berlin, Nov. 9th, 1918

THE KAISER SIGNS ACT OF ABDICATION IN PRESENCE OF HINDENBURG

Amsterdam, Saturday.

The Kaiser signed a letter of abdication this morning at Headquarters in the presence of the Crown Prince and Hindenburg. The Crown Prince signed a renunciation, shortly afterwards. Both are expected to take leave of the troops to-day. – Exchange.

Mr. H. W. Smith, the "Daily News" Special Correspondent in Holland, telegraphing yesterday afternoon, says :—

I have just received a message from a correspondent at Evsden on the South Limburg frontier, stating that the ex-Kaiser crossed into Holland in a motor car shortly after 11 o'clock this morning.

There has been much speculation in Holland for many months as to the likelihood of the ex-Kaiser seeking refuge in this country. Two months ago, rumours were current that preparations were being made at the Castle of Middachten north-east of Arnhem, which was said to have been purchased from the Bentinck.

The castle, whither the fallen monarch and his suite are now stated to be found. dates back to 1315, but has been repeatedly rebuilt and extended. It now consists of a quadrangle in brick, surrounded by a moat.

A message from Maastricht (5 miles north of Evsden states that the Kaiser is there, awaiting the decision of the Dutch Government as to his further movements. With him are the Kaiserin and the Crown Prince and their suite. They crossed the frontier without hindrance due to the fact that it is only weakly guarded by the Dutch. The German guards on the other side were withdrawn only yesterday.

HERR BALLIN DEAD

Rotterdam, Sunday.

The Hamburg correspondent of the "Nieuwe Rotterdamse Courant" telegraphs that Herr Ballin, the German shipping magnate, has died suddenly from syncope.

ANOTHER AIR V. C.

PILOT'S MAGNIFICENT STRUGGLE.

The Victoria Cross has been awarded to Capt. Ferdinand M.F. West, M. C., R.A.F., "in recognition of his outstanding bravery in aerial combat."

Capt. West is the airman who, while engaging hostile troops at a low altitude far over the enemy lines, was attacked by seven aircraft and early in the flight had one of his legs partly severed by an explosive bullet.

Lifting his disabled leg, which had fallen among the controls and rendered the machine unmanageable, he regained control of his aeroplane and, although wounded in the other leg, enabled his observer to drive away the enemy craft. Desperately wounded as he was, Captain West landed safely in our lines but fainted from exhaustion. On recovering consciousness he insisted on writing his report.

PEACE !

ARMISTICE SIGNED !

STATEMENT BY THE PREMIER.

Hostilities to cease at 11 o'clock to = day.

The long-expected news of an Armistice being declared has at last been received, and the following historical message has just been received:

The Armistice was signed at Five o'clock this morning, and hostilities are to cease on all Fronts at 11 a.m. to-day.

TO-DAY'S BRITISH OFFICIAL.

CAPTURE OF MONS.

CANADIAN TROOPS ENGAGED.

The following message from Sir Douglas Haig was issued in France at 10-19 a.m. to-day :

"Shortly before dawn this morning Canadian Troops of the First Army, under General Horne, captured Mons."

GENERAL FOCH'S MESSAGE TO THE ALLIED TROOPS.

The following message from Marshal Foch to the Commanders-in-Chief was transmitted to the wireless stations of the French Government :

"Hostilities will cease on the whole Front as from November 11th, at 11 a.m. French time).

"Allied Troops will not until further orders go beyond the line reached at that date and that hour.

"(Signed),
"MARSHAL FOCH."

The following message has been issued from German Plenipotentiaries to the German High Command :

"To be communicated to all authorities interested.

"Armistice was signed at five o'clock in the morning (French time), which comes into force at 11 a.m.

This page is a re-typed compilation of the War articles on page 3 of the 3rd edition of the Evening Swindon Advertiser from 11 Nov. 1918. Originals are now longer held as a newspaper archive and are available from Swindon Central Library, Local Studies Section on micro film.

France for only a short time. He is buried in Maubeuge-Centre Cemetery and is remembered on the Purton War Memorial, the Memorials in St Mary's Church and Swindon's Roll of Honour.

Also at the Sambre, the celebrated war poet Wilfred Owen, serving with the 2nd Battalion, Manchester Regiment, was killed in action on 4 November, during the crossing of the Sambre-Oise Canal.

Further Allied advances quickly followed, together with a general German retreat along the Meuse from 5 November. The same day Marshal Foch was placed in supreme strategic command of all forces operating against Germany. French forces recaptured Rethel and Mezières; United States forces captured Sedan; and Belgian troops reoccupied Ghent on 9 November. The British captured Maubeuge and Canadian forces retook Mons in Belgium on the morning of 11 November.

Armistice in the West

On 3 November, the Allied governments agreed to German proposals for an armistice based on acceptance of President Wilson's "14 Points" of January 1918.

With the military setbacks in the previous months and hunger and shortages back home, sailors in the German High Seas Fleet, based at Kiel, mutinied on 3 November. Soldiers and workers throughout northern Germany began to establish revolutionary councils on the Russian soviet model.

On the 5th, Wilson sent a final Note to the German Government indicating the Allies' acceptance of the armistice proposals. The German delegation arrived at Compiègne Forest in France, on 8 November. They were handed the armistice terms on board Ferdinand Foch's railway carriage headquarters.

While the final terms were being discussed, the German army withdrew its support for the Kaiser on 8 November. Revolution broke out in Berlin and on 9 November the Chancellor, Prince Maximillian, announced the Kaiser's decision to abdicate. Prince Maximillian became Regent while Friedrich Ebert of the Social Democratic Party (SDP) became Chancellor of the new German Republic.

On the 10th, the Kaiser crossed the frontier to live in exile in neutral Netherlands.

All this led to the conclusion of the Armistice which was signed on 11 November between the Allied and Germany. It was signed in Marshal Foch's special train at Compiègne. Hostilities on the Western Front ceased at 11a.m. (Paris Time) on the 11th day of the 11th month of 1918.

The news was too late for the morning newspapers, so the Evening Swindon Advertiser Standard was one of the first to carry the news. The illustration on page 190 shows the main stories from page 3 that day - pages 1 and 2 of course were solely advertisements at that time.

(As the archives are now held on microfilm, it has not been possible to reproduce the actual broadsheet newspaper page in any readable form,. So that the information there is at least readable, I have retyped the stories in a close representation of the layout and fonts used at the time. However, you may need a magnifying glass for some of the smallest print!)

German Front - Post-Armistice

One of the terms of the armistice was the complete removal of all German forces from occupied territories and the placing of the Rhineland under Allied occupation. While the Germans withdrew, the Allied armies commenced their march towards Germany. With no resistance, Belgian troops re-entered Brussels on 18 November. The Belgian Government was reinstated in Brussels on 21 November, with Léon Delacroix succeeding as Prime Minister. King Albert I made a triumphal procession through Brussels also on 21 November. He had commanded the Allied Army group in October's Courtrai offensive.

The last German troops left Belgium on 26 November but as they were withdrawing munitions and equipment, two German ammunition trains exploded in Hamont, Belgium on 21 November, killing 1,750.

The war may have been over but Purton men and their families were still seeing the consequences of war. **Charles William Parsons** was the son of Charles and Mary Anne Parsons, of Bentham Lane, Purton, though when he enlisted he was living in Wool, Dorset. He was serving with the 10th (Service) Battalion, King's Own Scottish Borderers when he died of pneumonia, aged 22, on 25 November 1918. He is buried in St André Communal Cemetery, Nord, France and is remembered on the Purton Parish War Memorial and the Memorials in St Mary's Church.

Elijah Cook was the son of Thomas and Ellen Cook of Pavenhill, Purton. He was serving with the 2/8th (Territorial Force) Battalion, Worcestershire Regiment with the 182nd Brigade. After the war ended, his Brigade was moved by train from Cambrai on 24 November for rest and retraining. As the journey continued on 26 November, the railway engine left the line, coaches violently collided and one of them was crushed. Elijah, aged 18, and 4 others were killed and six more were seriously injured. All 5 were originally buried in Cramont village near the crash site, but later the bodies were moved to Terlincthun British Cemetery, Pas-de-Calais, on the cliffs overlooking the English Channel. Elijah is remembered on the Purton War Memorial and the Memorials in St Mary's Church.

There were several inconsistencies in his records: he is recorded on the War Memorial as P. Cook, as Percy in the Memorial Book, and G. Cook on his headstone. Bob Lloyd brought these inconsistencies to the attention of the Commonwealth War Graves Commission who will replace or amend his headstone. These and other inconsistencies are covered in detail in Bob's book.

Following the 11 November Armistice, Russia cancelled the Treaty of Brest-Litovsk on 13 November.

Austro-Hungary

On 1 November, an independent government of Hungary was formed in Budapest now that Hungary was no longer part of the Austro-Hungarian Empire.

Unaware that the Austrian fleet had been handed over to the Yugo-Slav National Council on 31 October, next day two men of the Italian Navy planted mines on the side of a battleship, the former SMS Viribus Unitis, now renamed the Jugoslavija. They were discovered and taken prisoner. They informed the new captain that the explosives were set to go off at 6.30a.m. and the ship was evacuated. When the explosion did not happen when the time came, the captain returned to the ship with many sailors, believing that the Italians had lied. The mines exploded at 6.44a.m. sinking the Jugoslavija and killing between 300 and 400 of her crew. The ship under the name *Viribus Unitis* was the same ship that had carried the body of the assassinated Archduke Franz Ferdinand from Bosnia to Trieste in June 1914.

Slovene leaders took over the administration of the Duchy of Carniola (modern-day Slovenia) from Austria-Hungary on 2 November.

Edward John Woolford was the son of Daniel and Charlotte Woolford of 4 Cricklade Road, Purton and was serving in Italy with the 5th (Service) Battalion, 1/4th Royal Berkshire Regiment where they were fighting in the Vittorio Veneto campaign (commenced 24 October). On 1 November 1918, the Battalion received orders to attack Monte Catz at 02:00 and Monte Mosoiagh at 05:30. At 14.00 Battalion HQ was established on Monte Catz and companies were engaged in consolidating positions. 12 men had been killed in action that day or died of wounds. Edward, aged 26, was one of those who died of wounds on 1 November. He is buried in Barenthal Military Cemetery, Italy and remembered on the Purton War Memorial and the Memorials in St Mary's Church.

The Battle of Vittorio Veneto continued until 3 November. The Italian victory ended the war on that front and brought about the collapse of the Austro-Hungarian Empire. The Italians captured over 5,000 artillery pieces and more than 350,000 Austro-Hungarian troops. On the same day, Austria-Hungary signed an armistice with Italy at Villa Giusti near Padua and Italian troops occupied Trieste.

Hostilities between Austria-Hungary and the Allies ceased on 4 November under the terms of the 3 November armistice. Over the next few days, Italian naval forces occupied Antivari in Montenegro and Fiume (Rijeka).

Emperor Charles I of Austria abdicated on 12 November and the German-Austrian Republic (essentially the modern Austria) was proclaimed. The Hungarian Democratic Republic was declared on the 16th.

The Yugo-Slav National Council protested at the Italian occupation of Fiume on 17 November. Next day, Italy reinforced its garrison. United States troops entered Fiume on the 26th.

The War at Sea
On 2 November, SS Surada and SS Murcia were the last British merchant vessels to be sunk by submarine in the Mediterranean. In the last major naval engagement of the war, the British battleship HMS Britannia was sunk by a German submarine off Cape Trafalgar on 9 November with 50 men killed.

In accordance with the Armistice agreement at Compiègne, the German light cruiser SMS Königsberg entered the Firth of Forth on 15 November carrying naval delegates to arrange surrender of the German fleet. The first contingent of German submarines assembled off Harwich on 20 November and next day the German High Seas Fleet arrived in the Firth of Forth. 5 battlecruisers, 9 battleships, 7 cruisers, 49 destroyers and 176 submarines were surrendered to the British Grand Fleet. Between 25 and 27 November, they were moved under escort to Scapa Flow, Orkney for internment.

On the 26th, an Allied fleet took control of the remainder of the Russian Black Sea Fleet from Germany. That Fleet had been surrendered to Germany in 1917.

Africa
On 1 November a German force in East Africa under Colonel von Lettow-Vorbeck entered Northern Rhodesia (Zambia), attacked Fife, and captured Kasama by the 9th. On 13 November, the German force reached the Chambezi River where they received the news of the armistice. Hostilities in East Africa ceased on 14 November and a formal German surrender was signed on the 25th at Abercorn, Northern Rhodesia, (now Mbala, Zambia).

Ottoman Empire
On 12 November, the British and French Governments made a joint declaration of regarding the future of Syria and Mesopotamia.

An Allied fleet passed through the Dardanelles that same day and arrived on the 13th in Constantinople, which was placed under Allied Occupation. This was reinforced by the arrival of French troops on the 21st.

The British military government of Palestine began on 23 November.

Serbia and Yugoslavia
On 1 November, Serbian forces recaptured their capital, Belgrade, from Austrian forces and on the 6th King Peter re-entered the city from exile. A joint Yugo-Slav and Serbian government was formed on 7 November to control foreign and military affairs.

The Yugo-Slav National Council voted on 23 November for the formation of a common state to include Serbia and Montenegro together with the newly liberated territories.

Rumania
Allied forces crossed the Danube at Ruschuk on 10 November and entered Rumania. King Carol I announced that Rumania had taken up arms again on the side of the Allies. (Following the Russian exit from the war in 1917, Rumania had been occupied by the Austro-Hungarian Empire.)

On the 21st, the Greek, Serbian and Rumanian Governments announced their decision to strengthen the union between the three countries by all available means. These three had been in alliance during the 2nd Balkan War of 1913.

On 30 November, the Rumanian Government was re-established at Bucharest.

The New Republics
Poland, Latvia, Estonia and Czechoslovakia all formed new governments during November. But many of these new countries were born in a state of turmoil.

On 1 November, Ukraine declared war on Poland in dispute over territories in Galicia. The Polish-Ukrainian War continued until July 1919 with a Polish victory but with 25,000 casualties between them.   Between 21 and 23

November, Polish forces, swelled by volunteers and freed criminals organised a 3-day pogrom at Lwów in Galicia, massacring at least 320 Ukrainian Christians and Jews.

In Estonia, the Russian Red Army invaded on 28 November, starting the Estonian War of Independence and capturing Narva. The Commune of the Working People of Estonia was established as a Soviet puppet state in Narva on the 29th. The war lasted until February 1920, ending with an Estonian victory and an independent Estonian State.

Other News

The 1918 influenza epidemic spread from New Zealand to Western Samoa on 7 November on board the freighter SS Talune, killing 7,542 on the island by the end of the year (about 20% of the population).

Part 66: The Immediate Aftermath

Although the War ended in November 1918, men were only gradually demobilised. Some were still suffering from wounds received during the war; others contracted diseases in the chaotic post-war environment.

Edwin E Saunders was the son of George and Alice Saunders, of Greenhill. He had been serving with the 54th Brigade, Ammunition Column, Royal Field Artillery as a Shoeing Smith. Following service in Salonika, his brigade was fighting in Italy in the Vittorio Veneto campaign. On his return journey to England, he was taken off the train in which he was travelling, at St Germaine, France, on 24 November 1918. He died of pneumonia, aged 29, on 4 December 1918 in a Military Hospital. Edwin is buried in St-Germain-au-Mont-d'Or Communal Cemetery Extension, Rhone, France, and remembered on the Purton War Memorial and the Memorials in St Mary's Church. The Memorial Book incorrectly states that he was killed in action.

Esaw Hawcutt was the son of Mrs Mary Ann Hawcutt, Bruern, Kingham, Oxford and until his enlistment was employed by the Great Western Railway as a packer at Purton railway station. He was serving in France with the 186th Siege Battery, Royal Garrison Artillery and may have taken part in the bombardments during the 2nd Battle of the Somme (August to September 1918). On 9 September he was taken into hospital suffering from Peripheral Vascular Disease and invalided to UK on 26-27 September where he was admitted to Cambuslang War Hospital, Glasgow. On 22 November 1918, Esaw was sent to an auxiliary convalescence hospital with trench fever, later readmitted to Cambuslang on 2 January 1919 where he developed meningitis.

Esaw died aged 27 on 4 February 1919 at Cambuslang of trench fever and meningitis. He is buried in Milton-Under-Wychwood Churchyard.

Trench fever, also known as five-day fever, is a moderately serious disease transmitted by body lice. It infected armies in Flanders, France, Poland, Galicia,

Italy, Salonika, Macedonia, Mesopotamia, Russia and Egypt in the Great War. From 1915 to 1918 between one-fifth and one-third of all British troops reported ill had trench fever while about one-fifth of sick German and Austrian troops had the disease.

Frederick William Staley was the son of Henry George and Sarah Ann Staley of New Road, Purton. He was serving with the 1/4th Battalion Wiltshire Regiment, attached to the 75th Division in Palestine where he received a dangerous head wound. The 75th Division joined General Allenby's final offensive in the Battles of Megiddo in which, at the Battle of Sharon (19 September) the 75th Division was tasked with taking Miske and the trench system around the village of Et Tire. It is possible that Frederick was wounded in this action. He spent 4 months recovering in hospital before he was transferred to England. Frederick died aged 23 on 16 February 1919 in the 1st London General Hospital of those wounds. He was buried in Purton Churchyard on 22 February 1919 under a CWGC headstone. Frederick is remembered on the Purton War Memorial and the Memorials in St Mary's Church.

Albert Bunce was the son of William James and Ellen Elizabeth Bunce of Odd Time Cottage, Pavenhill, Purton. He was serving with the Labour Corps, 72nd Prisoner of War Escort Company. In the summer of 1916 a decision was made to keep German POWs on mainland Europe instead of transporting them all to England. Some of those kept on mainland Europe were formed into POW Companies of around 425 men (later enlarged due to the number of prisoners taken towards the end of the War). The POW Escort Companies included an Officer, NCOs and Other Ranks including cooks and ASC drivers. The POW's were worked and received pay, though not directly at the front or in work directly supporting the war effort due to the Hague Convention. The work that the POW companies completed took the strain away from the Corps previously employed to carry out many of the tasks such as the Royal Engineers and ASC.

Albert died, aged 20, on 11 April 1919 at Swindon Victoria Hospital. The cause of death is listed on his death certificate as (1) Acute Cellulitis (Bacterial infection) and (2) Septic Embolus. His step-mother Susannah Bunce was in attendance. Albert was buried in St Mary's Churchyard on 16 April, under a locally manufactured wooden cross with a brass inscription plate. He is remembered on the Purton War Memorial and in the Memorial Book in St Mary's Church.

The Purton branch of The Royal British Legion has campaigned for a CWGC headstone but he is not eligible nor for War Grave status because he did not die during the War or due to an injury or ailment caused by Military Service. Albert's Service Record and pension papers, which might provide evidence of a war death, were destroyed in the 2nd World War during a bombing raid that struck the National Military Archives.

Francis Charles Titcombe was the son of Mr and Mrs Charles Titcombe, Greenhill. He had served in France with the Royal Engineers and was discharged on 5 February 1917. Francis re-enlisted with the 3rd Battalion,

Wiltshire Regiment on 13 February 1919, with his occupation given as farrier. On 22 July 1919 on a Disability Claim Form, his unit was recorded as Cavalry Corps Bridging Park.

Francis was admitted to Cambridge Hospital, Aldershot on 31 December 1919 and over the following days his medical sheet records a rapid decline in health. On 12 January 1920 he was mumbling and incoherent, and became comatose at about 6p.m. He died, aged 31, at 11.55p.m. from (1) Influenza and (2) Pneumonia. His mother was present at his death. Francis is buried at Lydiard Millicent Churchyard, beneath a CWGC headstone. He is listed in the Memorial Book (Survivors list) in St Mary's Church, as Frank Titcombe, Royal Engineers.

Charles Reginald Edmonds was the son of Alfred and Alice Edmonds, Lydiard Green. He had served with the 5th Battalion, Wiltshire Regiment at Gallipoli in 1915. On 8 May 1919 he was transferred to Z class - the Class Z Reserve was a Reserve contingent of the British Army consisting of previously enlisted soldiers, now discharged. The first Z Reserve was authorised by an Army Order of 3 December 1918. When expected difficulties with German violations of the 1918 Armistice did not happen, the Z Reserve was abolished on 31 March 1920.

Charles died, aged 22, on 25 May 1920 of phthisis (tuberculosis) and was buried in Lydiard Millicent Church Cemetery under a CWGC headstone. Charles is recorded as an official War casualty.

Portugal
President Sidónio da Silva Pais was assassinated on 14 December and succeeded by João do Canto e Castro.

Part 67: Peace Treaties 1919-20

On 18 January 1919, the Paris Peace Conference was opened in the Great Hall of Mirrors in the Palace of Versailles. Symbolically, the date and location were significant: during the Siege of Paris in the Franco-Prussian War, the German princes had assembled in that same room to proclaim the Prussian King Wilhelm I as German Emperor, Kaiser Wilhelm I, on 18 January 1871.

Delegates from 27 nations assembled for the Conference although it was chiefly controlled by the Big Four major powers: France, Britain, Italy and the U.S.A. The fifth major power, Japan, only sent a former prime minister to the conference and so played a small role. The delegates were assigned to 52 Commissions which reported back to Conference on subject areas including the creation of a League of Nations, responsibility for the war, treatment of prisoners of war, international aviation and many others. The main conclusions were included in the Treaty of Versailles which also dealt specifically with Germany. Further treaties were created for the other defeated nations. The conference ended on 21 January 1920 when the inaugural meeting was held of the General Assembly of the League of Nations.

PARTITIONING OF GERMANY

Treaty of Versailles *(concerning Germany, signed 28 June 1919):*
Territorial Changes:

Germany lost all territorial gains made under the Treaty of Brest-Litovsk and the eastern European "protectorates" that Germany had established were given full independence. Moresnet and Eupen-Malmedy on the Belgian-German border were transferred to Belgium but with a plebiscite to determine the wishes of the people. The French coal industry had been mostly destroyed during the war, so Germany was to give the output of the Saarland coalmines to France in compensation for 15 years. During that period the League of Nations would control of the Saarland. A plebiscite would then decide sovereignty. Alsace and Lorraine, taken by Germany in the Franco-Prussian War, were returned to France. A plebiscite in Schleswig-Holstein would determine sovereignty between Germany and Denmark - Schleswig voted to join Denmark, Holstein for Germany.

Parts of Upper Silesia were ceded to Czechoslovakia and to Poland while a plebiscite would be held to determine the future of the rest of the province. Poland received control of the province of Posen (now Poznán) and Pomerelia (Eastern Pomerania) was transferred to Poland giving the new state access to the Baltic Sea. Danzig at the seaward end of this "Polish Corridor" became a Free City under the control of the League of Nations. A plebiscite was to be held in part of southern East Prussia while the Soldau area of East Prussia was transferred directly to Poland. Memel, between East Prussia and Lithuania was ceded to Lithuania.

Mandates:
Germany lost all its former colonies which became League of Nations mandates. Togoland and Kamerun (Cameroon) were transferred to French control. Ruanda and Urundi were controlled by Belgium, German South-West Africa (Namibia) by South Africa and German East Africa (renamed Tanganyika) by Britain. Portugal was given control of an area of German East Africa south of the Ruwuma River known as the Kionga Triangle (Quionga) which became part of Mozambique. German port concessions in Shandong, China, were passed to Japan, which was also given all German islands in the Pacific Ocean north of the equator. The German possessions south of the equator were granted to Australia, apart from German Samoa which was given to New Zealand.

Military Restrictions:
The treaty intended to make it impossible for Germany to take offensive action again so that other nations could disarm in safety. Germany was to hold a maximum army strength of 100,000 men and army organisation was controlled. The creation of paramilitary forces was forbidden under the treaty.

The Rhineland was demilitarised and all fortifications in the Rhineland were to be destroyed. To ensure compliance, the Rhineland was to be placed under Allied military occupation for a period of 15 years (to 1934). Germany was not to be allowed to take part in the arms trade. The German navy was only allowed six pre-dreadnought (i.e. old) battleships and six light cruisers, with tight limits on destroyers and torpedo boats, and an outright ban on submarines. Naval manpower was limited to 15,000.

The German Navy's High Seas Fleet had been interned at Scapa Flow since November 1918, with the Peace Conference to decide the fate of the ships. On 21 June 1919, the German officer in command at Scapa Flow took it upon himself to order the scuttling of the fleet, since the negotiation period for the treaty had lapsed and he had not received notification of a one-week extension to the deadline. 53 ships, representing the majority of the fleet, were sunk.

Reparations:
Germany was forced to accept responsibility for losses and damages caused by her aggression and that of her allies. Germany was to compensate the Allied powers financially with the exact amount to be determined by a Reparations Commission. The subsequent 1921 London Schedule of Payments required Germany to pay 132 billion gold marks (then $33 billion) in gold, commodities, ships or securities. In reality, the amount was 50 million Gold Marks in A and B bonds (then $12.5 billion).

Gold marks may not mean much to you and they didn't to me. So here is a comparison. Just before the war, Germany was on the gold standard and 1 kilogram of pure gold was fixed at 2790 marks. During the war, Germany came off the gold standard and the Allies didn't want any of the reparations paid in paper marks, which might be subject to inflation … no one was even thinking of the hyper-inflation that occurred later in the 1920s.

As I am writing this (10 August 2018), the BBC currency and commodity internet pages tell me that there are $1.2784 to £1 and 1 troy ounce of gold is valued at $1,216. Given that there are 32.15 troy ounces in a kilogram, that means 50 billion gold marks is worth:

1216 / 1.2784 x 32.15 / 2790 x 50 billion = £548 billion in 2018 money. That is an enormous number but represents a compromise put forward by Britain and Belgium compared with a much higher figure that France and Italy wanted, and a much more lenient figure from the USA. As another comparison, in April 2018, the US gold holdings in Fort Knox had a book value of slightly over $11 billion. *Source: Status Report of U.S. Government Gold Reserve. Current Report: April 30, 2018.*

As a further significance, the Treaty of Versailles was signed on the 5th anniversary of the assassination of Archduke Franz Ferdinand in Sarajevo on 20 June 1914.

Treaty of St-Germain-en-Laye *(concerning Austria, signed 10 September 1919):* Austria was also to admit its war guilt. Huge amounts of imperial Austrian territories were redistributed, much in line with changes already made at local level in 1918. Bohemia and Moravia became the economic heart of the new Czechoslovakia. Galicia and Lodomeria, which had been annexed from Poland by Austria in 1772, were given back to the re-established Polish Republic. Austrian Silesia was divided between Poland and Czechoslovakia, even though this placed a large German-speaking population in Bohemia and Sudetenland. Rumania received Bukovina.

The South Tyrol, predominantly German-speaking, and the Trentino were given to Italy. The Austrian coastal regions of Gorizia and Gradisca, the city of

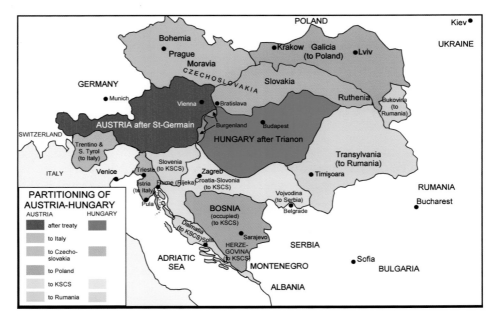

Trieste, the Istrian peninsula and several Adriatic islands of Dalmatia also became part of Italy. Mainland Dalmatia, Carniola and Lower Styria were given to the Yugoslav Kingdom of Serbs, Croats and Slovenes, together with Bosnia and Herzegovina.

The German-speaking Burgenland was transferred from Hungary to Austria.

Politics & Military Considerations:
The treaty forbade Austria from "compromising its independence", either directly or indirectly. This meant that Austria could not enter into political or economic union with Germany without League of Nations consent. It also meant they couldn't use their chosen name, German-Austria, and had to change it back to simply 'Austria'.

The Austrian Army was limited to a force of 30,000 volunteers with no conscription. The treaty covered many other political and economic issues that resulted from the break-up of the large empire, such as rail and river transport.

***Treaty of Neuilly-sur-Seine** (concerning Bulgaria, signed 27 November 1919)*:
Western Thrace was transferred to Greece, cutting off Bulgaria's access to the Aegean Sea, and a population exchange was arranged between the two countries. Bulgaria also lost land on its western border with the Kingdom of Serbs, Croats and Slovenes (later Yugoslavia), and was required to recognise that kingdom. Dobruja, occupied during the war, was returned to Rumania.

Bulgaria's army was limited to 20,000 men and the country was required to pay reparations of £100 million.

***Treaty of Trianon** (concerning Hungary, signed 4 June 1920)*:
As Hungary had already left the joint empire with Austria, its *de facto* borders at the start of the peace conference were defined temporarily as the cease-fire lines of November 1918. However, the Rumanian Army had already advanced beyond that line and the Allied powers required Hungary to acknowledge the new Rumanian territory gains. The Hungarian government was put in a position of being unwilling to accept the terms and of simultaneously being bound by the Conference constitution to accept them. The Hungarian leadership therefore resigned and power was seized by the Communist faction who set up a Soviet Republic and a Red Army.

The new Red Army moved into Slovakia and reached the new Polish border cutting off Czechoslovakia from any support from Rumania. A cease-fire was agreed on 1 July 1919 and the Hungarian Red Army began to leave Slovakia by 4 July. Hungary then attacked the Rumanian army at the River Tisza on 20 July but collapsed after only 5 days - *see map inside back cover*. The Rumanian army marched into the Hungarian capital, Budapest, on 4 August 1919.

The Hungarian government was restored to power by the Allies and their new delegation returned to the Paris Conference on 1 December 1919.

Slovakia was ceded to the new Czechoslovakia together with Ruthenia. The whole of Transylvania was ceded to Rumania and the Burgenland became part of Austria (see above). The Kingdom of Serbs, Croats and Slovenes (KSCS) gained Medimurje and part of the Slovene March (now Prekmurje). Additionally, Vojvodina was ceded to Serbia.

The Ottoman Empire
The disposition of the Ottoman Empire was confused by another regional war which will be dealt with in Part 69.

Part 68: Elections and Civil Wars

Britain & Ireland
The Representation of the People Act (1918) was signed into law in February 1918. Its provisions allowed all men over 21 years old the vote. Although women were allowed to vote for the first time, it only included women over 30 years old and who held £5 of property or had husbands who did. It made residency in a specific constituency the basis of the right to vote there - but men who had residence or a business in more than one could register to vote in both. In November 1918, the Parliament (Qualification of Women) Act 1918 was passed, allowing women to be elected into the House of Commons.

Immediately after the Armistice, a General Election was called for the whole of the United Kingdom to be held on 14 December 1918. Because of the delay in collecting votes from men serving overseas, the actual count was held on 28 December.   In Britain it resulted in a landslide victory for Lloyd George's coalition government which had replaced Asquith's last elected government in December 1916.

The only woman to be elected to parliament was the Sinn Féin candidate for Dublin St Patrick's, Constance Markievicz. However, she chose not to take her seat at Westminster in line with the abstentionist policy of Sinn Féin. (The first woman to take her seat in the House of Commons was Nancy Astor on 1 December 1919, following a by-election in Plymouth Sutton after her husband resigned the seat.)

The election result was a totally different matter in Ireland.   The Irish Parliamentary Party was defeated and retained only 6 out of 105 Irish seats. The overwhelming winner of the election was the nationalist Sinn Féin party with 70% of the seats. Their MPs demanded not only the Home Rule enacted in 1914 (and delayed by the war) but full independence. Sinn Féin set up its own parliament, the Dáil Éireann, and declared Ireland an independent republic. The north of Ireland was still in favour of the union with Great Britain and so Britain passed a Fourth Home Rule Bill in 1920. This was to create two new parliaments, one in Northern Ireland and the other in the South. The Northern Ireland parliament was established in 1921 for the 6 Unionist counties of Ulster, Cavan, Monaghan and Donegal electing for the south.

Meanwhile, the Irish Republican Army (IRA) fought a guerrilla war (Irish War of Independence or Anglo-Irish War) from 1919 to 1921 against the British security forces in Ireland. The conflict started when two members of the armed British police force, the Royal Irish Constabulary (RIC), were shot dead on 21

January 1919 in Tipperary by members of the IRA. In September 1919, the British government outlawed the Dáil and Sinn Féin and the conflict intensified with the IRA ambushing RIC and British Army patrols, attacking their barracks and forcing isolated barracks to be abandoned. The British increased the strength of the RIC with British recruits, the "Black and Tans". Their poor discipline and reprisals against civilians made their presence deeply resented.

A ceasefire was agreed on 11 July 1921 which led to the Anglo-Irish Treaty of 6 December 1921 which ended British rule in the south of Ireland. The south became a self-governing Dominion a year later and was named the Irish Free State.   In June 1922, disagreement between republican factions over the political settlement led to an 11-month-long Irish Civil War.

The Russian Civil War
After Imperial Russia collapsed in 1917, power was seized by the Bolshevik party under Vladimir Lenin. With the severe terms of the Treaty of Brest-Litovsk, Germany had taken control of many of the countries formerly in the western part of the Russian Empire including Finland, the Baltic states, White Russia (Belarus) and Ukraine. While the Great War continued, it was in the interests of the Allied Powers to try to get Russia back into the war against Germany. The Allies encouraged monarchist groups and landed armies in Russia towards that cause. The grouping was known as the Whites as opposed to the Bolshevik Reds.

While the Reds controlled Petrograd, Moscow and the land between, the allies landed forces to help the Whites at Murmansk and Archangel in the far north and Vladivostok on the Pacific coast in the east. Britain had also landed armies in Georgia and Azerbaijan in the southern Caucasus to prevent Germany and its Turkish allies from accessing the large oil reserves in the region. A Czech army captured and interned in Siberia had taken over the area, turning the tables on their captors and controlled the centre of the Trans-Siberian Railway.

Admiral Alexander Kolchak, the former Lord High Admiral of Russia, had set up a provisional counter-revolutionary government in Ufa, some 700 miles east of Moscow. His government was recognised by the disparate White groups, the Czechs and the Allies. It was funded by gold raided by the Czech Legion from Russia's bullion reserves at Kazan which was used to pay for the advances made by the Whites.

Having taken Perm, Kolchak's forces moved forward in April 1919 to Tsaritsyn (Stalingrad, Volgograd) on the River Volga. With the British advancing from the north, Kolchak was in a position to advance towards Moscow. A coordinated attack by both forces against the Bolsheviks might have been successful but never happened. The Whites lost what might have been their best opportunity to defeat the Bolsheviks. Instead, the Red Army secured Tsaritsyn and began to push the Whites back eastwards. With the Great War won in the west, Britain and the other Allies had little incentive to stay in Russia and withdrew all forces shortly afterwards.

Leon Trotsky, the Communist Military Commissar in the civil war, was willing to accept any help he could get including using ex-tsarist officers to give the inexperienced Red Army the military guidance they lacked. Although Red Army morale was high, Trotsky knew that it could all evaporate with their first major defeat, so advance was essential. If a commander in Trotsky's army succeeded he was promoted, but if he failed and survived, he paid the price. The Red Army didn't lack recruits: Lenin had ordered that food supplies went first to the soldiers and those behind in the cities would only get what was left.

The Whites on the other hand were an uncoordinated grouping that seldom agreed with one another and, despite Kolchak's lead, had no sole commander at army level. They were also renowned for their ill-treatment of the people in the areas they controlled. With the Whites having no support from the land, nor from the Allies, the Red Army drove Kolchak and his forces back to Siberia. He surrendered to the Communists and died in their custody. White forces in the south of Russia were evacuated from the Crimea from November 1920 onwards.

The Polish-Ukrainian War of 1920-21 challenged Bolshevik plans in the west. Trotsky's Red Army, freed from problems with the Whites, attacked Poland in support of the Ukraine, broke through the Polish lines and advanced on Warsaw. While the Poles counter-attacked, Lenin decided to cut his losses and signed the Treaty of Riga on 18 March 1921. 10 million Ukrainians and Belarussians ended up under Polish rule. The Russian civil war carried on against groups in the east and south until 25 October 1922, but it was the Treaty of Riga that secured the western borders and therefore the future of the Soviet Union government under Lenin.

Part 68: Greece and Turkey

The Ottoman Empire captured Constantinople in 1453, bringing an end to the Byzantine, or Eastern Roman, Empire. Following their war of independence (1821-32), the Greeks began to see in the decline of the Ottoman Empire a chance to rebuild their Byzantine past. Even today, a Greek will call himself Romios *(Ρομιός, Roman)*. This rebuilding became known as "The Great Idea" *(Μεγάλη Ιδέα, Megali Idea)*. Later territorial gains during the Balkan Wars and the acquisition of Crete, reinforced the idea.

At its height the Great Idea included the return of Constantinople (Istanbul) to Greece as its capital together with the Hagia Sophia Cathedral *(Holy Wisdom)*, plus large areas of western Anatolia. In 1918, there were sizeable ethnic Greek populations in Anatolian Turkey, especially in the province of Smyrna (Turkish Izmir).

The Treaty of Sèvres *(concerning the Ottoman Empire, signed 10 August 1920)* The treaty stipulated that Turkey would renounce all non-Turkish territory and cede it to Allied administration. Land in the eastern Mediterranean and beyond became British Mandated Palestine and Iraq, and French Syria and Lebanon.

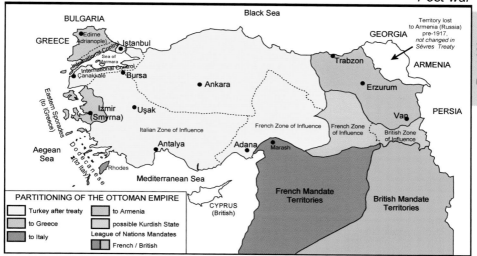

In Anatolia, a large area in the north west centred on Erzurum was given to Armenia. An Inquiry was to be instituted to determine responsibility for the Armenian Genocide in which up to 1.5 million Armenians died between 24 April 1915 and 1917. There were provisions for the possible creation of a Kurdish state in the south east, notably with most of the province of Van but without the city of Van itself which was in the Armenian partition. The city has a large Kurdish population but was historically associated with Armenia.

Greece received the territory around Izmir (Smyrna in Greek) and almost the whole of Eastern Thrace up to a few miles from Istanbul, including Edirne (Greek Adrianopolis). Since Turkey renounced almost all the offshore islands, those in the Aegean were given to Greece, while the Dodecanese islands, which Italy occupied after the Italian-Turkish War of 1912, were formally ceded to Italy.

In anticipation of the treaty terms, Greek forces began landing at Smyrna in May 1919 with Allied naval protection, ostensibly to safeguard the local ethnic Greek population from Turkish reprisals. The Greeks quickly established a bridgehead and secured Smyrna and the surrounding area. During the summer of 1920, before the signing of the treaty, Greek forces penetrated some 130 miles east of Symna as far as Uşak and northwest towards Bursa.

Turkish War of Independence
The terms of the Sèvres treaty were harsh on Turkey and nationalist feelings were heightened. Mustafa Kemal had been the Ottoman commander of the 7th Army in Palestine during 1918. He resigned from the Ottoman Army on 8 July 1919 and the Ottoman Caliphate government issued a warrant for his arrest. In September 1919, he assembled a congress of all Turkish parties opposed to the Caliphate and the Allies and was appointed head of its executive committee. In December 1919 elections were held for the Ottoman

Parliament which resulted in a landslide victory for the Association for Defence of Rights for Anatolia, led by Kemal. The Istanbul parliament was dissolved by British forces on 18 March 1920. New elections were held establishing a new Parliament in Ankara, titled the Grand National Assembly (GNA), with Kemal as the Speaker. There were now effectively two opposing authorities.

On 10 August 1920, the Ottoman Grand Vizier signed the Treaty of Sèvres. The opposing GNA stripped the signatories of the treaty of their citizenship and this started the Turkish War of Independence. Kemal and the GNA gathered a National Army to fight against the Caliphate army and its Allied occupation force support. The GNA faced French and Armenian forces in the east and the Greeks advancing from Smyrna in the west. In January 1920, the National Army advanced east to Marash where they were victorious over the French-Armenian Legion. Between 5,000 and 12,000 Armenians are estimated to have been massacred after the battle.

By August 1921, the Greek army was defeated by Kemal's forces at the Sakarya River, 50 miles from Ankara (23 August -13 September 1921). The Allies proposed to modify the Treaty of Sèvres in the face of Kemal's successes, but the proposal was rejected. In August 1922, Kemal launched an all-out attack on the Greek lines at Afyonkarahisar in the Battle of Dumlupınar, halfway between Ankara and Smyrna, pushing the Greeks back. Turkish forces regained control of Smyrna on 9 September 1922. The Greek and Armenian quarters of Smyrna were destroyed in the Great Fire of Smyrna on 14 September.

Because of the chaos of the fire, estimates of Greek and Armenian deaths vary widely between 10,000 and 100,000. Between 50,000 and 400,000 Greek and Armenian refugees were crammed onto the waterfront to escape from the fire and were forced to remain there with no facilities for two weeks, before Allied ships could evacuate them.

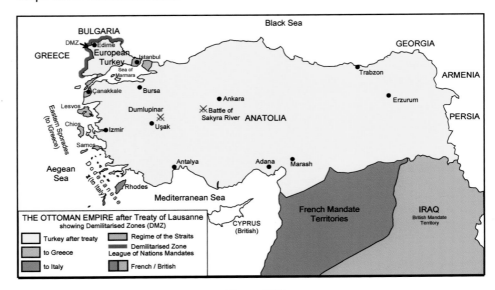

The Treaty of Lausanne (*concerning the Ottoman Empire, signed 24 July 1923*):
Peace talks were resumed at Lausanne, Switzerland, on 20 November 1922. In view of massacres by both sides in the War of Independence, the treaty provided for the protection of the Greek Orthodox Christian minority in Turkey and the Muslim minority in Greece. However, a population exchange had already occurred under a Convention that had been agreed between Greece and Turkey. Most of the territorial changes outside Anatolia made under the Treaty of Sèvres were restated.

Apart from the Anatolian offshore islands, Greece lost the territorial gains from Sèvres at Smyrna and in Western Thrace (European Turkey). Armenia was not to retain the former gains at Erzurum and Trabzon, and the border was reinstated at the pre-1914 line. Kurdish aspirations in the south east were rejected.

A more limited Regime of the Straits was created in order to protect the rights of international shipping through the Dardanelles via the Sea of Marmara and the Bosporus connecting the Aegean to the Black Sea. This was controlled under the League of Nations until 1936.

Postscript
King Constantine I of Greece was deposed by the army on 27 September 1922 and was succeeded by his son, George II. After a failed royalist coup in October 1923, the Revolutionary Committee sent George into exile in Rumania on 19 December 1923 and he was officially deposed on 25 March 1924 when a Greek Republic was declared. The monarchy was restored on 25 November 1935 and George II returned to the Greek throne.

In 1934, the Turkish Parliament granted Mustafa Kemal the surname Atatürk, meaning "Father of the Turks", in recognition of the role he played in building the modern Turkish Republic.

Part 70: Spanish 'Flu

The 1918 influenza pandemic started in January 1918 and lasted until December 1920 in several distinct waves of infection. It was an unusually deadly pandemic, caused by the H1N1 influenza virus. It was transported to most parts of the world, infecting some 500 million people and resulting in the deaths of between 50 and 100 million people, between 3% and 5% of the world's population at that time. That made it one of the deadliest natural disasters in human history. In Britain, a quarter of the population was affected and the death toll was 228,000.

Because it started in wartime, newspaper reports of its spread were censored for reasons of public morale in Germany, Britain, France, the United States and other belligerent nations. Spain was a neutral country whose papers weren't banned from reporting the disease as it spread there. In particular, the severe illness of King Alfonso XIII raised interest levels and gave the impression that Spain was particularly badly affected. As a result, the virus was popularly called Spanish 'Flu.

This particular strain was unusual in several ways. Most influenza outbreaks are at their worst in winter, but this one occurred in the northern hemisphere in summer and autumn. Additionally, 'flu epidemics tend to kill the young, the elderly or those already suffering other weaknesses - this one mainly killed young adults who were otherwise in full health.

Several explanations were put forward for the high mortality rates:
- that this was a variant of the virus with particularly aggressive characteristics;
- that its effect on the body was to cause an overreaction of the body's immune system (cytokine storm) causing rapid respiratory failure;
- that the overreactive immune systems in young adults attacked them more aggressively just because their immune systems were strong to start with.

More recent investigations suggested that the virus itself was not especially more aggressive but wartime conditions put the patient more at a disadvantage due to malnutrition, overstretched medical facilities and poor hygiene.

But again, if it were a more aggressive strain, its effects could be explained by wartime necessities. In peacetime, the way people respond would weaken the strain - those who become only mildly ill would continue their daily lives, passing on to others around them the milder strain. Those badly affected would stay at home and the stronger strain wouldn't spread further. In the wartime trenches, soldiers mildly ill did stay where they were - in the trenches - and passed on the mild form. But those showing the more severe symptoms were packed onto crowded trains or other transports and sent to crowded field hospitals where the strain was passed on to staff and to patients who were there for other conditions.

The symptoms of the most aggressive strains developed very quickly and it was said that those well and healthy at breakfast could be dead by tea-time. Within hours of feeling symptoms of tiredness, fever and headache, some victims would rapidly develop pneumonia and start turning blue, indicating a shortage of oxygen. They would then struggle for air until they suffocated to death. Although hospitals were overwhelmed with patients, there were no treatments available for the 'flu itself, nor were there any antibiotics at that time for the pneumonia that went with it.

The peak wave of the outbreak hit Britain at the end of the war when people *were* on the move again. Troops began travelling home by train from France and the 'flu spread from railway stations to the centres of cities, and onwards to the suburbs and the countryside. Prime Minister David Lloyd George contracted it but survived. (Other famous survivors were the cartoonist Walt Disney and Kaiser Wilhelm II, as well as Alfonso of Spain.)

As always with such epidemics, those who survive the first wave of infection build up an immunity. So, when the second and subsequent waves passed through a community, the proportion of the population infected decreased as did the severity. The pandemic died out in due course but left a death toll higher than that of the Black Death of 1347 to 1351.

Part 71: Weimar and the Rise of Fascism

German Post-War Government

Germany was governed by the Council of the People's Deputies (CPD), from November 1918 to January 1919, under the leadership of President Friedrich Ebert. Elections were held in December 1918 for a National Assembly to write a new constitution for the German Republic.

Germany's many and opposing political factions ranged from radical left-wing groups, including the Spartacist League and the Communists, to those wanting to restore the monarchy. The far-right blamed civilian defeatism for the loss of the war and promoted this "stab in the back" theory. Ebert made an agreement with the Supreme Army Command, now led by General Wilhelm Groener to ensure that the CPD and its successor Assembly could maintain control. The Ebert-Groener pact was that the government would not reform the army if the army agreed to protect the state. The army thereby stayed under the command of the officer class, even though the army structure was supposed to have been re-organised under the Versailles treaty terms.

Causes of discontent with the government, included:
* continuing food shortages of the 1920s;
* a depreciating currency;
* the national humiliation attached to acceptance of "war guilt" at Versailles;
* the loss of territory at Versailles and the military occupation of the Rhineland.

In January 1919, the Spartacist Uprising tried to establish a communist state, with bloody street fights between government and insurrectionist paramilitaries. Two leading Spartacist-Communists, Rosa Luxemburg and Karl Liebknecht, were arrested then beaten and shot in custody.

The National Assembly met in Weimar, 140 miles south-west of Berlin, rather than Berlin itself so as not to fuel further riots. A new constitution was adopted on 11 August 1919 which defined Germany as a federal semi-presidential constitutional republic.   The capital and seat of government remained at Berlin. (The term "Weimar Republic" was not used at the time, only post-1933 to define it as a former constitutional era.)

Hyperinflation

By 1931, when reparations payments were cancelled, Germany had paid 20 billion gold marks out of the 50 billion of the 1921 London Schedule of

Payments. 12.5 billion was cash in dollars from loans from New York banks. The rest was goods such as coal and chemicals, or from assets like railway equipment.

In the early post-war years, inflation was already growing at an alarming rate, but the government simply printed more Paper Marks. By 1923, the Republic claimed it could no longer afford the reparations payments and defaulted on some payments. In response, French and Belgian troops occupied the Ruhr, Germany's key industrial region, taking control of mining and manufacturing. An eight-month-long strike further damaged the economy.

Strikers were paid benefits by the state, but Germany had no international trade to pay for it. Instead more money was printed. Payments within Germany were being made with paper money which became increasingly worthless. The nominal value of debts within the country stayed the same, so businesses were able to repay originally huge bank loans in the worthless currency. Inflation led to pay rises for workers sometimes raised and paid twice within a day and the circulation of money spiralled. To save paper, which was the only thing of value about them, banknotes and postage stamps were overprinted to a thousand times their original value.

On 15 November 1923, a new currency, the Rentenmark, was introduced, backed by the value of land used for agriculture and business. The Rentenmark was established at a rate of one trillion Papiermark for one Rentenmark, making one U.S. dollar equal to 4.2 Rentenmark. Reparation payments were resumed, and the Ruhr was returned to Germany.

The Beer Hall Putsch

Among many uprisings, on 8 November 1923 the National Socialist German Workers Party (NSDAP), led by Adolf Hitler, staged the Beer Hall Putsch (Munich Putsch). 3000 NSDAP members, under the leadership of Adolf Hitler, marched into the centre of Munich and attempted to take over the Bavarian state government and capture the Bavarian prime minister Gustav von Kahr at a meeting at a beer hall in Munich. The Bavarian police put down the putsch and 16 Nazis and 4 police officers were killed. Hitler was arrested and sentenced to five years in prison for treason. He served less than eight months in a comfortable cell, with many visitors before his release on 20 December 1924. Hitler dictated *Mein Kampf* in prison laying out his ideas and future policies. From that time Hitler focused on legal methods of gaining power.

The Rise of Hitler

In 1929, the start of the depression in the United States also hit Germany. American banks withdrew their loans to German companies, and unemployment grew rapidly. In the September 1930 general election, the Nazi Party* (NSDAP) won 19% of the vote and entered the Reichstag for the first time. Government had only been possible up until then under a fragile coalition system, which

The term "Nazi" was a British invention and was never used in Germany. I use it here for simplification.

became unworkable; the last years of the Weimar Republic saw even more political instability. In the July 1932 elections the Nazis won 37% of the vote and became the largest party in the Reichstag. Three short coalition Chancellorships of Brüning, von Papen and Schleicher were followed by Hitler's election to Chancellor on 30 January 1933. By early February, Hitler's government began to clamp down on opposition groups inside and outside the Reichstag.

Hitler blamed the Communists for the Reichstag Fire of 27 February 1933 and used the state of emergency to obtain President Hindenburg's assent for the Reichstag Fire Decree the following day. The decree invoked Article 48 of the Weimar Constitution and "indefinitely suspended" a number of constitutional protections of civil liberties, allowing the Nazi coalition government to take swift action against political dissidents.

The 5 March 1933 elections were preceded by Nazi exploitation of Germany's radio and aviation to sway the electorate. Even so this election yielded a smaller majority of 16 seats for the coalition. Returned to power, Hitler put forward to the Reichstag and Reichsrat (upper house) the Enabling Act as a Constitutional Amendment giving the German Cabinet, in effect Hitler himself, the power to enact laws without the involvement of the Reichstag. It was passed in both houses on 24 March 1933 and was signed by President Paul von Hindenburg later that day. The powers were to last four years unless renewed by the Reichstag. The combined effect of the Enabling Act and the Reichstag Fire Decree transformed Hitler's government into a legal dictatorship.

- - - - -

Italy and the Rise of Mussolini

Before the war, Benito Mussolini had been a committed member of the Socialist Party, but he was also a nationalist and a journalist. He had formed his own newspaper and wrote strongly in favour of Italy entering the Great War on the Allies' side. The Socialist Party had a policy of neutrality and his divergent views ultimately led to his being expelled from the party. As an Italian Nationalist he wanted to unify a country split by regional loyalties. Italy entered the war in 1915 and Mussolini volunteered with the Bersaglieri corps in which he served with distinction on the front. He was severely injured in 1917 and was forced to leave the army.

Although on the victorious side, Italy's war casualties were very high and the country had been impoverished by the war effort. Mussolini founded the Italian Fascist Party, which combined a mix of socialism and nationalism. The Party soon had mass appeal based on Mussolini's call for all Italians to unite and overcome their class differences. Many war veterans joined the Party and many who were unemployed were formed by Mussolini into squads who became known as "Blackshirts", a formidable paramilitary force.

The Italian government was weak with the democratic parties unable to work together, and the church and state were similarly split on many issues. Many in the civil service and the army were sympathetic with the aims and ideology represented by Mussolini. Also, with the rise of communism and lawlessness, the intimidation of the Blackshirts seemed to offer security to the middle class.

All these effects helped the rise of the Fascist Party to popularity.

However, the Fascists only won 35 seats in the election of 1921, far fewer than the Socialists. Amid continued unrest, strikes and government unpopularity, the Fascists made their "March on Rome": 30,000 Blackshirts travelled from all over Italy to demand the resignation of the Prime Minister and a change of government. Throughout this the Blackshirts were well drilled and disciplined and seen to be a force that represented law and order against the Communists and Socialists.

Mussolini had feared that there would be bloodshed and that the army would fire on the marchers as they reached Rome. Instead the government did resign and Mussolini was offered the Prime Ministership which he accepted. The monarchy, army, landowners, industrialists and the Catholic Church appeared to have been so concerned about an imminent Communist revolution that they let the Fascists take power, believing they could manage Mussolini. Even when he set about creating a one-party state, Mussolini did not interfere with the interests of the conservative elite who had helped him to power.

In 1926, Mussolini survived 4 assassination attempts after which all other parties were outlawed. An electoral law abolished parliamentary elections and instead the Grand Council of Fascism would select a list of candidates to be approved by plebiscite. Officially, the Grand Council could remove Mussolini from office. In reality, only Mussolini could summon the Grand Council and determine its agenda. He was now the undisputed leader of Italy and known as "Il Duce", (The Leader).

Part 72: Remembrance

National Remembrance

It is not within the scope of the current work to discuss the full extent of Remembrance within Britain, the Empire and the rest of the world. We have obvious symbols and institutions to this day that were set up in the years immediately following the War: the Cenotaph in Whitehall; the Tomb of the Unknown Warrior in Westminster Abbey; the Royal British Legion; the Imperial (now Commonwealth) War Graves Commission; the Ceremony of Remembrance at the Royal Albert Hall.

Purton Remembrance

Cenotaphs, war memorials or "wayside crosses" to commemorate the fallen of the Great War didn't just happen. They weren't installed by the government but were paid for by local voluntary public subscription. The word cenotaph comes from two Greek words meaning empty (kenos) tomb (taphos).

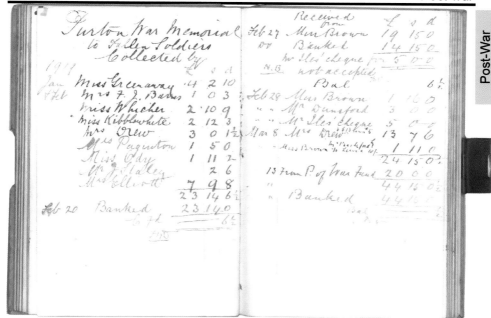

The hostilities of the Great War ended on 11 November 1918 and by January 1919 thoughts were on the consequences. Purton Museum holds the account book of the Purton War Memorial Fund, which shows the names of the Treasurers of the fund over the years on the front cover. But it also shows that it was a book started for a different, though related, purpose as it starts off being called the Purton Prisoners Food Fund of which the first Treasurer was A. Durnsford (May to October 1915). The purpose of the charity was to send food parcels to Prisoners of War held by the enemy. In November 1916, the role was taken up by F.W. Drew who continued through to 1919, when on 1 January 1919 the charity was renamed the Purton War Memorial Fund. His handwriting carries on in the book until 17 April 1919 after which another hand writes entries up to March 1920. All these entries are in fountain pen and there is still a sheet of pink blotting paper folded inside the book.

The names of donors recorded inside are those you would expect - all the typical names of Purton people that have survived across the years: landowners, tradesmen, workmen, they are all there. By the end of October 1918, £417 16s 4½d had been collected and used to pay for food parcels.

The book carries over towards the Purton War Memorial Fund and hands a balance of £20 across to the new fund. By March 1920, £235 10s 0d had been collected and that is presumably what the Cenotaph cost to order and erect.

Also in the Museum's collection is a copy of the Order of Service for the "Unveiling and Dedication of Wayside Cross, Erected in Memory of the Men of this *Parish who in the Great War gave their lives for us. Sunday 26th*

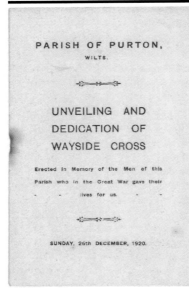

PARISH OF PURTON,
WILTS.

❖—❖—❖

UNVEILING AND

DEDICATION OF

WAYSIDE CROSS

Erected in Memory of the Men of this
Parish who in the Great War gave their
- - lives for us. - -

❖—❖—❖

SUNDAY, 26th DECEMBER, 1920.

December 1920". The service started with the hymn "O Valiant Hearts" followed by prayers. The Chairman of the Parish Council, J. Haskins, Esq., then called upon Colonel Canning C.M.G., to unveil the Cross after which the hymn "For all the Saints" was sung.

The cross was then dedicated and the roll of the names inscribed upon the cross were read by the Chairman of the Parish Council and an address was delivered by the Revd R. Cowie, C.F. The hymn "Son of God" was followed by more prayers, the blessing and The Last Post. Wreaths were then laid by representatives of the Service Men, the Parish Council, the Mothers of Purton and the School Children after which The Reveille was sounded. After a short silence, everyone cried "God Save the King".

On Remembrance Sunday, a service is still held every year in memory of the dead of the Great War, of the Second World War (whose names have been added) and of all conflicts since. This is organised by the Purton Branch of the Royal British Legion.

National Damage and Change

Beyond the deaths and injuries of so many, what had been a vibrant world of the Edwardian days was in many ways destroyed. The 1920s and 30s were a time of belt-tightening for many as the world economy struggled to come to terms with the massive changes that resulted.

Every theatre of war saw enormous ruin as the economies of nations had been devoted to destroying their neighbours rather than building themselves. In Britain and Germany, neither of their home territories were on the front line, so physical damage to property was limited to naval and air force attacks which, though serious in their own right, did not compare with billions of shells being fired from land-based artillery. Much of Belgium and France north and east of Paris was completely obliterated over distances some 200 miles east to west and 150 miles north to south. We can draw an equivalence to say Dover to Cardiff (east-west) times Southampton to Derby (south-north).

So many men had been killed that it was said that a generation had been lost. Certainly, from my own family memory, it resulted in large numbers of women who were either widowed or who could never marry. The maiden aunts were many in number.

As with the population in general, so with the great houses. So many of their staff had been called up, and either killed or saw other possibilities, that they never managed to get their servants back in sufficient numbers to keep the houses going. Many of the great houses fell to ruin, others were eventually taken over by the military or the National Trust and its forerunners. Collectors bought the contents as perhaps exampled by the wonderfully eclectic collection at Snowshill Manor, near Broadway in Gloucestershire.

Toll of War

There really is no point in remembering the dead if one doesn't also look at the cost of all that happened in terms of both loss of life for the dead and debasement of life for the living.

The following table makes stark reading:

Countries	Total Mobilised	Killed & Died	Wounded	Prisoners and Missing	Casualties	Casualties % of Mobilised
Allied Powers						
Russia	12,000,000	1,700,000	4,950,000	2,500,000	9,150,000	76.3
France	8,410,000	1,357,800	4,266,000	537,000	6,160,800	76.3
British Empire	8,904,467	908,371	2,090,212	191,652	3,190,235	35.8
Italy	5,615,000	650,000	947,000	600,000	2,197,000	39.1
United States	4,355,000	126,000	234,300	4,500	364,800	8.2
Japan	800,000	300	907	3	1,210	0.2
Romania	750,000	335,706	120,000	80,000	535,706	71.4
Serbia	707,343	45,000	133,148	152,958	331,106	46.8
Belgium	267,000	13,716	44,686	34,659	93,061	34.9
Greece	230,000	5,000	21,000	1,000	17,000	11.7
Portugal	100,000	7,222	13,751	12,318	33,291	33.3
Montenegro	50,000	3,000	10,000	7,000	20,000	40.0
Total	42,188,810	5,152,115	12,831,004	4,121,090	22,104,209	52.3
Central Powers						
Germany	11,000 000	1,773,700	4,216,058	1,152,800	7,142,558	64.9
Austria-Hungary	7,800,000	1,200,000	3,620,000	2,200,000	7,020,000	90.0
Turkey	2,850,000	325,000	400,000	250,000	975,000	34.2
Bulgaria	1,200,000	87,500	152,390	27,029	266,919	22.2
Total	22,850,000	3,386,200	8,388,448	3,629,829	15,404,477	67.4
All Belligerents						
Grand Total	65,038,810	8,538,315	21,219,452	7,750,919	37,508,686	57.6

Source: Historical Atlas of the Twentieth Century
Matthew White - First World War Casualties
Note: columns will not add up as many will be in more than one category.

Purton's figures by comparison are summarised as follows, using figures from Bob Lloyd. The total number of men in the Purton Military list is 530. Of those 94 were killed of whom 55 are recorded on the Purton War Memorials and 39 not so listed. By checking entry by entry in Bob's work, I have come up with a figure of 55 wounded in addition to those killed. So, the comparison is as follows:

	Total Mobilised	Killed & Died	Wounded	Prisoners and Missing	Casualties	Casualties % of Mobilised
Purton	530	94	55	*included**	149	28.1
British Empire	8,904,467	908,371	2,090,212	191,652	3,190,235	35.8
Total Allies	42,188,810	5,152,115	12,831,004	4,121,090	22,104,209	52.3
Total Belligerents	65,038,810	8,538,315	21,219,452	7,750,919	37,508,686	57.6

Note: The Purton figures for Prisoners and Missing are included in either killed or survived so are not compared.

Purton's casualties, however horrific, are blessedly lower than the averages.

War Wounded

Throughout the account of the war years in this series, it has been natural to focus on those who died during the war itself or who died perhaps years afterwards from injuries sustained. It is all too easy to forget those who were wounded, sometimes horribly, and lived with those disabilities all the rest of their lives.

Strangely, while the general ratio of wounded to killed is about 2:1 to 3:1, Purton's is the other way around: more like 1:2. Unless there is a massive under-reporting in the figures, this can only be related to how the military actions that Purton men fought in were somehow "different" from others. This is outside the scope of the current work, and I leave it to others to establish a rationale.

Full List of Purton War Wounded:
(in alphabetical order by surname)

This list includes those men with Purton connections known to have suffered injuries during the war other than those killed or died in service, for which see the main body of the work Earlier war injuries to those later killed are included here.

Francis Percy Bathe
10 April 1917: Gunshot wound.
13 September 1917: Taken back on strength till end of war.

William Stanley Bathe
29 October 1917: gassed at Ypres.
19 November 1917: Admitted Fairfield Court Military Hospital Eastbourne with Trench fever and effects of being gassed. Struck off battalion strength.
19 December 1917: Transferred to convalescence Hospital in Epsom. Pneumonia.
4 May 1918: Developed trench fever and returned to Canada 23/09/1918
2 November 1918: Discharged with disabilities: (1) Myalgia and (2) gas with partial loss of musculature to back, arms, legs and Bronchitis. Medically unfit for further Service.

Edward Boyekin Bletso
14 April 1918: Wounded in action, gunshot wound right ankle at Battle of Hazebrouck, a phase of 4th Battle of Ypres. Missing in action, confirmed POW.
19 November 1918: Repatriated to England, ex POW.

Bertram George Brown
4 October 1914: (RN) Wounded by shrapnel shell in Defence of Antwerp, shrapnel entered back of the left thigh and passed through the muscles lodging under the skin on the inside of thigh. Escaped Antwerp to England. Shrapnel removed at Gosport Naval Hospital by [operation]. Was not returned to unit.

Daniel George Bull
25 October 1914: Gunshot wound to left thigh with 1st Battalion Wilts
28 October 1914: Transferred to England. Transferred to 5th Battalion Wilts.
31 August 1916: Killed in action at Basra.

Wilfred Eggleton Cook
15 September 1914: Gunshot wound right leg, from sniper fire.
23 September 1914: Returned to England.
24 September 1914 to 21 July 1920: based in UK and employed as Battalion Tailor, no longer fit for active service (with 3rd Battalion from 19 January 1915).

William A Coward
25 September 1915: Shell wound to shoulder at Hooge, Belgium, with 1st Wilts, and hospitalised at Boulogne.
27 April 1916: Posted to 2nd Wilts, Poulainvile, France.
28 October 1916: Admitted to hospital, cause not stated.
Later transferred to the Royal Engineers (as Sapper).

James Curtis
1916: Believed wounded with 5th Wilts in Mesopotamia (Iraq).
23 May 1918: Discharged not fit for further War Service aged 29.

John Davies
31 March 1915: With British Expeditionary Force, France.
20 April 1916: Hospitalised to London suffering a hernia, ruptured whilst building a trench parapet.
6 July 1917: Discharged, no longer physically fit for War Service.

Thomas Driscoll
18 October 1916: Wounded at Flers, France, with 2nd Wilts. Returned to Battalion.
9 April 1917: Wounded in action, attacking Hindenburg Line. Returned to Battalion.

Henry George Eacott
24 October 1914: Shell wound to back, with 1st Wilts at Neuve-Chappelle, France. Treated at No.7 Field Ambulance and admitted to hospital.
29 November 1914: Returned to UK on HMHS Carisbrook Castle.
3 August 1915: Discharged due to wounds.

Thomas Henry Embury
17 May 1915: Wounded in action, with 2nd Wilts at Rue De L'Epinette trenches, France. Hospitalised.
18 June 1915: Returned to Battalion

26 September 1915: Wounded in action in Battle of Loos. Transferred to UK 4 Oct 1915.

18 December 1915: Returned to 2nd Wilts who were at Le Mesge, France.

18 October 1916: Killed in action near Flers, France.

Albert Victor Fishlock

25 September 1915: Wounded in action, with 1st Battalion Monmouth Regiment, gunshot wound (shrapnel) to hand, thigh and chest. Returned to England and hospitalised.

6 October 1916: Hospitalised again in Blackburn.

28 January 1917: Returned to France.

7 August 1917: Wounded in action, but remained on duty.

11 June 1918: Posted to Machine Gun Corps.

8 October 1918: Killed in action, aged 20.

William George Garlick

06/11/1916: Wounded with Australian Imperial Force. Shell fragment in left side (France). Assessed in Rouen and admitted to hospital in Etaples, 19 November 1916.

27 November 1916: Rejoined Battalion.

14 April 1917: Sick in hospital and admitted to hospital in Rouen, 24 April 1917.

27 April 1917: Returned to England, Eastleigh Hospital with Trench fever.

22 November 1917: Rejoined Battalion, France.

11 May 1918: Admitted to hospital with "Trench fever" and to Rouen Hospital, Influenza, 13 November 1918.

6 June 1918: Rejoined Battalion.

3 October 1918: Wounded in action, gunshot wound left thigh and convalesced at Buchy, 10 ~October 1918.

22 November 1918: Rejoined Battalion. Returned to Australia September 1919.

Ernest John Godwin

09/01/1917: Wounded in action with Australian Imperial Force at Haifa. Gunshot wound left arm.

1 March 1917: Mentioned in General Murray"s Dispatches (London Gazette).

10 May 1917: Admitted to the Citadel Hospital in Cairo.

10 August 1919: Disembarked in Australia - in Egypt he had suffered 3 bouts of malaria.

Louis Walter Gough

24 August 1915: Serving with 37th Divisional Artillery. Admitted to hospital with a hernia. Discharged from hospital on 21 September 1915

Readmitted to hospital, hernia, and discharged to convalescent Depot, 16 October 1915.

30 October 1915: Posted 29th Brigade, 4th Division. Then via several re-postings discharged 13 May 1916 discharged, as under enlistment age. Age on discharge was 17 years and 11 days, 15 years when enlisted.

Albert Greenaway

14 August 1914: Arrived in Rouen, France with 1st Wilts.

30 September 1914: Admitted to 7thField Ambulance at Braine and returned England 11 October 1914.

9 February 1915: Returned to France with 2nd Wilts, in field from 9 March 1915.

26 March 1915: Wounded in the trenches at Estaires, France.

1 April 1915: Returned to Battalion from hospital.
22 July 1916: Wounded owing to passing a lorry full of explosives at the moment when it was blown up by a shell.
7 August 1916: Posted to 6th Wilts, Kemmel, France.
18 January 1919: Returned England. Demobilised, placed on Reserve (Class Z).

William Charles Griffen
29 December 1914: With 7th Battalion Berks
4 October 1915: Discharged from hospital - reason not known.
3 November 1916: Mediterranean Expeditionary Force, Salonika, with 12th Battalion Hampshire Regiment.
18 September 1918: Wounded in action, Salonika. Discharged from hospital 28 Oct 1918.
18 April 1919: To England for demobilisation.

Arthur James Gunter

17 May 1915: Wounded in action with 2nd Wilts, Rue De L`Epinette trenches, France.
19 May 1915: To England. After recovering from wounds, transferred to Hampshire Regiment.
June 1916: Wounded in Egypt, in hospital at Mohasain.
24 April 1919: Discharged.

Esaw Hawcutt

22 August 1917: Royal Garrison Artillery, France. To hospital with influenza, to 26 August 1917.
6 December 1917: Hospitalised with poisoned hand until 31 December 1917.
29 February1918: Returned to France.
9 September 1918: To hospital with Peripheral Vascular Disease. Invalided to England.
27 September 1918: Admitted to Cambuslang War Hospital.
22 November 1918: Sent to auxiliary convalescence hospital with trench fever.
2 January 1919: Re-admitted to Cambuslang where he developed meningitis.
4 February 1919: Died in Cambuslang War Hospital, Glasgow: Trench fever and meningitis.

Ernest Reuben Hewer
30 May 1915: Arrived in France, Royal Field Artillery.
1 December 1916: Hospital (Foot). Transferred to hospital at Le Treport. 19 Dec 1916
6 January 1917: At convalescence Depot.
February 1917: Base Depot postings.
8 February 1919: Demobilised in England

Montague Matthew Hicks
7 August 1915: Arrived Gallipoli with 7th Battalion Royal Dublin Fusiliers (Sulva Bay). Withdrew to Salonika, late September 1915.
23 September 1916: Wounded with gunshot wound left shoulder (River Struma, Balkans). Admitted to hospital, Salonika, then 8 October 1916 to hospital in Malta.
19 February 1917: Re-joined Battalion.
22 August 1917: Hospital, Salonika with dysentery.
22 October 1917: Transferred with Battalion moved to Egypt
6 June 1918: Battalion returned to England.

20 June 1918: Hospital with malaria.
16 October 1918: Embarked for Murmansk (Syren) British North Russia Expeditionary Force (NREF) with 6th Battalion Yorkshire regiment.
4 March 1919: Joined Archangel Elope NREF.
23 August 1919: Arrived England for demobilisation.

Edward Holder
28 December 1914: In France with 1st Wilts. Admitted to Casualty Clearing Station Bailleul with Bronchial Catarrh and fever. Returned to England.
27 April 1915: Returned to France and rejoined 1st Wilts at Dickebushe, Belgium.
12 June 1915: Wounded in head in accident involving a grenade at Ypres, along with 2 dead and 23 others wounded.
15 June 1915: Returned to England to hospital.
18 November 1915: Posted to various non-active positions.
29 January 1919: Demobilized. Disability listed due to gunshot wounds, loss of left eye and mandible (jaw) right hand side.

Walter Hunt
17 July 1917: Wounded with 2nd Battalion Royal Marine Light Infantry with a gunshot wound to the face, while in support of working and burial parties.
20 July 1917: Invalided back to the UK.
2 December 1917: Returned to Battalion.
27 March 1918: Killed in action, Aveluy Wood.

John Huntley
26 March 1918: Base Hospital le Treport. Leg wounds. With Royal Artillery.
2 February 1919: 110th Battery.
24 February 1919 Demobilized. Address given was 2 Cricklade Road, Purton.

Reginald Charles Iles
6 September 1915: Arrived in France, with the Royal Engineers, aged about 18. Served in Salonika.
21 April 1918: The Royal Air Force was formed, and Reginald enlisted 20 July 1918.
20 October 1918: Hospitalised after aeroplane accident.
10 December 1918: Unfit, fit only for light duty.
18 April 1919: Transferred to unemployed list and demobilised.

John Jefferies
25/07/1917: Gunshot wound (shell) abdomen and right arm (severe). In France with 1st Battalion Royal Welch Fusiliers.
7 August 1917: Returned to England, presumably for hospitalisation and convalescence.
20 September 1918: Transferred to Service Corps Mechanical Transport Company.
1 February 1919: Demobilised.

Reginald Walter Kempster-Lamb
23 September 1915: At Gallipoli, aged 18. Served later with Battaion in Egypt and Palestine.
5 July1918: Serving in Flanders with West Somerset Yeomanry. Gunshot wound neck and right shoulder.
11 July to 22 November 1918: Reading War Hospital with shell wound to neck.
1 April 1919: Demobilised.

Albert Tom King
8 July 1916: Serving with 1st Wilts. Gunshot wounds to right calf, knee, forearm, wrist, hand, back and left thumb. Usna Hill, Leipzig Salient, Battle of the Somme.
21 August 1917: Discharged due to wounds.

Clayton Large
23/07/1917: Serving with 1st Wilts, Ypres, Belgium. Admitted to Casualty Clearance with gunshot wounds to arm, face and back.
24 July 1917: Admitted to 15th General Hospital, injuries described as "mild".
14 April 1919: Demobilised to Reserve (Class Z).

Robert Jacob Merchant
19 to 21 March 1917: Training in England with Canadian Expeditionary Force. Admitted to Bramshott Military Hospital (rheumatism). Convalesced to 16 May 1917, Red Cross Hospital Buxton, then posted to reserve Battalion.
16 August 1917: Wounded at Longmoor camp whilst under training instruction on trench raids. Contusions to head and body caused by "mine explosion".
5 September to 8 October 1917: Hospital, Epsom.
28 March 1918: SOS 4th reserve, transferred overseas to 47th Battalion British Columbia Regiment.
18 August 1918: Amiens. Gunshot wound (shrapnel wound back), punctured lung. Admitted to Casualty Clearing Station where shrapnel was removed.
29 August 1918: Transported to England (Hammersmith, Epson, Witley and Rhyl).
15 February 1919: Discharged, medically unfit.

Cecil John Mildenhall
14 September 1916: With 4th Battalion Canadian Infantry on Somme front (from 8 September). Gunshot wounds left thigh and foot. Admitted to hospital at Wimereux.
15 September 1916: Reported "dangerously ill, may be visited".
16 September 1916: Died of wounds aged 27. Gunshot wounds, left thigh, left foot, gas gangrene.

George Henry Charles Mills
20 November 1916: Mobilised as a Baker, K (Supply) Company, Aldershot.
25 February to 9 March 1918: Hospital, Aylesbury (Heart trouble).
27 February 1919: Discharged, no longer physically fit for War Service.

Robert Mills
14/ May 1918: Serving with 7th Wilts since September 1915. Discharged, not fit for further War service, aged 22, due to wounds.

Thomas Morgan
26 September 1914 Serving with 1st Berks in action East of Ypres at Hooge. Admitted to hospital at St Nazaire. Transferred to England - "sick".
17 June 1917 Medical board, loss of left eye and amorousness of right eye. (The original date for this injury is given as 07 April 1913 in Wootton Bassett, caused by a piece of steel from a toy cannon.
28 June 1917 Discharged, being no longer physically fit for service.

William Frederick Nethercote
10 October 1915: With 6th Wilts in France. "Wounded in action, caused by explosion". Admitted 58th Field Ambulance. Then hospital at Rouen.
7 to 17 January 1916: Hospital with defective vision, again 12 to 15 March 1916.

23 June 1917: Transferred to Royal Engineers, Sapper with carpentry skills.

18 February 1919: To UK. Medical board, claim for defective vision due to 1915 injuries. Board decision that eyesight had worsened since explosion but did not directly cause loss of sight.

Joseph New

6 April 1918: Admitted to Rockhampton Hospital "wounded". Had been serving with 9th (Service) Battalion Rifle Brigade, France since 1915.

26 November 1918: Demobilized.

Albert Painter

29 July 1916: Serving with 25th Battalion Australian Imperial Force. Gunshot wound to buttock (severe), Battle at Pozieres. Admitted to St Johns Ambulance.

13 August 1916: Transferred to England to hospital in Leicester.

5 October 1916: discharged from 1/5th NG Hospital to Port Down.

19 November 1916: Returned to France rejoining Battalion.

7 January 1918: England on leave, returned to France 24 January 1918.

9 May 1918: To 7th Field Ambulance "sick". Transferred to Rouen.

28 May 1918: Rejoined the Battalion.

10 June 1918: Killed in action at the Third Battle of Morlancourt.

Thomas Painter

13 October 1914: Serving with 1st Wilts. Wounded, gunshot wounds to left shoulder and thigh, at River Loisne.

22 October 1914: Evacuated to England, hospital in Lincoln.

21 November 1914: Wounds healed.

28 December 1914: Re-admitted to hospital with rheumatism, unable to walk further than 100 yards.

30 June 1915: Discharged, no longer physically fit for War Service - rheumatism and sciatica caused by wounds.

Edward Ernest Francis Albert Parsons

18 September 1914: Posted to 7th (Service) Battalion Royal Dublin Fusiliers.

31 March 1915: Seriously ill in Dublin Hospital with pneumonia.

10 July 1915: To Mediterranean Expeditionary Force, arrived Gallipoli 7 August. Later to Salonkia.

2 September 1917: To Egypt, for service in Palestine.

21 March 1918: Involved in Accident - no details.

24 May 1918: Returned to UK for treatment of malaria.

2 June 1916: With Battalion to France.

5 July 1918: On leave to Purton.

17 July 1918: Admitted Chiseldon Hospital - no details.

April 1919: Demobilised.

29 November 1919: Cricklade Court, petty crimes for neglecting his children (Purton Wilts). Offence dated 25/11/1919. Sentenced to 2 months jail. Wife sent to the Workhouse. No information as to how this might have helped the children.

Ernest Ponting

18 March 1915: Arrived in France with Royal Field Artillery.

12 December 1917: London Gazette reports award of Military Medal. The Herald reported (October 1917) that "Ponting has been in France for two years and eight months and has gone through fierce fighting. Mr and Mrs Ponting are very proud of the

Military distinction and the family have just received news that their eldest son has been slightly wounded whilst serving in France".

One wonders how "slight" a wound might be that was associated with the Military Medal

James Pound
31 October 1914: With 1st Wilts. Wounded in action.
9 November 1914: Transferred to UK with gunshot wound to right groin and left finger.
10 February 1915: Re-joined Battalion at Locre, Belgium,
12 March 1915: Killed in action aged 26, at Kemmel, Belgium.

John Mervyn Prower
8th Canadian Battalion (90th Winnipeg) 2nd Canadian Infantry Brigade on mobilization at Valcartier Camp.
03/10/1914 Embarked for England.
9 February 1915: To France with 8th Battalion, 2nd Canadian Infantry Brigade, and served at 2nd Battle of Ypres.
1915: Promoted to temporary Major, then Brigade Major.
1 January 1916: Mentioned in Despatches, now Captain 8th Battalion.
14 January 1916: Awarded Distinguished Service Order .
3 August 1916: Promoted temporary Lieut-Colonel.
4 January 1917: Mentioned in Sir Douglas Haig`s Despatches for distinguished and [gallant] service and [adherence] to duty in the field.
1917: Served at Vimy Ridge, 3rd Ypres (Passchendaele), Mentioned in Despatches.
1 January 1918: Awarded Bar to the DSO.
30 April 1918: Appointed Colonel, Commandant of the Canadian Corps of Infantry school.
12 May 1918: Sidecar accident, travelling as passenger in a sidecar between Hesdin and Aubin St,Vast. The sidecar collided with an RAF tender, the RAF vehicle having swerved to the wrong side of the road.
16 May 1918: Hospital in Amiens, then transferred to England, hospital in Sidcup with lower fractured jaw, left ear badly torn.
5 October 1918: Discharged from hospital, appointed GSO 2, HQ Canadian Corps.
After the War he was kept on in service in India, later as Brigadier in command of the Quebec permanent force. Lord Tweedsmuir later gave him the position of head of the Imperial War Graves commission in September 1938 when he held the rank of Brigadier General.

Wilfred Rawlinson
Served on various Royal Navy ships from August 1914 to 7 March 1916 when he was invalided out.

William John Read
07/10/1916 Date of Embarkation, British Expeditionary Force.
08/10/1916 Joined No3 Infantry Base Depot.
15/10/1916 Transferred to 1st Battalion Wiltshire Regiment. The 1st Battalion was on the Somme near Thiepval.
17 November 1916: Serving with 1st Wilts on Somme near Thiepval. Enteritis. Admitted to hospital, discharged 28 November 1916.
10 March 1917: To hospital, ICT (Inflammation of Connecting Tissue) Legs. Admitted 77th FA.
12 April 1917: Returned to Battalion.

13 April 1917: Trench Fever. Admitted No3 General Hospital, then to England, Trench Fever.

16 August 1917: Discharged, "no longer physically fit for War Service" (chronic Rheumatism).

Edmond St.John Richardson
27 November 1914: Serving with Royal Wiltshire Yeomanry, training on Salisbury Plain. Discharged (Rheumatism).

Ernest Abraham Rivers
13 June 1916: Serving with Royal Engineers.
28 September 1917: Discharged, no longer physically fit for War Service. No other details.

Herbert Mayo Hick Robson
26 November 1914: With Royal Wiltshire Yeomanry. Discharged, medically unfit.

Ernest Charles Rumming
19 January 1915: Serving with 2nd Wilts. Influenza, admitted to hospital at Rouen.
5 February 1915: Suffering from synechia (eye condition where the iris adheres to either the cornea or lens), admitted to the 9th General Hospital Rouen. Diagnosed as effect of an old eye injury.
13 February 1915: To Infantry Base Depot at Rouen, then to Battalion.
16 March 1915: Re-admitted to hospital.
1 May 1915: Returned to England.

Albert James Parsons Salter
Royal Marine Light Infantry, initially mobilised to Mediterranean Expeditionary Force.
13 November 1916: Shell wound, left leg, in action in France. Transferred to UK 24 November 1916.
16 June 1917: Returned to BEF, France.
26 October 1917: Bullet wound, right arm at Ypres, Belgium. Transferred to UK 30 October 1917.
17 March 1919: Discharged, general character, very good.

Leslie Victor Selby
1 June 1915: Arrived France with Royal Field Artillery.
29 October 1916: Hospital - no details.
6 April 1918: ~With 41st Division, Battle of the Ancre. Admitted 49th Field Ambulance, gassed. To hospital at Etaples.
13 July 1918: Left Convalescent Hospital, Eastbourne, and posted to Reserve.

Fred Selwood
7 February 1915: With 1st Wilts. Wounded, shell wound foot, Kemmel Belgium. Admitted to 7th Field Ambulance.
1 March 1915: Gunshot wound left foot "slight". To hospital, Boulogne, then UK.
14 February 1916: With 5th (Service) Battalion Wiltshire Regiment via Port Said to Basrah, Mesopotamia.
8 or 9 April 1916: Gunshot wound left thigh. The Battalion was at Faliyeh.
26 July 1916: Malaria.
5 November 1917: Transferred to Royal Engineers.
1 July 1919: Demobilized.

Richard Stanley Selwood
27 September 1916: Serving in France with 4th Australian infantry Division.
8 October 1916: Wounded in the field (shell shock) at Dickebusch.
1 December 1916: Released from CCS, fit to re-join unit.
7 June 1917: Killed in action at Mesines Ridge.

Walter John Selwood
22 October 1917: To France and posted 2/5th East Lancashire Regiment.
12 April 1918: Returned to England, to hospital Newcastle-on-Tyne.
2 August 1918: Discharged," no longer physically fit for war service".

William Shailes
11 December 1914: Arrived in France with 1st Wilts. Served at Locre, Belgium.
27 September 1916: Discharged due to wounds - no further details.

William Slade
11 December 1916: Left Southampton to Salonika. Served with 273rd Railway construction Company.
7 September 1917: Admitted 40th CCS with malaria, then to 18th Stationary Hospital.
17 September 1917: Returned to unit.
28 May 1918: Admitted to 31st CCS with jaundice.
2 August 1918: Re-joined unit.
19 October 1918: Admitted 2/3 Field Hospital.
2 December 1918: To 49th General Hospital, then to hospital (Malta 6 December) with Dysentery.
30 January 1919: Invalided to UK.
3 May 1919: Demobilized.

Herbert Henry Stone
4 November 1916: Posted to 1/4th Wiltshire Regiment to India.
15 September 1917: Transferred with Regiment to Egypt.
November 1917: Palestine. Fell ill with high temperature (104°F / 40°C) and admitted to 33rd Field Clearance Station. From there via several staging hospitals to Alexandria and to Mustapha Convalescence Hospital. He was then returned to unit.
15 March 1919: Returned to UK.
12 April 1919: Demobilised.

Frank Sutton
25 March 1915: Serving with 1st Wilts. Admitted to 7th Field Ambulance at Locre, suffering from boils [possibly from gassing at Hill 60 near Ypres].
15 April 1915: Admitted to 8th FA at Dickebusche (boils); transferred to rest camp.
29 April 1915: Admitted to 3rd Stationary Hospital, Boulogne, then to England, chest deformity. After recovery re-joined Battalion now in Mesopotamia.
30 March 1917: The Battalion was at Deltawa. Frank died of wounds, aged 18.

Albert Telling
The North Wilts Herald reported that Albert Telling (Gloucestershire Regiment) was recovering in a Hospital in France. He had received shrapnel wounds to his right leg and head whilst in Italy.

Francis Charles Titcombe
17 August 1914: To France with Royal Engineers.
10 September 1914: Admitted to hospital.

16 December 1915: Returned to Unit from Hospital - note 15 months.
5 February 1917: Discharged for re-enlistment.
13 February 1919: Re-enlisted.
22 July 1919: Disability claim form. Unit recorded as Cavalry Corps Bridging Park.
31 December 1919: Admitted to Cambridge Hospital, Aldershot. Over the following days his medical sheet records a rapid decline in health.
12 January 1920: Mumbling and incoherent. Comatose about 6pm, Died 11:55pm from (1) Influenza (2) Pneumonia.

William Titcombe
2/1 Wessex Royal Engineers.
00/11/1915 Weymouth.
8 February 1916: With 503rd Field Company Royal Engineers (2/1st Wessex), in France.
12 March 1918: Admitted to hospital (foot or leg injury).
22 March 1918: Discharged from hospital.
19 December 1918: Re-admitted to hospital.
29 December 1918: To England, from 2nd Australian General Hospital.
5 March 1919: Demobilized.

Harry William Tuck
4 July 1917: To France, 1st Battalion Dorset Regiment.
2 November 1917: To Field Ambulance sick, dysentery.
14 January 1918: Re-joined Battalion.
25 March 1918: Wounded. Admitted to 91st Field Ambulance, gunshot wound face. then to 36th Casualty Clearing Station, gunshot wound right eye.
7 May 1918: Re-joined Battalion.
5 August 1918: To Field Ambulance. Injuries to right leg and right hand.
29 August 1918: Re-joined Battalion.
8 April 1919: Stationed at Bonn, Germany.
19 April 1919: Home for discharge.

Henry Edgar Tuck
7 June 1917: Serving with Machine Gun Corps. Wounded in action, gunshot wound to foot. Admitted to 108 Field Ambulance.
12 June 1917 Transferred to UK.
18 February 1919: Discharged from MGC to Reserve (class Z).

Arthur S. Wheeler
In April 1917, the Swindon advertiser and North Wilts Herald ran a story of interest. The piece reported that that a soldier named Arthur Wheeler had been in hospital for 11 months after suffering wounds at the Somme. He had been serving with the 10th Battalion Lincolnshire Regiment when injured in the right hand. The damaged hand was removed at Aldershot where he was recovering in September 1916.

Jesse Wheeler
16 September 1916: Serving with 28th Battalion Canadian Expeditionary Force. Wounded, shell wound face (shrapnel).
13 October 1916: Admitted 1st Australian General Hospital, Rouen. Then to Shoreham on Sea, Bethnal Green, then Bromley by 30 October 1916.
7 November 1916: Discharged from hospital.
7 February 1917: Taken back on Battalion strength, Base Depot Le Havre.

2 May 1917: Re-joined unit in the field. In what capacity, not known.
18 May 1919: To Canada and demobilsed.

Oliver Wheeler
7 February 1917: Serving with 28th Battalion Canadian Expeditionary Force..
10 July 1917: To No.18 General Hospital Amiens, with bronchitis. Then to Convalescence Hospital at Cayeux.
7 November 1917: Admitted to No1 Canadian Field Hospital, shell wound (shrapnel) left arm and hand, shoulder, side penetrating, Ypres.
13 November 1917: Transferred to No5 General Hospital, Rouen, dangerously ill.
2 February 1918: To England, Royal Victoria Hospital Netley, then Hospital Epsom.
6 October 1918: To Convalescent Hospital, Liverpool.
30 October 1918: Invalided to Canada, Moose Jaw Convalescent Hospital, Saskatchewan.
7 February 1919: Discharged.

Stanley Willoughby
3 November 1915: In transit with Army Service Corps bound for Gallipoli on troop ship HMT Woodfield. The ship was torpedoed and sunk by an Austro-Hungarian submarine Spain. Stanley was reportedly wounded by shrapnel in his arm.
Two lifeboats got off and the survivors were landed at Melilla on the coast of Spanish Morocco. 45 British and 9 Arabs were later recorded as being in the hands of Spanish Authorities. The interned men were later moved to Malaga where they were harshly treated and regularly threatened that they would be shot.
12 February 1916: Escaped from Malaga, Spain. Arrived in UK 21 February 1916.
17 June 1916: Discharged, being no longer physically fit for War Service. Suffering from neurasthenia, which might be classed as Post Traumatic Shock Disorder today.
22 October 1917: Medical at Chisledon Camp; anaemic with neurasthenia, 30% disability.
In later years, his family did once try to ask and record his story but he shook so badly they had to stop. He would only say, "Feel this" to his daughters, asking them to feel the shrapnel in his arms.

Henry Woodward
28 November 1914: Discharged from 2nd Wilts, "no longer fit for Military Service". The disability described as a hernia, reappearing after first occurrence whilst serving in South Africa 1913.

Frederick Woolford
13 December 1914: Serving in France and Belgium with 1st Canadian Mechanical Transport CASC. Divisional Ammunition Supply Column.
28 July 1915: Admitted to No2 Canadian Field Ambulance, then Hospital Bailleul. Wounded at Steinwench, being thrown from a loaded wagon, large contusion to scalp requiring 22 stitches.
30 July 1915 No8 Casualty Clearing Station before transfer to rest Station at Mont des Cats. Injury described as gunshot wound, head (scalp), then transferred to Le Treport.
13 August 1915: East General Hospital Brighton.
1 October 1915: Transferred to Convalescent Hospital Epsom.
29 October 1915: Discharged, proceeded to Depot.
9 March1916: Considered fit for clerical work CASC.
16 July 1916: Canadian Army Service Corps Transport Depot, Shorncliff.

22 September 1918: Returned to Canada. No suitable war employment in England.
4 September 1919: Discharged being medically unfit, aged 55 years old.

Francis Woodhouse Worley
1 March 1917: Posted 4th Wilts.
30 April 1917: Transferred to Labour Corps Company 628 (Sutton Veny).
16 August 1917: Discharged being no longer physically fit for War Service, heart trouble aged 18 years 8 months.

The Unveiling & Dedication of the Wayside Cross, Purton,
Sunday 26th December 1920, courtesy Purton Museum

Part 73: Echoes that Live On

It is said of the Great War that five great empires entered the war, but only one emerged intact:

Austria-Hungary was dissected by the victorious powers and ceased to be in its former imperial sense. The successor states of Austria and Hungary were created as democracies.

The immediate enthusiasms of the liberated Austro-Hungarian Slav provinces that formed Czechoslovakia in the north and Yugoslavia in the south had already seen divergences of politics before the end of the Second World War but were constrained during the Communist post-war era. Once that hold was released, Czechoslovakia spilt in two comparatively amicably while Yugoslavia ceased to be during a series of acrimonious wars in the 1990s.

The Ottoman Empire was also split up with the successor state of Turkey to be a democracy. Other potential democracies were created in their wake: Syria, Lebanon, Iraq and Palestine. The Hejaz in the south of Arabia was never going to be a democracy but it was owed a debt for the raising of the Arab Revolt.

Palestine, created after the war, was under British control as a League of Nations Mandate. Its foundation however was at odds with the Balfour Declaration of 1917 which sought to create a Jewish homeland within its borders. As early as 1920, conflict began in Mandatory Palestine between the Arab population and the minority Jewish community which had lived there for many generations. The situation was further exacerbated by the migration of European Jews to Palestine in several waves during the inter-war years and after WW2. By 1945 the Jewish population had increased to 33% of the total of Palestine. The creation of the state of Israel and the Arab-Israeli War that occurred at the end of the British Mandate period widened the issue into the regional Arab-Israeli and Sunni-Shi'a conflicts that we still see today.

Much of today's terrorism can be laid at the door of the creation of new states after the Great War without consideration of the local issues and with boundaries that bore little resemblance to communities.

Germany was ambushed and tied up, to prevent it "ever going to war again". Any dissection was minimal in terms of land area, but major in terms of reparations and rules under which it was to operate. In fact, that only raised resentment and was a leading cause of the Second World War.

Russia had been a strict autocracy for so long before the war that it effectively self-destructed. The pressure relief from partial democratisation in the 1900s wasn't enough to prevent revolution and civil war. After the civil war, harsh autocracy returned under state dictatorship until the end of the Soviet era. Wars for independence erupted in Georgia, Nagorno-Karabakh, Abkhazia, South Ossetia, and the Caucasus in the 1990s even until the brief Russo-Georgian War of August 2008. Russia annexed the Crimea from Ukraine in 2014 and the entire length of the border between Russia and Ukraine is still disputed.

The British Empire was the only empire of the five that survived the war.

It was unique among the other empires in being a democracy though still with a long way to go in the development of universal suffrage and civil liberties. George V was only King-Emperor in name as the prime minister ran the country with powers limited by parliament. The Empire itself referred mainly to India. The five dominions were self-governing - Canada, Newfoundland, Australia, New Zealand and the Union of South Africa - and each found increased national pride from its experience of the war.

Apart from the sheer cost of war, the main changes in the short term in Britain had been on the cards even before the war: the home rule of Southern Ireland and votes for women. Being a democracy, a general election was held as soon as the war was over: the war government was re-elected by a landslide.

The **United States** had a policy of neutrality or "isolationism" before its entry into the Great War but in its involvement in Europe the country showed itself a strong new player on the world stage. However, once the war was over, the US returned to isolationist policies until going to war again in WW2, again forced by enemy attacks.

The League of Nations

When the League was set up in 1920, its primary aim was to prevent wars through collective security and disarmament and settling international disputes through negotiation and arbitration. Other fields covered by its Covenant concerned labour conditions, rights of native inhabitants, human and drug trafficking, the arms trade, global health, prisoners of war, and protection of minorities in Europe. The League lacked its own armed force and depended on the victorious Great Powers of the Great War to enforce its resolutions, which they were often reluctant to do.

The credibility of the organisation was weakened since the United States did not ratify the treaty and so never joined the League. The Soviet Union joined late and by the time of the Second World War had left again as had Japan, Italy and Spain among others. The League lasted for 26 years and was replaced by the United Nations after the Second World War.

The Geneva Convention & The Geneva Protocol

A Swiss businessman, Henry Dunant had visited wounded soldiers after the Battle of Solferino (1859), in the Second Italian War of Independence, and wrote of the horrors of war and the lack of facilities, trained medics, and medical aid available. He proposed the setting up off a permanent relief agency for humanitarian aid in times of war and a treaty to recognise the agency's neutrality to allow it to work in a war zone. The agency became the International Red Cross in Geneva. In 1864 an international conference agreed the Geneva Convention to cover the rights and treatment of sick and wounded soldiers in the battlefield. Henry Dunant won the first Nobel Peace Prize in 1901 for these achievements.

The Geneva Convention was updated in 1907, when Britain signed it for the first time, and a new conference was established in 1927 in light of the Great

War experiences and provided additional rights for Prisoners of War in addition to those provided by the 1907 Hague Convention.

As the Geneva Convention did not deal with the conduct of war itself, a conference in Geneva in 1925 was held under the terms of the 1907 Hague Convention for the Supervision of the International Trade in Arms and Ammunition and in Implements of War. The 1925 "Geneva Protocol" for the "Prohibition of the Use in War of Asphyxiating, Poisonous or other Gases, and of Bacteriological Methods of Warfare" was added to the Hague Convention. This covered the use of chemical and biological weapons in international armed conflicts, but did not cover their production, storage or transfer in the 1925 version. The Protocol came into effect in 1928 under the oversight of the League of Nations.

Violations of the Geneva Protocol have occurred. Japan used chemical weapons against Taiwan in 1930; Italy used mustard gas against Abyssinia in 1935; and Japan used chemical weapons against China from 1938 to 1941. Saddam Hussein used several different chemical agents against Iran during the 1980-88 Iran-Iraq War and against Iraqi rebels in instances such as the Halabja chemical attack.

Since production and stockpiling of chemical weapons was not against the terms of the Protocol, Britain, the United States and Germany all produced huge quantities of chemical weapons ready for use. Neither side used them fearing the terrible retaliation that would have resulted. An American ship carrying chemical weapons was sunk in an air raid at Bari, in Italy, in 1943. The resultant release of mustard gas caused many deaths. After the Second World War, thousands of tons of shells and containers with chemical weapons were dumped at sea by the Allies.

During the Syrian Civil War and associated conflicts, both sides have accused each other of using chemical weapons. Although the United Nations has confirmed the use of chemical weapons, they did not investigate which side had used them. However, because the weapons were used within Syria's own borders, rather than between separate countries, nasty as it was it fell outside the scope of the Geneva Protocol.

The Wiltshire Regiment

The Regiment lost so many men by April 1918, that the 2nd Battalion was amalgamated into one command with the 2nd Berks. The Commands were eventually restored but it was a forerunner of the two regiments' being amalgamated in 1959 into the Duke of Edinburgh's Royal Regiment (Berkshire and Wiltshire). This too was amalgamated in 1994 with the Gloucester Regiment to form the Royal Gloucestershire, Berkshire and Wiltshire Regiment (RGBWR) renamed the RGBW Light Infantry in July 2005. Further changes amalgamated the Devonshire and Dorset Regiment, the Royal Green Jackets and The Light Infantry into a new large regiment - The Rifles - formed in 2007 with 5 regular and 3 reserve battalions.

The 1st Battalion The Rifles memorialises the Wiltshire Regiment link as it was formed from the 1st Battalion The Devonshire and Dorset Light Infantry, and 1st Battalion The Royal Gloucestershire, Berkshire and Wiltshire Light Infantry.

"Great War" or "First World War"

From time to time during the writing of this series in Purton Magazine, I have been asked 'what is the difference between the Great War and the First World War'. The answer lies in the chronology.

When the present Queen came to the throne, she had the name and regnal number Elizabeth II. Queen Elizabeth of Tudor times gained the number "I". Similarly, during the Great War the conflict was simply known as "the War" in Britain as it was a European war when it started. By the time the United States joined in, the War had already spread far and was known there as "the World War".

At the end of the war, when it came to remembrance and commemoration of the dead, the term "The Great War" came into usage to give expression to the scale of the sacrifice made.

However, as early as 18 February 1919, the Oxford English Dictionary attributes "World War No. 2" to the Manchester Guardian in an article considering a "future war arising out of the social upheaval ... from the First World War". OED gives another citation for "World War II" from the 11 September 1939 issue of Time Magazine. In the German language, Count Tisza had prophesied the term *Weltkrieg* in July 1914 - *see Part 13.*

It perhaps most telling that, on the signing of the Treaty of Versailles in June 1919, Marshal Ferdinand Foch of France stated "this [treaty] is not peace. It is an Armistice for twenty years." He was correct, the Second World War started on 3 September 1939, 20 years, 2 months and 5 days after his prophecy.

"Shell Shock" and Combat Stress

Shell shock was a term coined in World War I to describe the type of post-traumatic stress disorder many soldiers suffered during the war (before PTSD itself was a term). It is a reaction to the intensity of the bombardment and fighting that produced a helplessness appearing variously as panic and being scared, or flight, an inability to reason, sleep, walk or talk. The term has entered into popular imagination and memory and is often identified as the signature injury of the War.

In 1915, the British Army in France categorised patients depending on the perceived cause of shell shock and shell concussion. If the cause was seen as being from action by the enemy, the patient would rank as "wounded" and was allowed to wear a "wound stripe" on his arm and received a pension on demobilisation. But if the man's breakdown did not follow a shell explosion, it was not thought to be "due to the enemy". His file would be labelled "Sick" and he would not be entitled to a wound stripe or a pension.

By June 1917, all British cases of shell shock were evacuated to a nearby neurological centre and were labelled as NYDN - "not yet diagnosed nervous". It appeared that between 4-10% of shell-shock cases were due to physical causes ('commotional'), and the rest were 'emotional'. Shell shock was therefore not to be seen as a valid disease: it was banned as a diagnosis and mention of it was censored, even in medical journals.

Alternatively, the effects of shell shock could be interpreted on the front line as cowardice or "lack of moral fibre". During the war, 306 British soldiers were executed for cowardice; many of whom were victims of shell shock. On 7 November 2006, the Government of the United Kingdom gave them all a posthumous conditional pardon and they are commemorated at the *Shot at Dawn Memorial* at the National Memorial Arboretum in Staffordshire.

In World War II and thereafter, diagnosis of "shell shock" was replaced by that of Combat Stress Reaction, a similar but not identical response to the trauma of warfare and bombardment.

Combat Stress was formed in 1919, as the Ex-Servicemen's Welfare Society, and is a registered charity in the United Kingdom offering therapeutic and clinical community and residential treatment to former members of the British Armed Forces who are suffering from a range of mental health conditions; including post-traumatic stress disorder (PTSD). Combat Stress makes treatment available free of charge for all ex-servicemen who are suffering with mental illness.

Currently, the organisation is helping almost 6,000 people who are ex-servicemen aged from 19 to 97. Combat Stress are treating 971 ex-servicemen who served in Afghanistan and 1,185 who served in Iraq (Gulf War I and Gulf War II). On average, it takes 13 years for an ex-serviceman to make first contact with Combat Stress for advice, help, and treatment; however, those who served in Iraq and Afghanistan are approaching the charity more speedily.

Support is currently being given to those who suffer from clinical depression, raised anxiety states, substance abuse (drug and alcohol) and post-traumatic stress disorder (PTSD). This support is delivered throughout the United Kingdom through three treatment centres at Ayr (Hollybush House), Newport in Shropshire and Leatherhead (Tyrwhitt House), along with community outreach teams.

Kohima Epitaph - written in 1916

When you go home, tell them of us and say,
For your tomorrow, we gave our today.

The words are attributed to John Maxwell Edmonds (1875-1958), inspired by Simonides. Edmonds had put them into a collection of 12 epitaphs for the First World War in 1916.

According to the Burma Star Association the words were used for the Kohima Memorial as a suggestion by Major John Etty-Leal, the GSO II of the 2nd Division, who was also a classical scholar.

The Thermoplyae Epitaph. Simonides, c. 480 BC

Ὦ ξεῖν', ἀγγέλλειν Λακεδαιμονίοις ὅτι τῇδε
κείμεθα, τοῖς κείνων ῥήμασι πειθόμενοι.

Oh stranger, tell the Spartans that
we lie here, obedient to their ways.

Bibliography

Purton & The Great War: A Study of a Wiltshire Parish and The Great War (CD edition) - *Bob Lloyd, 2014.*

The Balkans - *Misha Glenny (Granta Publications, 1999)*

Bismarck: A Life - *Jonathan Steinberg (Oxford University Press, 2011)*

Catastrophe: Europe goes to War 1914 - *Max Hastings (William Collins, 2013)*

The Causes of World War One - *Firstworldwar.com (firstworldwar.com/origins/causes.htm)*

Christmas Truce: The Western Front December 1914 - *Malcolm Brown & Shirley Seaton (Macmillan, 2014)*

English History: 1914-1945 - *AJP Taylor (Oxford University Press, 1965)*

Evening Swindon Advertiser microfilm archive (Swindon Central Library, Local Studies Section)

Fighting on the Home Front: The Legacy of Women in World War One - *Kate Adie (Hodder & Stoughton, 2013)*

Great Britain's Great War - *Jeremy Paxman (Viking, 2014)*

The History of Italy - *Charles L. Killinger (Greenwood Press, 2002)*

Modern Greece: A Short History - *CM Woodhouse (Faber & Faber 1986)*

Portugal During World War 1 - *Wikipedia (en.m.wikipedia.org/wiki/Portugal_during_World_War_I)*

Purton's Past: *Alec Robins - Purton Historical Society, 1991, ISBN 0951714201*

When God made Hell: British Invasion of Mesopotamia and the Creation of Iraq 1914-1921 - *Charles Townshend (Faber & Faber, 2011)*

When this Bloody War is Over: Soldiers' Songs of the First World War - *Max Arthur (Piatkus, 2001)*

Wiltshire Regiment - *Wikipedia (en.wikipedia.org/wiki/Wiltshire_Regiment)*

The Wiltshire Regiment in 1914-1918 - *www.1914-1918.net/wilts.htm*

Various timelines on Internet, including:
Wikipedia (en.m.wikipedia.org/wiki/1914 and ditto through .../1918)
History Learning Site (historylearningsite.co.uk/world-war-one/timeline-of-world-war-one)
www.1914-1918.net/chronology
www.firstworldwar.com/timeline
www.historyorb.com/events
www.greatwar.co.uk/timeline

As a good read, set from the perspective of a Turkish village from the start of the Great War, through Gallipoli to the burning of Smyrna:
Birds without Wings - *Louis de Bernières (Vintage, 2005)*

Acknowledgements

I am grateful to Purton Magazine for running the original articles for this series every month from August 2013, when I started by introducing the background causes of the Great War.

I am also immensely grateful for the help I have gained from the amazing in-depth research of Bob Lloyd into all men with Purton connections who were involved in the military in the war.

The philosophy of the current project has been to convert Bob's directory by personal name into a journal showing how Purton people were affected by the war, month by month as it progressed. I am also grateful to those who have contributed the "My Family's War" articles recording their own family's memories.

Index

Agadir Crisis: 27
Aisne, 1st, battle: 44, 46
Aisne, 2nd, battle: 118, 127
Aisne, 3rd, battle: 170
Alsace-Lorraine: after
    Franco-Prussian War 10;
    Versailles 198
Amman, 2nd battle: 184
Amiens, battle: 179
Ancre, battle: 165
Arras, battle: 127
Artois, 1st battle: 55
Artois, 2nd battle: 70
Avre, battle: 165
Ayun Kara, battle: 146
Bailey, Frederick: 180
Bapaume, battle: 180
Bartlett, Richard: 137
Beassant, Richard: 173
Beaurevoir Line, battle: 184
Belgium: invaded 42;
    government restored 191
Bismarck: in German
    Unification 8
Blackford, John: 134
Bolimov, battle: 60
Booker, William: 79
Bridgman, Arthur: 127
Broodseinde, battle: 141
Brown, Arthur: 161
Brown, Herbert: 138
Brown, John: 182
Bulgaria, armistice: 183
Bull, Daniel: 105
Bullecourt, battle: 129
Bunce, Albert: 196
Bunce, Arthur: 77
Burgess, Francis: 167
Butcher, George: 167
Caldwell, Nelson: 71
Cambrai, 1st battle: 144,
    148
Cambrai, 2nd battle: 185
Cantigny, battle: 170
Caporetto, battle: 142

Casement, Sir Roger: 97,
    98, 105
Cavell, Edith: 82
Cer, battle: 43
Champagne, battles: 127,
    177
Christmas truce: 56, 58
Ciply (Mons), battle: 43
Cocos Islands, battle: 54
Conscription: 87, 167
Cook, Elijah: 192
Coronel, battle: 54
Ctesiphon, battle: 86
Curtis, Edward: 104
Damascus: 188
Daniels, Frederick: 145
Dash, Percy Edward: 95
Delville Wood, battle: 105
Dilman, battle: 72
Dobropolje, battle: 183
Dogger Bank, battle: 60
Drury, Henry: 46
Dunsford, Leonard: 115
Easter Rising: 97, 134, 170
Edmonds, Charles: 197
Edmonds, William: 166
Embury, Thomas: 110
Epéhy, battle: 182
Eveleigh, William: POW
    166, died 186
Fátima, visions: 131, 137,
    143
Festubert, battle: 71
Fisher, Herbert: POW 49,
    died 153
Fishlock, Albert: 185
Fiume: 187, 193
Flers-Courcellete, battle:
    107
Foch, Marshal Ferdinand:
    Minister for War 129;
    Western Front 160,166,
    179; Supreme Command
    191; Armistice 191;
    Versailles verdict 232
Fourteen Points: 153, 155

Franco-Prussian War: 9, 10
Franz Ferdinand,
    Archduke: assassination
    35
French, Sir John: 33, 87;
    Ireland 170
Fromelles, battle: 104
Gallipoli: 69, evacuation 88
Gaza, 1st battle: 126
Gaza, 2nd battle: 128
Gaza, 3rd battle: 143, 146
German spring offensive:
    160
Gibbs, Henry: 104
Gravenstafel, battle: 69
Green, Mervyn: 166
Grimes, Robert: 110
Haelen, battle: 43
Haig, Sir Douglas: C-in-C
    Army 87; Somme 113;
    Field Marshal 120;
    3rd Ypres 144; Backs to
    wall 166
Haines, Stanley: 110
Haines, William: 148
Haldane reforms 30
Harrison, Ernest: 182
Havrincourt, battle: 182
Hawcutt, Esaw: 195
Hayward, Albert: 127
Hedges, Edward: 119
Hedges, Percy: 141
Heligoland Bight, battle: 44
Hicks, George: 146
Hill 70, battle: 137
Hindenburg Line, battle:
    182
Hitler: wounded 110; Iron
    Cross *(2nd class)* 53, *(1st
    class)* 177; Nazism 210
Hooge mine: 76
Hundred Days offensive:
    179
Hunt, Walter: 160
Imbros, battle: 152

Irish Home Rule: 33, 37, 96, 168, 202, 230
Isonzo Campaigns: 74, 92, 106, 112, 117, 130, 140, 142
Jefferies, Reginald: 49
Jerusalem, battle: 146, 149
Jones, Reginald: 179
Jordan, William: 153
Jutland, battle: 99
Kemmel, 2nd battle: 167
Kibblewhite, Charles: 43
Kibblewhite, Ernest: 77
Kiel mutiny: 191
Kitchener, Lord: Omdurman 22; Gallipoli 83, 85; death 101
Kolubara, battle: 56
Kut-al-Amara: 88, 90, 95, 116, 119
:Land Army: 120
Lander, Charles: 167
Lane, Frederick: 165
Lane, John: missing 160, died POW 165
Lawrence of Arabia: 76, 101, 112, 119, 136, 188; DSO 154
Le Cateau, battle: 44
Leach, Albert: 179
Lewis, Albert: 160
Lewis, Harry: 121
Liège, battle: 43
Litten, Frederick: 119
Lloyd George, David: SS for War 104; Prime Minister 115; 1918 election 202; Spanish Flu 208
Loos, battle: 79
Lovelock, Victor: 169
Lusitania, RMS: 63, 74, 92; sinking 63
Lys, battle: 166
Malacca Straits, battle: 50
Malmaison, battle: 142
Mărășești, battle: 138
Marne, 1st battle: 46
Marne, 2nd battle: 177, 179

Martin, Ernest: 152
Martin, Herbert: 185
Martin, Tom: 75
Masurian Lakes: 1st battle 43; 2nd 64
Matthews, Alfred: 186
Matthews, Harry: 104
Matthews, Percy: 73
May Island, battle: 152
McNellee, Edward: 177
Megiddo, battles: 184, 196
Merchant, Frank: 174
Messines Ridge, battle: 131
Mildenhall, Cecil: 107
Mills, Edward: 186
Mills, Frederick: 77
Morlancourt, 3rd battle: 173
Mughar Ridge, battle: 146
Munitions accidents: Barnbow 149; Black Tom NJ 104; Eddystone PA 128; Faversham 97; Halifax N-S 149; Hamont (Belg.) 192; HMS Natal 89; HMS Vanguard 136; Hooley Hill 133; Kawachi 178; Kingsland NJ 120; Low Moor 105; Morgan NJ 189; Oakdale PA 171; Silvertown 120; Uplees 97; White Lund 143
Mussolini: 55, 211
Neuve-Chappelle, battle: 66
New, William: 184
Nicholas II, Tsar: 24, 31, 35, 114; assassination 178
Noyon, 2nd battle: 180
Nun's Copse, battle: 53
Oakley-Brown,Valentine: 185
Ogburn, Charles: 98
Ottoman Empire: Rise & Decline 10; armistice: 188
Paginton, George: 77
Painter, Albert: 173

Parsons, Albert: 87
Parsons, Charles: 192
Passchendaele, battle: 141
Pershing, Gen. John: Mexico 95, 102, 122; France 130, 132, 134, 142
Pétain, Marshal Philppe: 55; Verdun 92; Chief of Staff 127; Commander in Chief 129
Piave, battle: 175
Poison gas: 60, 69, 79, 101, 137, 170, 231
Polygon Wood, battle: 139, 141
Portugal: entente 27; Africa 76; Expeditionary Force 94, 119, 132, 149, 166; government 149, 172; Versailles 199
Pound, James: 65
Pozières Ridge , battle: 105
Price, Mervyn Harry: Médaille Militaire 176
Princip, Gavrilo: assassin 39; sentenced 50 death 169
Przasnysz, battle: 64
Purton wounded: 216
Race to the Sea: 46, 48
Ramadi, battle: 136
Rasputin, Grigori: 25, 40, 116
Rationing: 147, 177
Red Baron: *see Richthofen*
Reparations: after Franco-Prussian War 10; Versailles 199
Richardson, Mervyn Stronge: letters 58, death 93
Richthofen, Manfred von: 108, 168
Riga, battle: 139
Royal Air Force: founded 168
Rumming, Geoffrey: Gallipoli 69; death 145

Rijeka: *see Fiume*
Sadarapat, battle: 172
Sainsbury, William: 166
St Quentin Canal, battle: 182
Saunders, Edwin: 195
Scapa Flow: US fleet 149; German internment 193; scuttling 199
Scarpe River, battle: 129
Schleswig-Holstein: Danish-Prussian disputes 9; Versailles 198
Schlieffen Plan: 29, 42; deadline missed 47
Selwood, Richard Stanley: 132
Selwood, Thomas: 119
Sharon, battle: 196
Shopland, Herbert: 101
Skra-di-Lagen, battle: 172
Skuse, Charles: 186
Smith, Sidney: 77
Smyrna: 204
Somme, 1st battle: 101, 103
Somme, 2nd battle: 180, 181
Staley, Frederick: 196
Suffragism: 34, 36, 157, 202; Reform Acts 21;

Norway 98; Russia 135; USA 147
Sutton, Frank: 125
Sutton, Frederick: 166
Tafileh, battle: 154
Tangier Crisis: 27
Tanks: 80, 107
Tannenburg, battle: 43
Tel Asur, battle: 161
Thiepval Ridge, battle: 110
Titcombe, Francis: 196
Treaty of Lausanne: 207
Treaty of Neuilly-sur-Seine: 201
Treaty of Sèvres: 204
Treaty of St-Germain-en-Laye: 200
Treaty of Trianon: 201
Treaty of Versailles: 198
Trieste: 74, 112, 150, 193; St Germain 201
Tuck, William: 104
United States: isolationism 35; neutral 42; Lusitania 72; Mexico 94; Haiti 104 Zimmerman telegram 120, 122; declares war 124; first battle 170
Vardar, battle: 183
Verdun, battles: 105, 110, 113, 115, 137

Vimy Ridge: 100, 127
Vistula River, battle: 50
Vittorio Veneto, battle: 187; Austrian collapse 193
Vizer, George: 169
War deaths: 215
Webb, Mervyn: 185
Western Front, armistice: 191
Williams, Edward: 124
Wilson, President Woodrow: 35, 120, 124; War address 127; Fourteen Points 153, 155
Windsor, House of: 136
Wipers Times: 157
Women's Institute: 86
Woolford, Edward: 193
Woolford, Herbert: 184
Woolford, Joseph: 189
Ypres, 1st battle: 49
Ypres, 2nd battle: 69
Ypres, 3rd battle: 134
Ypres, 4th battle: 166
Ypres, 5th battle: 182
Yser, battle: 49
Zimmerman telegram: 120, 122